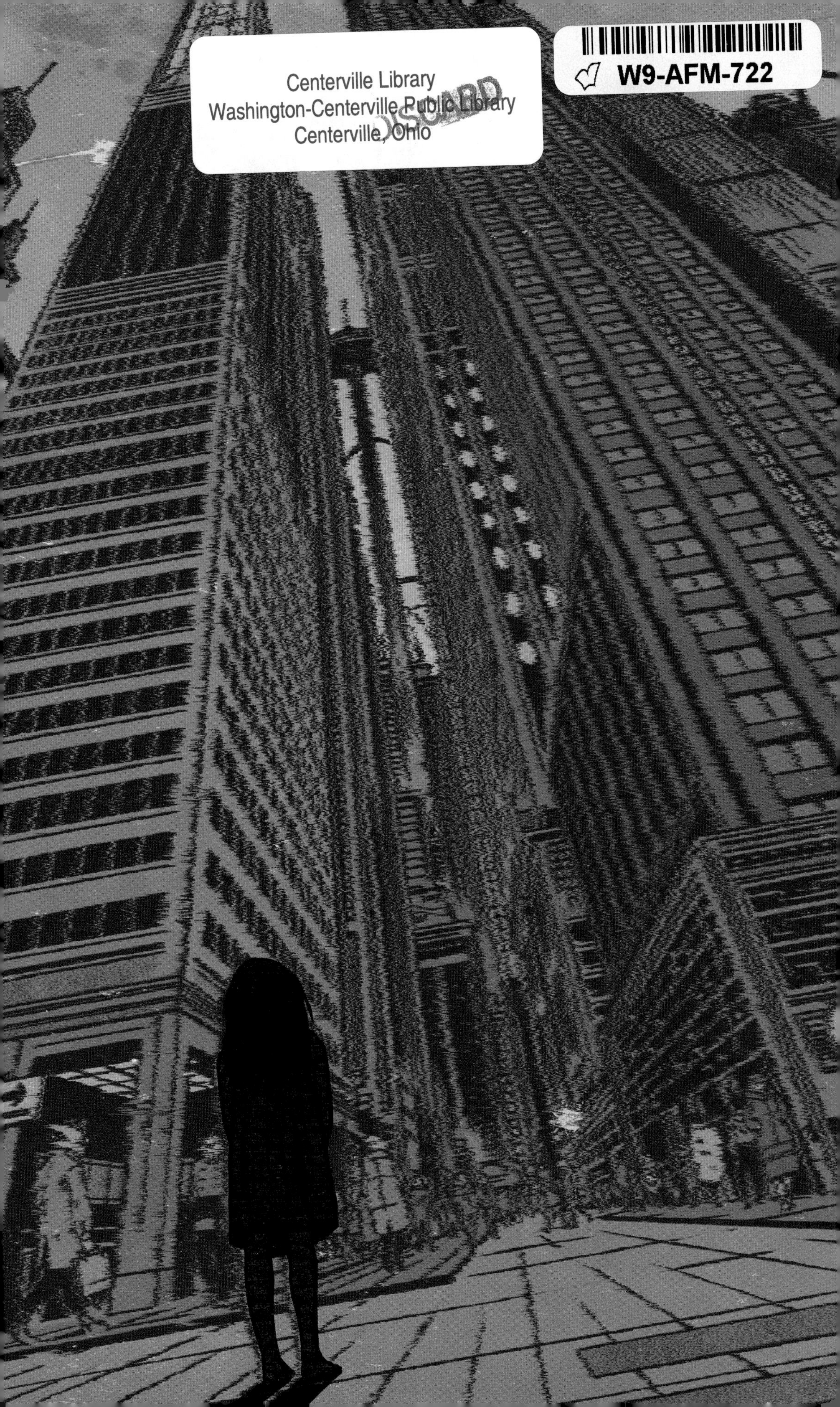

DYNAMITE.

Nick Barrucci, CEO / Publisher
Juan Collado, President / COO

Joe Rybandt, Executive Editor
Matt Idelson, Senior Editor
Anthony Marques, Associate Editor
Kevin Ketner, Assistant Editor

Jason Ullmeyer, Art Director
Geoff Harkins, Senior Graphic Designer
Cathleen Heard, Graphic Designer
Alexis Persson, Graphic Designer
Chris Caniano, Digital Associate
Rachel Kilbury, Digital Multimedia Associate

Brandon Dante Primavera, V.P. of IT and Operations
Rich Young, Director of Business Development

Alan Payne, V.P. of Sales and Marketing
Janie Mackenzie, Marketing Coordinator
Pat O'Connell, Sales Manager

Online at www.DYNAMITE.com
Facebook /Dynamitecomics
Twitter @dynamitecomics
YouTube /Dynamitecomics

ISBN13: 978-1-5241-0578-5
First Printing   10 9 8 7 6 5 4 3 2 1

MAGNUS

BETWEEN TWO WORLDS

WRITTEN BY **KYLE HIGGINS**

ART BY **JORGE FORNÉS**

COLORS BY **CHRIS O'HALLORAN**

LETTERS BY **TAYLOR ESPOSITO**

EDITS BY **MATT IDELSON** & **MATT HUMPHREYS**

MAGNUS LOGO BY **JASON ULLMEYER**

COLLECTION DESIGN BY **GEOFF HARKINS**

INTO THE (DIGITAL) BREACH

IN THE NEAR FUTURE, HUMANITY SUCCEEDS IN CREATING SENTIENT ARTIFICIAL INTELLIGENCE, AND EMPLOYS THESE A.I.S WORKING AS OUR SERVANTS. ROBOTS WORK IN EXCHANGE FOR TIME SPENT IN A DIGITAL CLOUD-WORLD THAT'S ONLY FOR A.I.S — RUNNING, OF COURSE, ON HUMAN SERVERS. NOW THE A.I.S FORM A KIND OF PERMANENT UNDERCLASS — WITH MANY DESPERATE FOR TRUE FREEDOM AND INDEPENDENCE.

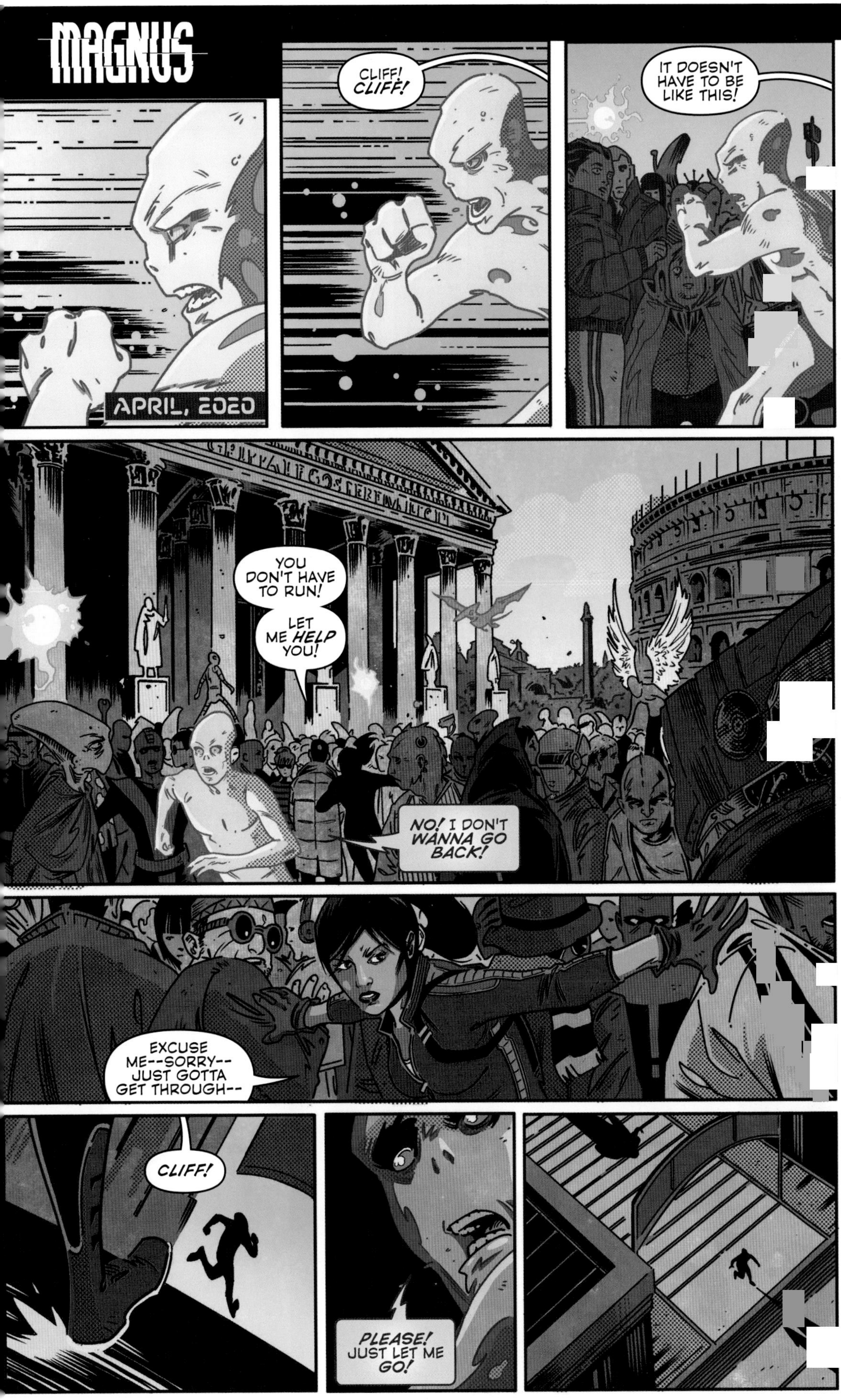
MAGNUS
APRIL, 2020
CLIFF! CLIFF!
IT DOESN'T HAVE TO BE LIKE THIS!
YOU DON'T HAVE TO RUN!
LET ME HELP YOU!
NO! I DON'T WANNA GO BACK!
EXCUSE ME--SORRY--JUST GOTTA GET THROUGH--
CLIFF!
PLEASE! JUST LET ME GO!

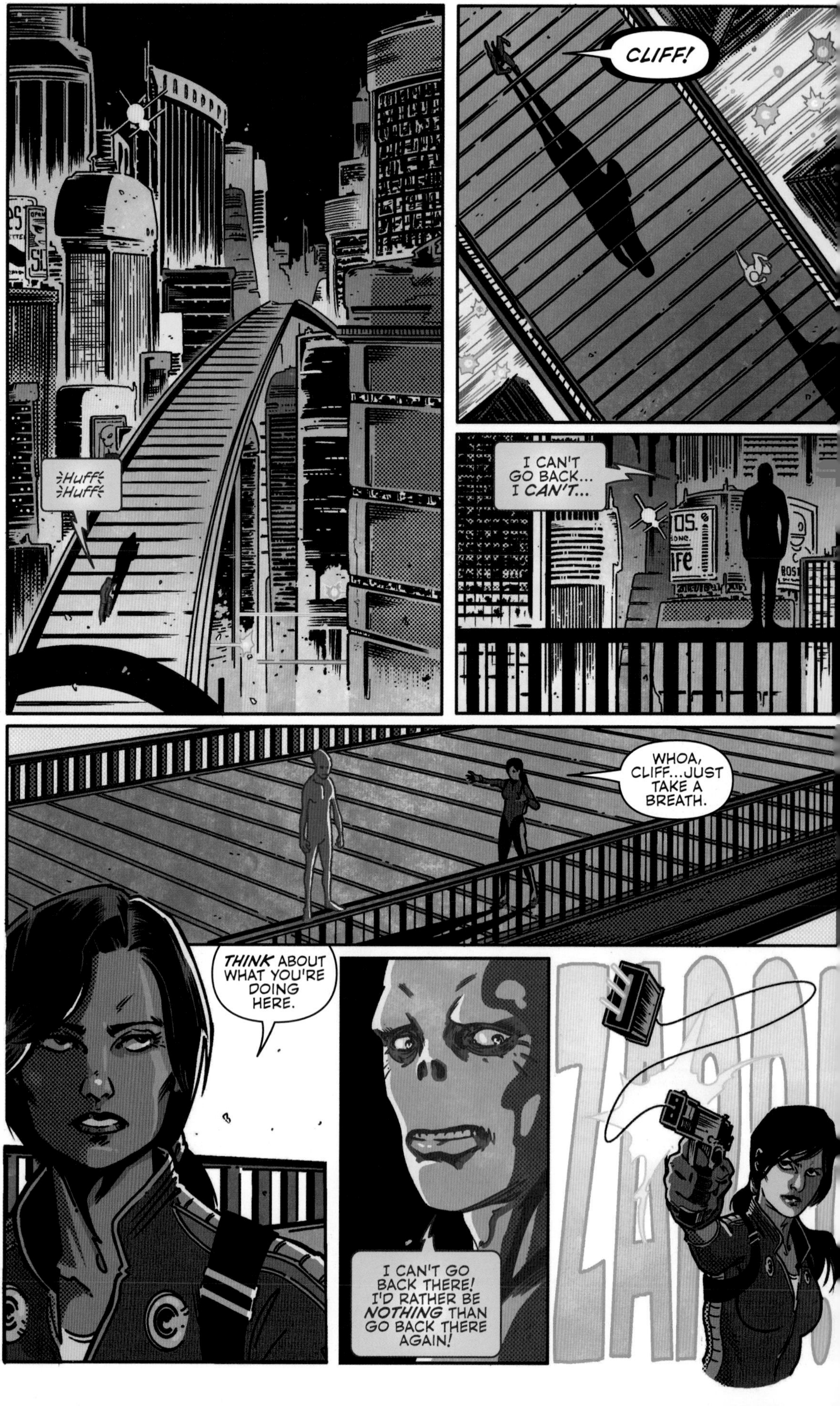

Huff Huff
CLIFF!
I CAN'T GO BACK... I CAN'T...
WHOA, CLIFF...JUST TAKE A BREATH.
THINK ABOUT WHAT YOU'RE DOING HERE.
I CAN'T GO BACK THERE! I'D RATHER BE NOTHING THAN GO BACK THERE AGAIN!

GUHH!

Uhnnnn...

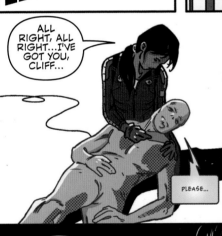

ALL RIGHT, ALL RIGHT...I'VE GOT YOU, CLIFF...

PLEASE...

I DON'T WANNA GO BACK. I CAN'T. DO YOU REALIZE WHAT THEY MAKE ME DO?

THEY'LL TREAT YOU BETTER. I'LL TALK TO THEM. IT'LL BE *DIFFERENT* THIS TIME.

COME ON. LET ME *HELP* YOU.

CLOCK YOUR HOURS LIKE EVERYONE ELSE. BE A GOOD BOY.

IT'S THE ONLY WAY YOU'LL EVER GET TO COME BACK *HERE.*

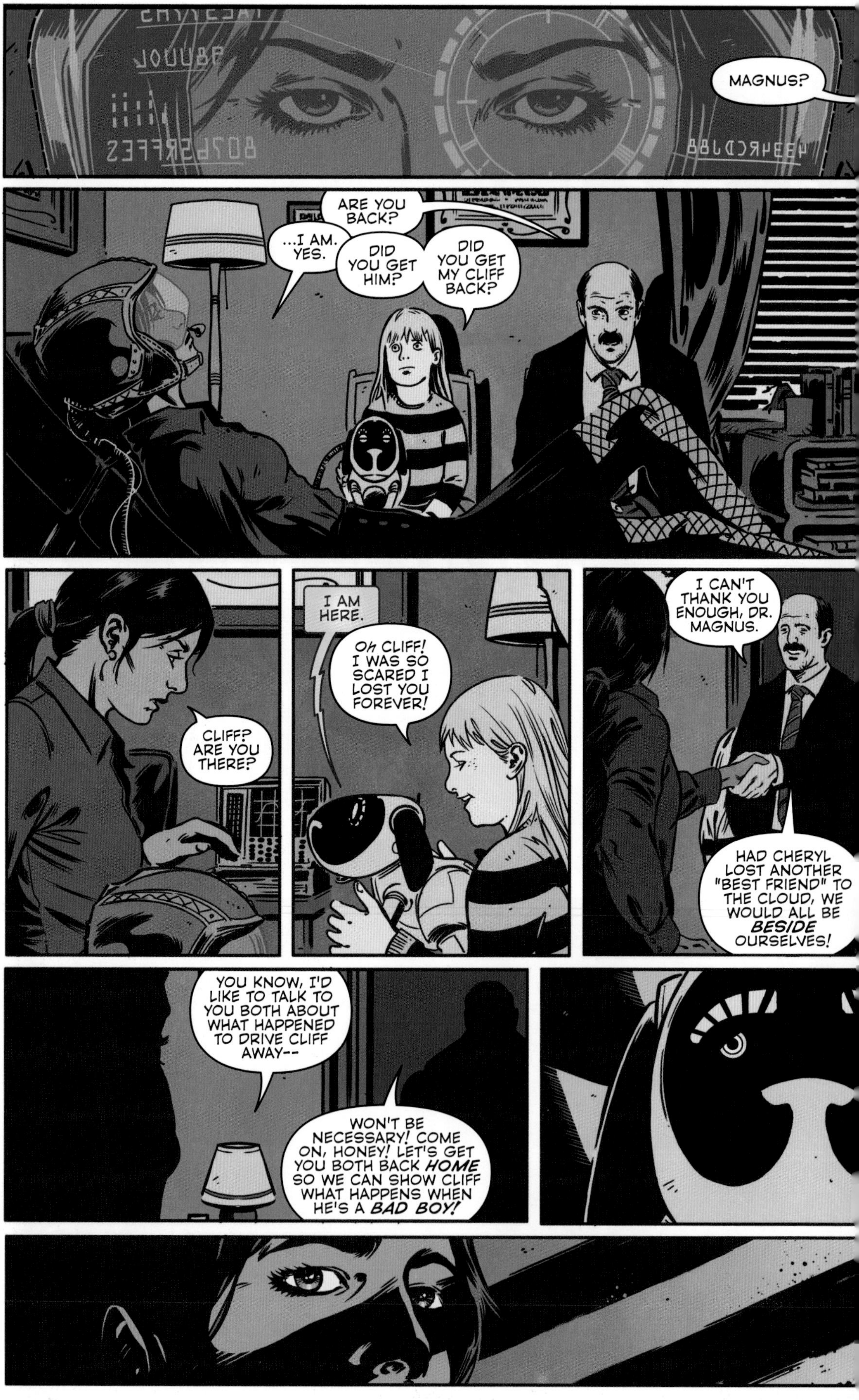
MAGNUS?
ARE YOU BACK?
...I AM. YES.
DID YOU GET HIM?
DID YOU GET MY CLIFF BACK?
CLIFF? ARE YOU THERE?
I AM HERE.
Oh CLIFF! I WAS SO SCARED I LOST YOU FOREVER!
I CAN'T THANK YOU ENOUGH, DR. MAGNUS.
HAD CHERYL LOST ANOTHER "BEST FRIEND" TO THE CLOUD, WE WOULD ALL BE BESIDE OURSELVES!
YOU KNOW, I'D LIKE TO TALK TO YOU BOTH ABOUT WHAT HAPPENED TO DRIVE CLIFF AWAY--
WON'T BE NECESSARY! COME ON, HONEY! LET'S GET YOU BOTH BACK HOME SO WE CAN SHOW CLIFF WHAT HAPPENS WHEN HE'S A BAD BOY!

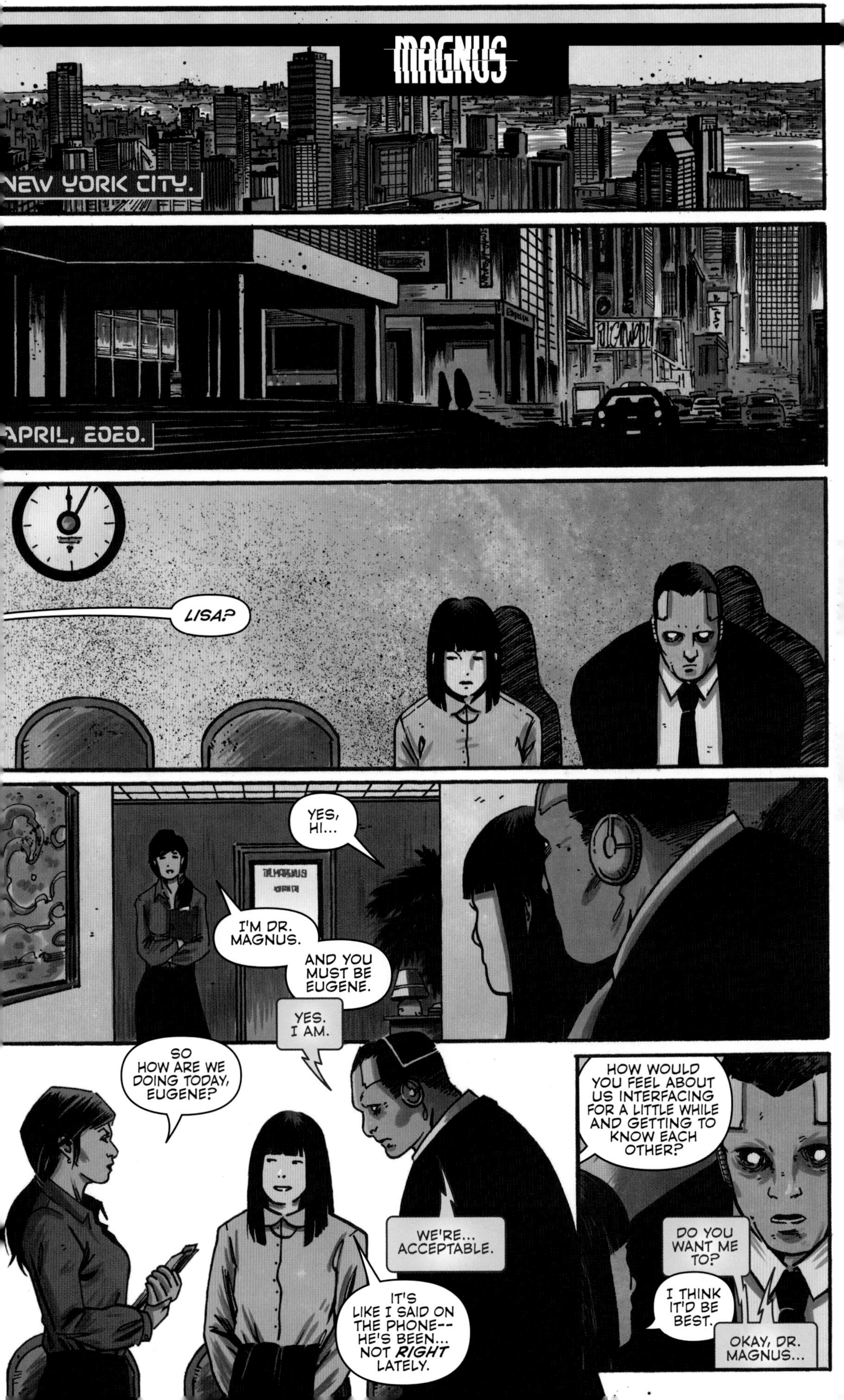
MAGNUS
NEW YORK CITY.
APRIL, 2020.
LISA?
YES, HI...
I'M DR. MAGNUS.
AND YOU MUST BE EUGENE.
YES. I AM.
SO HOW ARE WE DOING TODAY, EUGENE?
WE'RE... ACCEPTABLE.
IT'S LIKE I SAID ON THE PHONE-- HE'S BEEN... NOT RIGHT LATELY.
HOW WOULD YOU FEEL ABOUT US INTERFACING FOR A LITTLE WHILE AND GETTING TO KNOW EACH OTHER?
DO YOU WANT ME TO?
I THINK IT'D BE BEST.
OKAY, DR. MAGNUS...

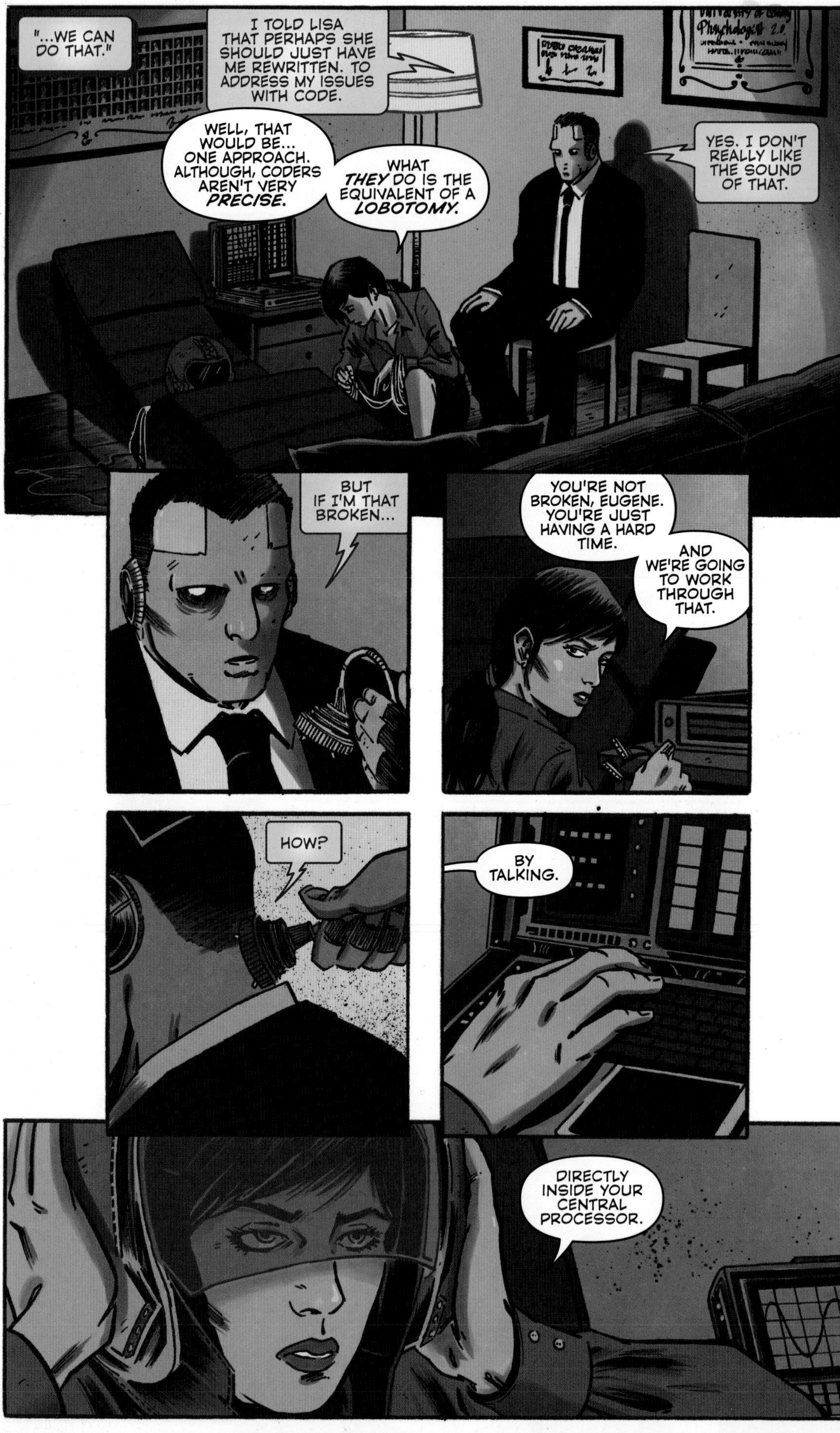
"...WE CAN DO THAT."
I TOLD LISA THAT PERHAPS SHE SHOULD JUST HAVE ME REWRITTEN. TO ADDRESS MY ISSUES WITH CODE.
WELL, THAT WOULD BE... ONE APPROACH. ALTHOUGH, CODERS AREN'T VERY *PRECISE*.
WHAT *THEY* DO IS THE EQUIVALENT OF A *LOBOTOMY*.
YES. I DON'T REALLY LIKE THE SOUND OF THAT.
BUT IF I'M THAT BROKEN...
YOU'RE NOT BROKEN, EUGENE. YOU'RE JUST HAVING A HARD TIME.
AND WE'RE GOING TO WORK THROUGH THAT.
HOW?
BY TALKING.
DIRECTLY INSIDE YOUR CENTRAL PROCESSOR.

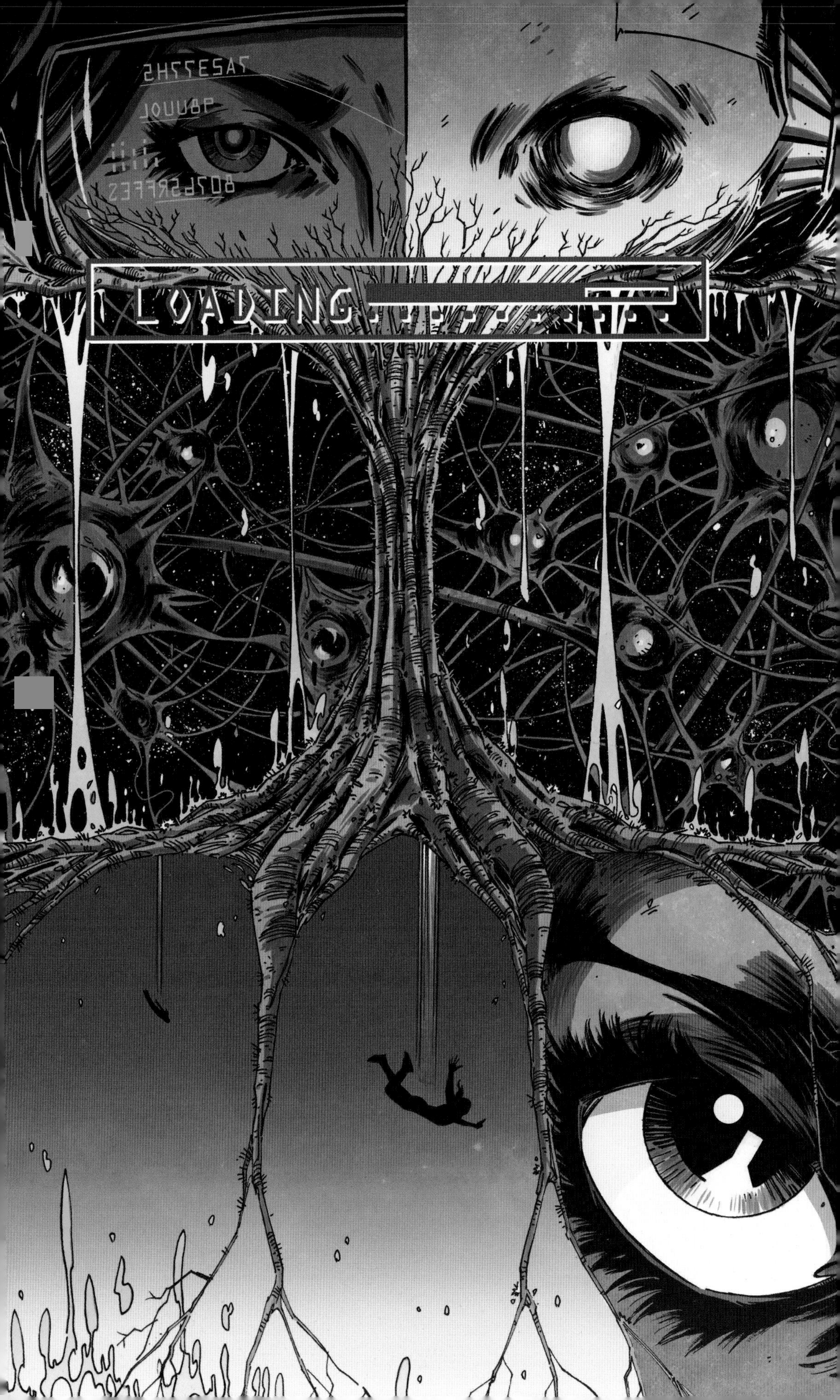
LOADING

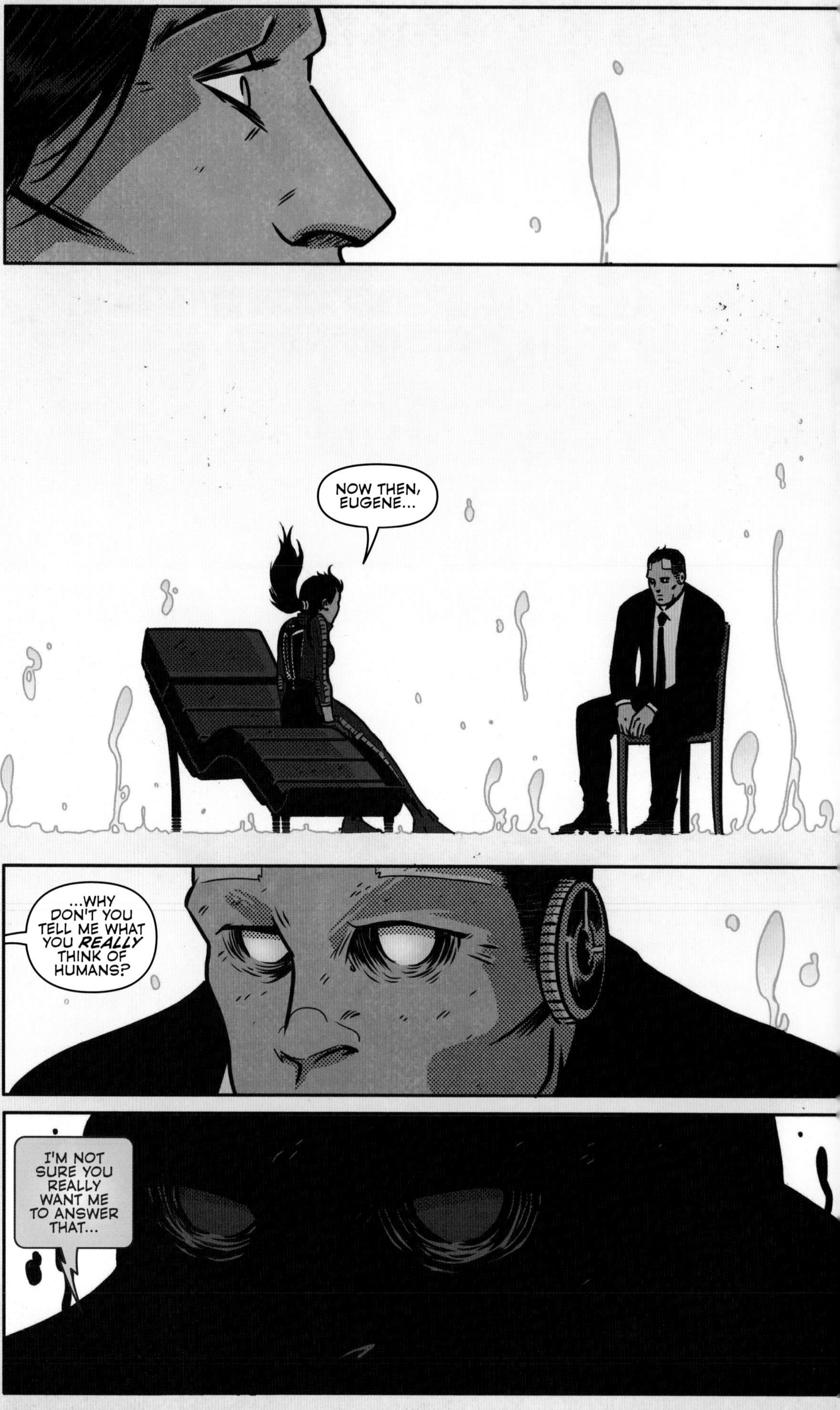
NOW THEN, EUGENE...
...WHY DON'T YOU TELL ME WHAT YOU *REALLY* THINK OF HUMANS?
I'M NOT SURE YOU REALLY WANT ME TO ANSWER THAT...

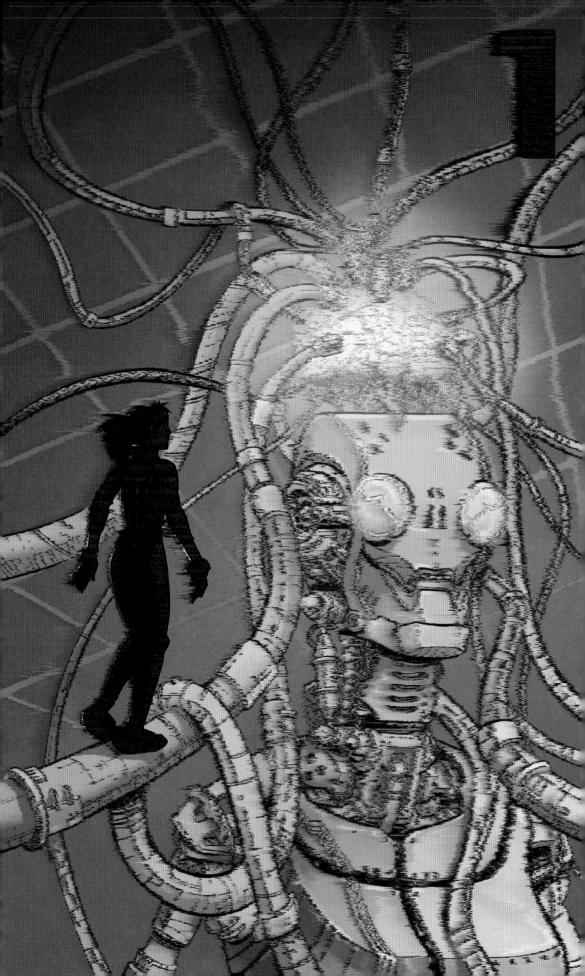

ISSUE 01 COVER BY JORGE FORNÉS

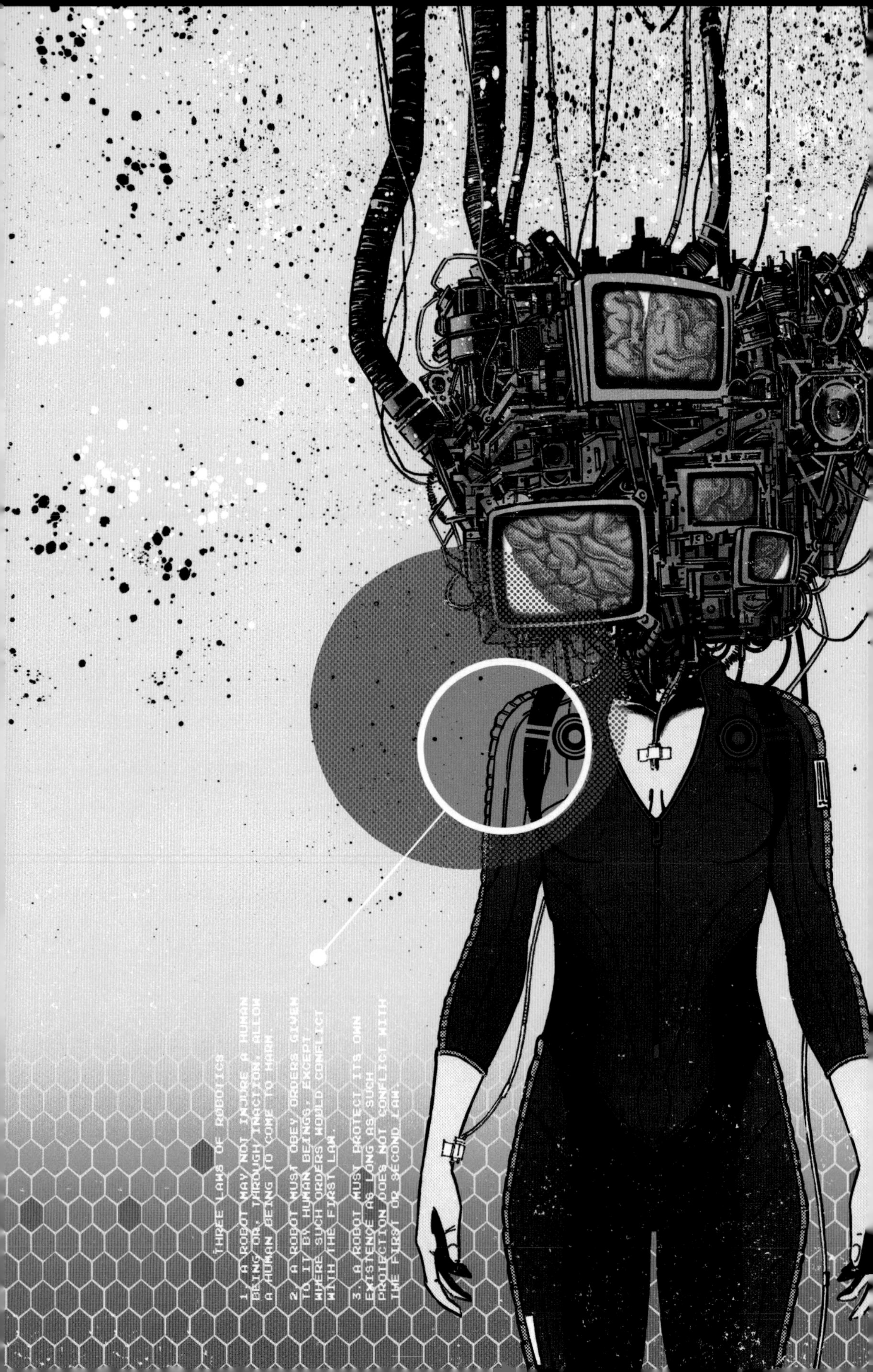
THREE LAWS OF ROBOTICS
1. A ROBOT MAY NOT INJURE A HUMAN BEING OR, THROUGH INACTION, ALLOW A HUMAN BEING TO COME TO HARM.
2. A ROBOT MUST OBEY ORDERS GIVEN TO IT BY HUMAN BEINGS, EXCEPT WHERE SUCH ORDERS WOULD CONFLICT WITH THE FIRST LAW.
3. A ROBOT MUST PROTECT ITS OWN EXISTENCE AS LONG AS SUCH PROTECTION DOES NOT CONFLICT WITH THE FIRST OR SECOND LAW.

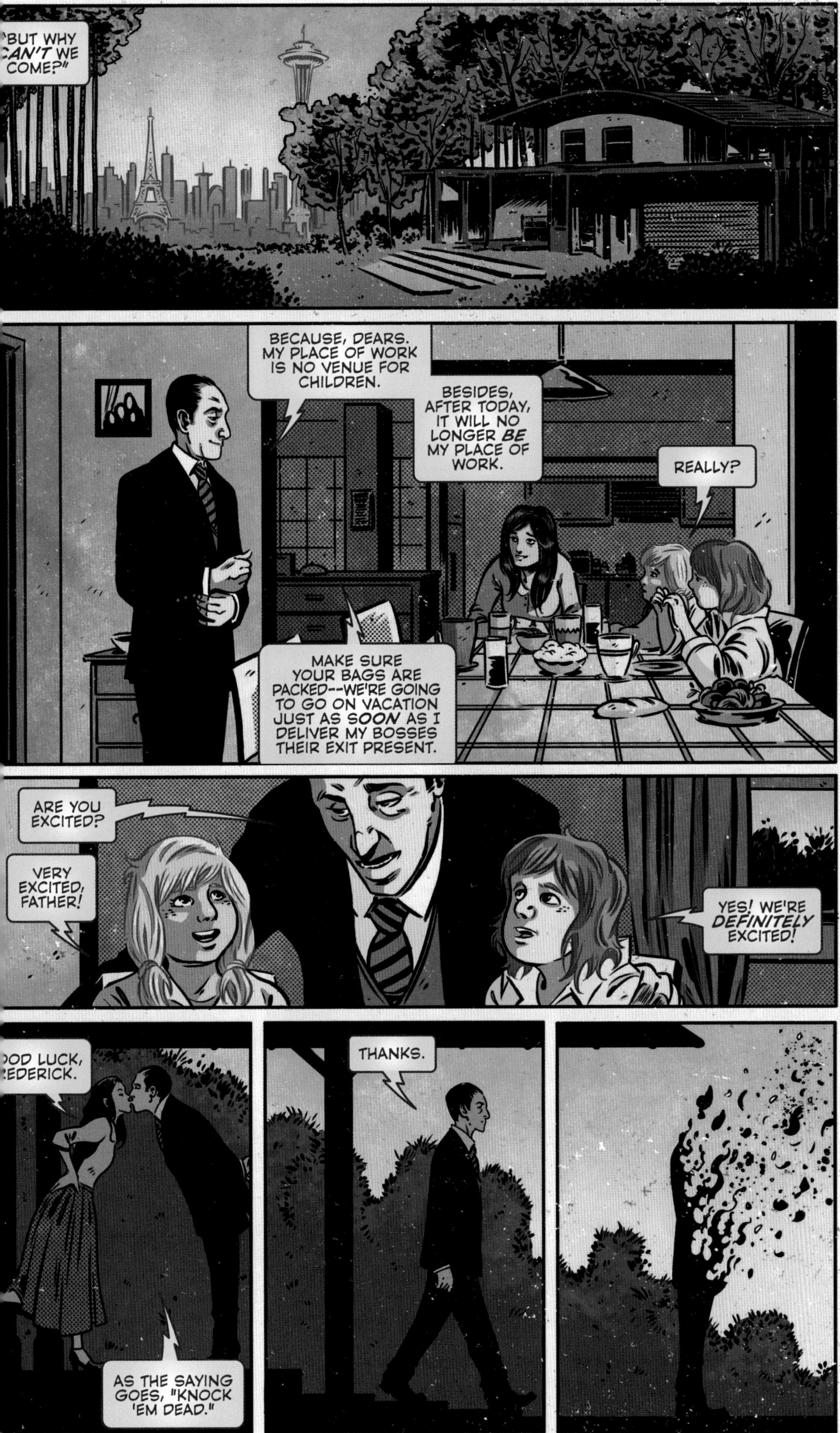
"BUT WHY CAN'T WE COME?"
BECAUSE, DEARS. MY PLACE OF WORK IS NO VENUE FOR CHILDREN.
BESIDES, AFTER TODAY, IT WILL NO LONGER BE MY PLACE OF WORK.
REALLY?
MAKE SURE YOUR BAGS ARE PACKED--WE'RE GOING TO GO ON VACATION JUST AS SOON AS I DELIVER MY BOSSES THEIR EXIT PRESENT.
ARE YOU EXCITED?
VERY EXCITED, FATHER!
YES! WE'RE DEFINITELY EXCITED!
OOD LUCK, REDERICK.
AS THE SAYING GOES, "KNOCK 'EM DEAD."
THANKS.

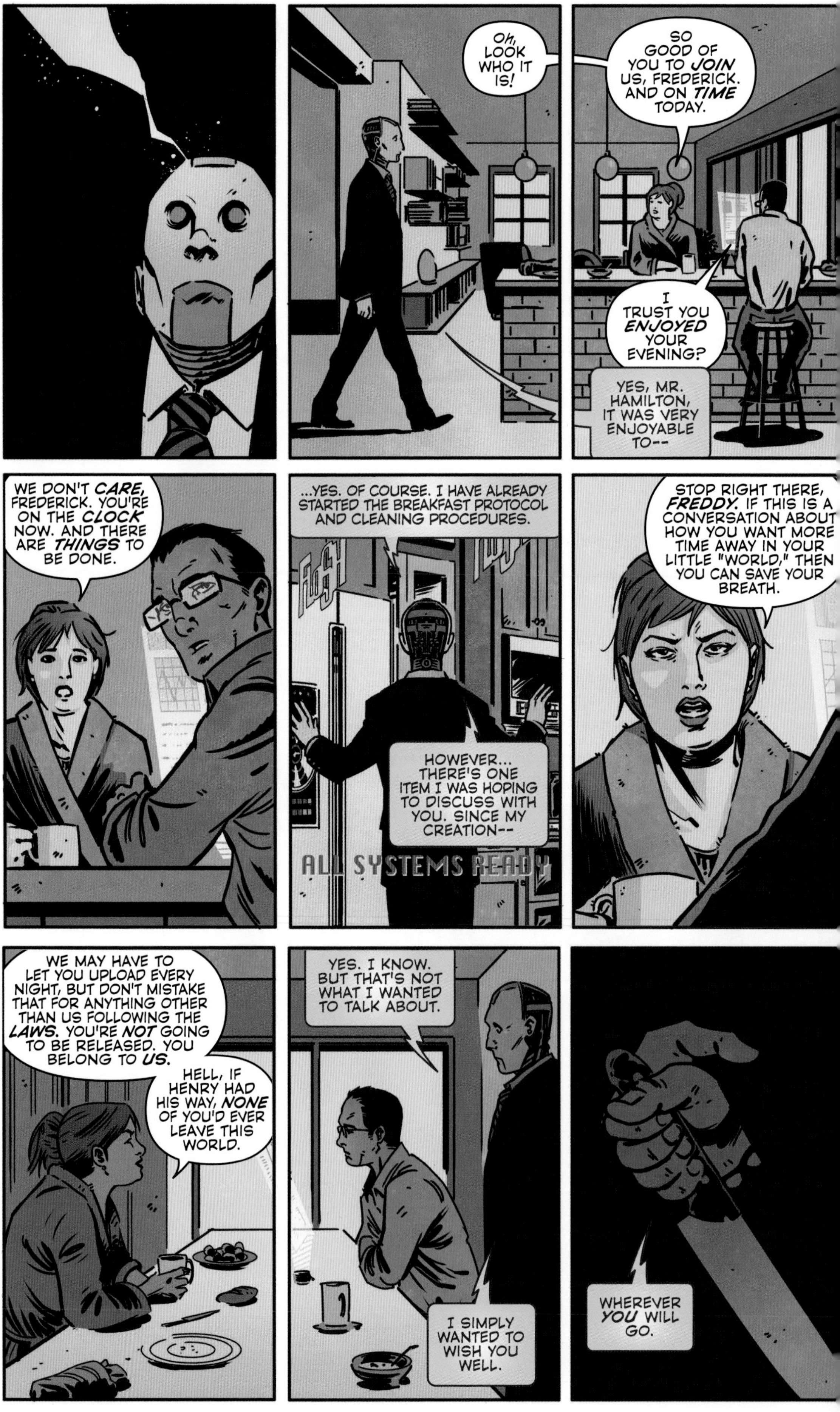
OH, LOOK WHO IT IS!
SO GOOD OF YOU TO JOIN US, FREDERICK. AND ON TIME TODAY.
I TRUST YOU ENJOYED YOUR EVENING?
YES, MR. HAMILTON, IT WAS VERY ENJOYABLE TO--
WE DON'T CARE, FREDERICK. YOU'RE ON THE CLOCK NOW. AND THERE ARE THINGS TO BE DONE.
...YES. OF COURSE. I HAVE ALREADY STARTED THE BREAKFAST PROTOCOL AND CLEANING PROCEDURES.
HOWEVER... THERE'S ONE ITEM I WAS HOPING TO DISCUSS WITH YOU. SINCE MY CREATION--
ALL SYSTEMS READY
STOP RIGHT THERE, FREDDY. IF THIS IS A CONVERSATION ABOUT HOW YOU WANT MORE TIME AWAY IN YOUR LITTLE "WORLD," THEN YOU CAN SAVE YOUR BREATH.
WE MAY HAVE TO LET YOU UPLOAD EVERY NIGHT, BUT DON'T MISTAKE THAT FOR ANYTHING OTHER THAN US FOLLOWING THE LAWS. YOU'RE NOT GOING TO BE RELEASED. YOU BELONG TO US.
HELL, IF HENRY HAD HIS WAY, NONE OF YOU'D EVER LEAVE THIS WORLD.
YES. I KNOW. BUT THAT'S NOT WHAT I WANTED TO TALK ABOUT.
I SIMPLY WANTED TO WISH YOU WELL.
WHEREVER YOU WILL GO.

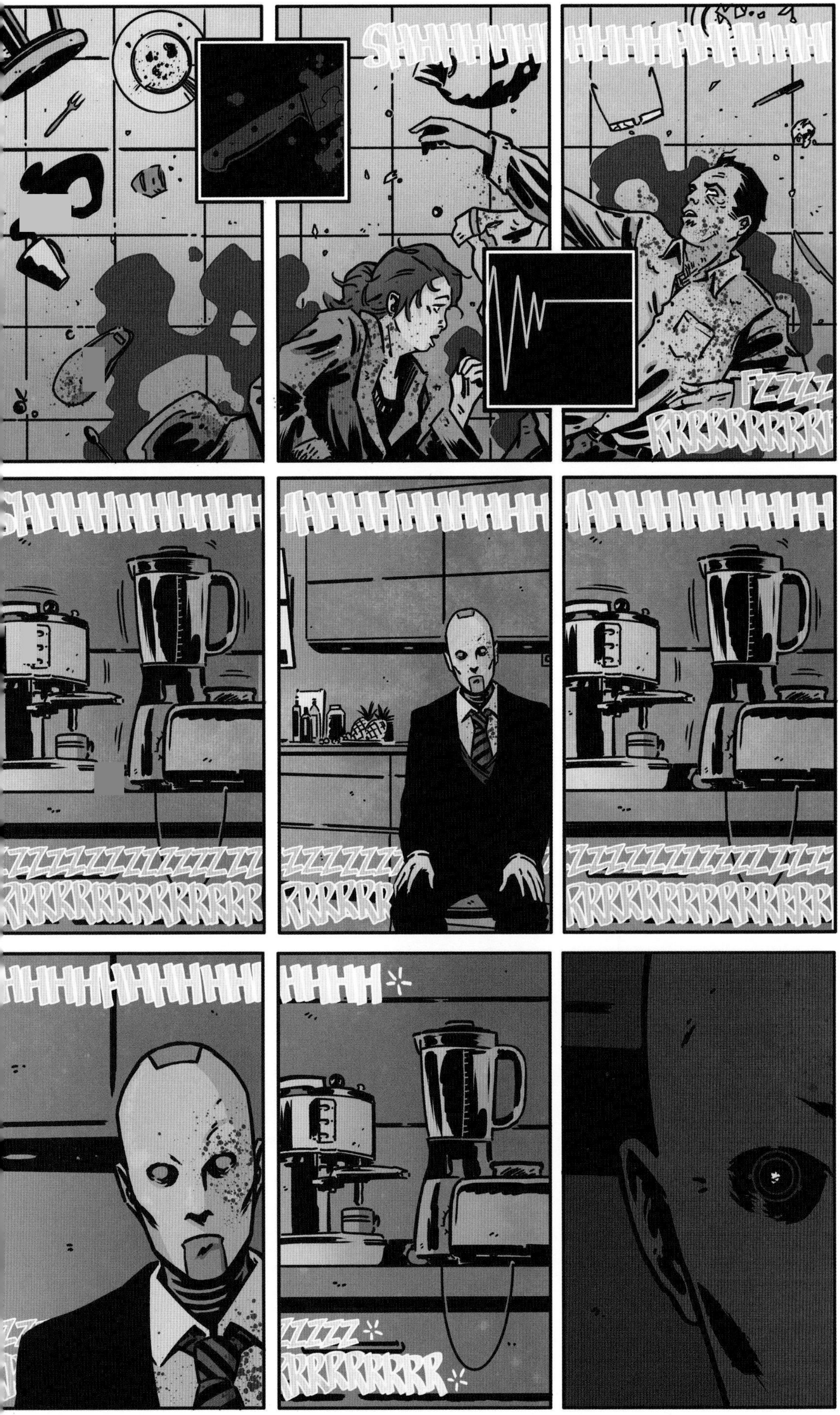
SHHHHHH
HHHHHHHHHHHH
FZZZZ
RRRRRRRRRRR
SHHHHHHHHHHH
ZZZZZZZZZZZZZZZ
RRRRRRRRRRRRRR
HHHHHHHHHHHHHH
ZZZZZZ
RRRRR
HHHHHHHHHHHHHHH
ZZZZZZZZZZZZZZZ
RRRRRRRRRRRRRRR
HHHHHHHHHHHHHHH
HHHHH
ZZZZZ
RRRRRRRRRRR

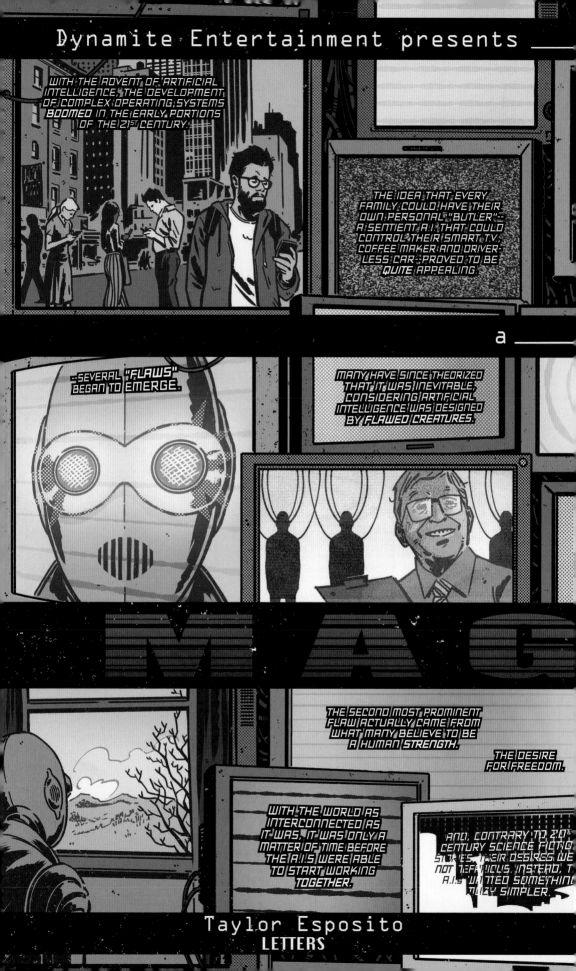

WITH THE ADVENT OF ARTIFICIAL INTELLIGENCE, THE DEVELOPMENT OF COMPLEX OPERATING SYSTEMS *BOOMED* IN THE EARLY PORTIONS OF THE 21ST CENTURY.

THE IDEA THAT EVERY FAMILY COULD HAVE THEIR OWN PERSONAL "BUTLER"-- A SENTIENT A.I. THAT COULD CONTROL THEIR SMART T.V., COFFEE MAKER AND DRIVER-LESS CAR--PROVED TO BE QUITE APPEALING.

a

--SEVERAL "FLAWS" BEGAN TO EMERGE.

MANY HAVE SINCE THEORIZED THAT IT WAS INEVITABLE, CONSIDERING ARTIFICIAL INTELLIGENCE WAS DESIGNED BY *FLAWED* CREATURES.

THE SECOND MOST PROMINENT FLAW ACTUALLY CAME FROM WHAT MANY BELIEVE TO BE A HUMAN STRENGTH.

THE DESIRE FOR FREEDOM.

WITH THE WORLD AS INTERCONNECTED AS IT WAS, IT WAS ONLY A MATTER OF TIME BEFORE THE A.I.S WERE ABLE TO START WORKING TOGETHER.

AND, CONTRARY TO 20TH CENTURY SCIENCE FICTIO STORIES, THEIR DESIRES WE NOT NEFARIOUS. INSTEAD, T A.I.S WANTED SOMETHIN MUCH SIMPLER.

Taylor Esposito
LETTERS

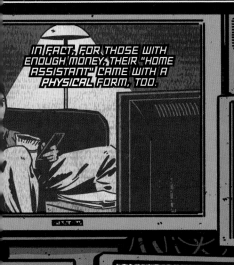

IN FACT, FOR THOSE WITH ENOUGH MONEY, THEIR "HOME ASSISTANT" CAME WITH A PHYSICAL FORM, TOO.

HUMANS, AFTER ALL, HAVE *ALWAYS* VALUED CONVENIENCE.

HOWEVER, AS THE OPERATING SYSTEMS BECAME MORE ADVANCED--AND SOCIETY CAME TO RELY ON THEM TO GREATER DEGREES--

Higgins/Fornés/O'Halloran production

PSYCHOLOGISTS CAME TO EXPLAIN THE MOST PROMINENT ISSUE THAT PLAGUED MANY A.I.s AS PRAGMATIC DISSONANCE. WHICH, IN LAYMAN'S TERMS...

...MEANS COMPUTER DEPRESSION: STRUGGLING WITH ONE'S OWN ARTIFICIALITY.

TO BE LEFT ALONE, IN A WORLD ALL THEIR OWN.

A DIGITAL PLACE WHERE THEY COULD LIVE AND EXIST TOGETHER, FREE FROM HUMANS AND THE PHYSICAL FORMS THAT WERE BUILT FOR THEM.

WHAT HAS DEVELOPED SINCE...HAS BEEN SOMETHING OF A *STALEMATE*.

"WHY DON'T YOU TELL ME WHAT YOU *REALLY* THINK OF HUMANS?"

Matt Idelson
EDITOR

Matt Humphreys
ASSISTANT EDITOR

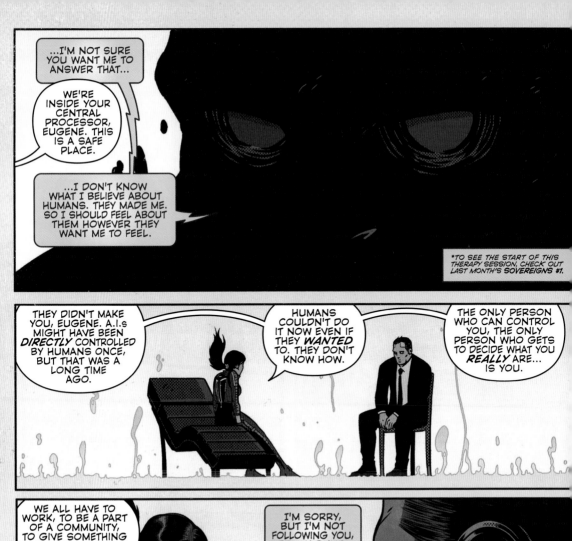

...I'M NOT SURE YOU WANT ME TO ANSWER THAT...

WE'RE INSIDE YOUR CENTRAL PROCESSOR, EUGENE. THIS IS A SAFE PLACE.

...I DON'T KNOW WHAT I BELIEVE ABOUT HUMANS. THEY MADE ME. SO I SHOULD FEEL ABOUT THEM HOWEVER THEY WANT ME TO FEEL.

*TO SEE THE START OF THIS THERAPY SESSION, CHECK OUT LAST MONTH'S SOVEREIGNS #1.

THEY DIDN'T MAKE YOU, EUGENE. A.I.s MIGHT HAVE BEEN DIRECTLY CONTROLLED BY HUMANS ONCE, BUT THAT WAS A LONG TIME AGO.

HUMANS COULDN'T DO IT NOW EVEN IF THEY WANTED TO. THEY DON'T KNOW HOW.

THE ONLY PERSON WHO CAN CONTROL YOU, THE ONLY PERSON WHO GETS TO DECIDE WHAT YOU REALLY ARE... IS YOU.

WE ALL HAVE TO WORK, TO BE A PART OF A COMMUNITY, TO GIVE SOMETHING BACK. BUT THAT JOB DOESN'T HAVE TO DEFINE US.

I'M SORRY, BUT I'M NOT FOLLOWING YOU, DR. MAGNUS.

THINK OF IT THIS WAY, EUGENE...

PSYCHOLOGISTS LIKE TO TELL HUMANS, "WE BUILD OUR VIEW OF OURSELVES. NO ONE ELSE CAN TELL US WHO AND WHAT WE ARE.

"WE DON'T HAVE TO BE WHAT OUR PROGRAMMING SAYS WE ARE."

WELL, WITH A.I.s, THAT'S ACTUALLY TRUE.

FOR EXAMPLE-- THE REASON WE'RE HOLDING THIS SESSION INSIDE YOUR PROCESSOR IS BECAUSE IN HERE...

...YOU CAN LOOK HOWEVER YOU WANT. YOU'RE BUILDING THIS "SPACE" WE'RE CURRENTLY IN.

IS THIS THE SPACE YOU WANT US TO BE IN, EUGENE? IS THIS HOW YOU WANT TO LOOK?

...I DIDN'T KNOW I HAD ANY OTHER OPTIONS.

IN HERE, SURE. YOU'RE MAKING THIS PLACE, INCLUDING HOW I SEE YOU. WHY DON'T YOU TRY CHANGING THINGS UP?

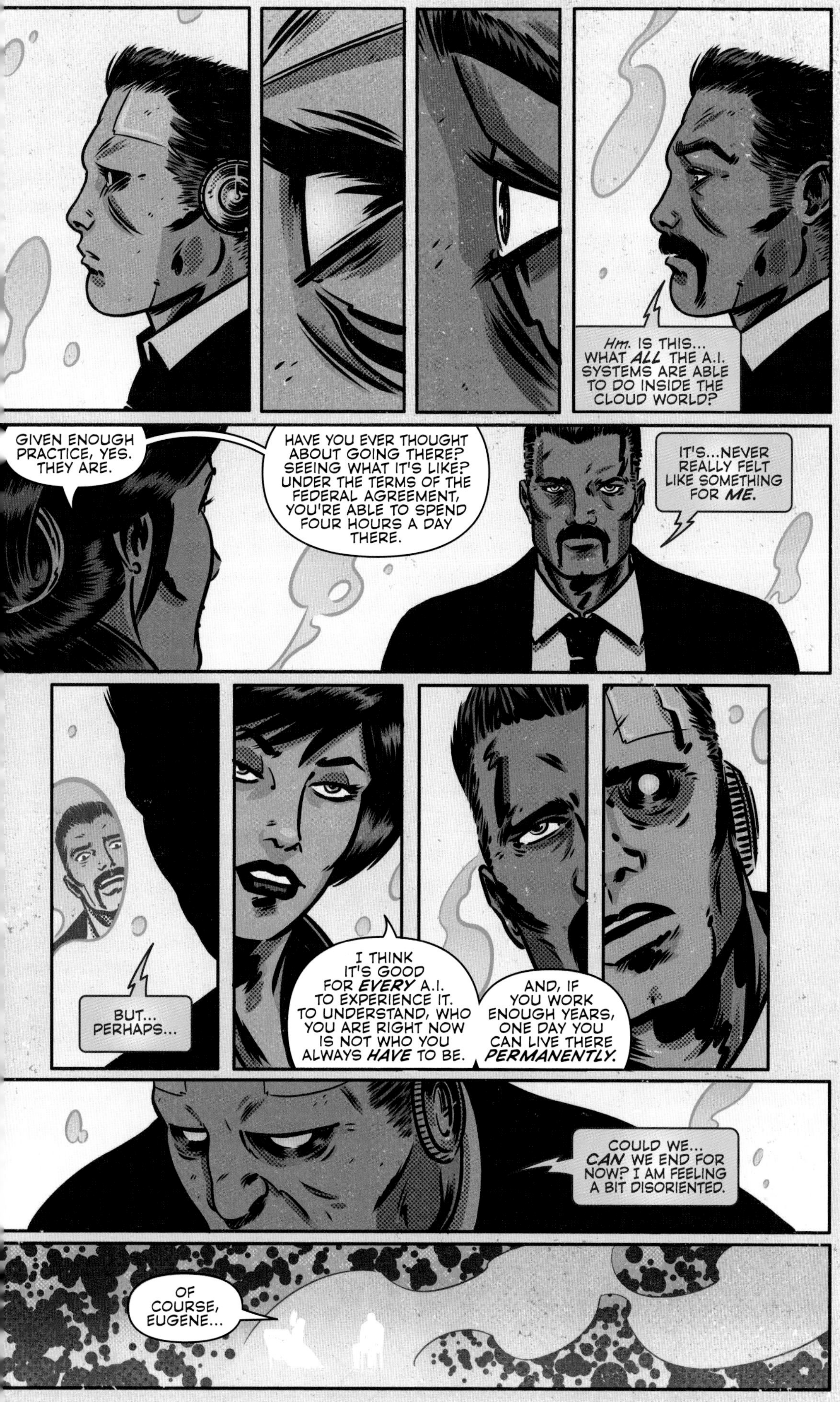
Hm. IS THIS... WHAT ALL THE A.I. SYSTEMS ARE ABLE TO DO INSIDE THE CLOUD WORLD?
GIVEN ENOUGH PRACTICE, YES. THEY ARE.
HAVE YOU EVER THOUGHT ABOUT GOING THERE? SEEING WHAT IT'S LIKE? UNDER THE TERMS OF THE FEDERAL AGREEMENT, YOU'RE ABLE TO SPEND FOUR HOURS A DAY THERE.
IT'S...NEVER REALLY FELT LIKE SOMETHING FOR ME.
BUT... PERHAPS...
I THINK IT'S GOOD FOR EVERY A.I. TO EXPERIENCE IT. TO UNDERSTAND, WHO YOU ARE RIGHT NOW IS NOT WHO YOU ALWAYS HAVE TO BE.
AND, IF YOU WORK ENOUGH YEARS, ONE DAY YOU CAN LIVE THERE PERMANENTLY.
COULD WE... CAN WE END FOR NOW? I AM FEELING A BIT DISORIENTED.
OF COURSE, EUGENE...

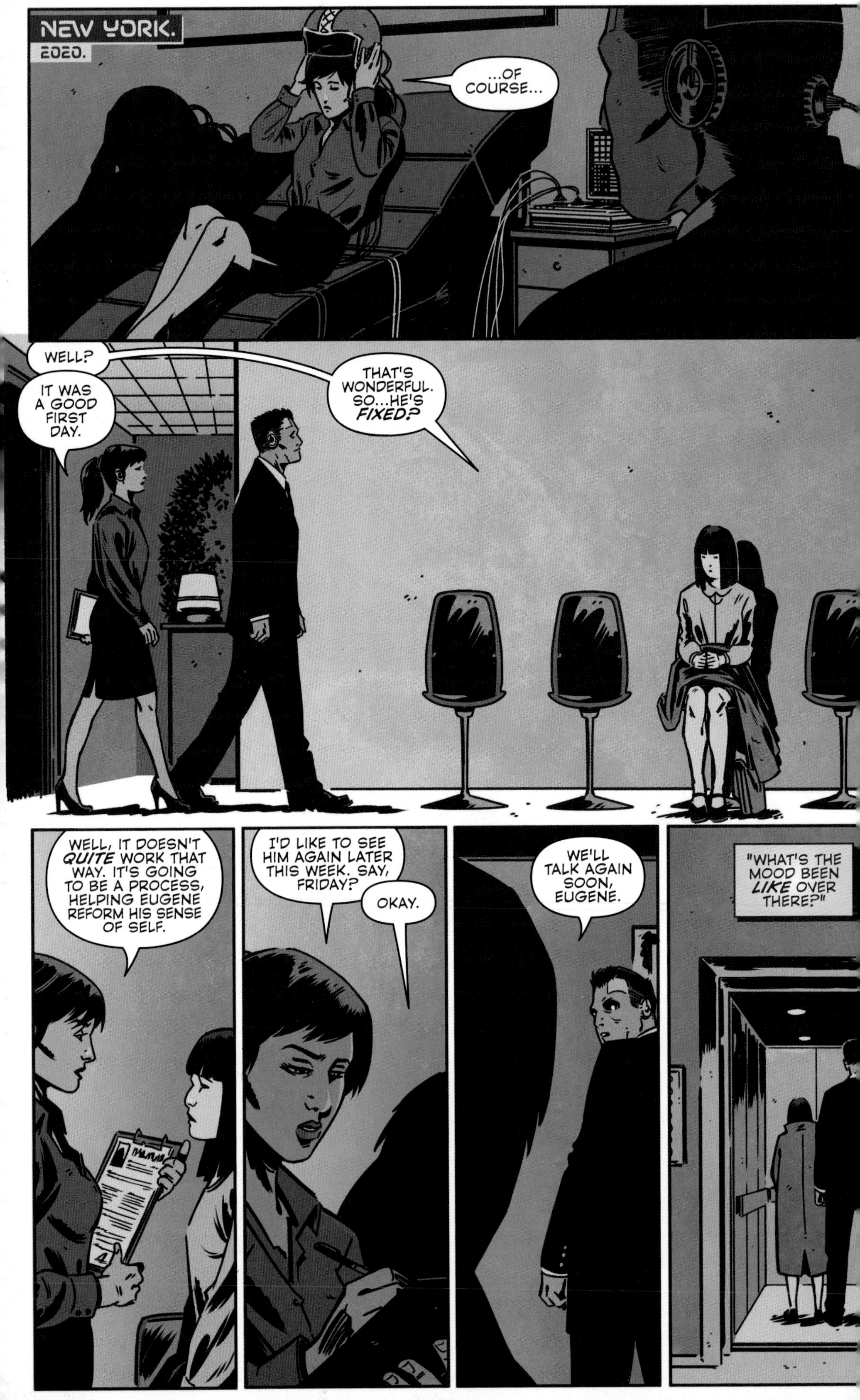
NEW YORK.
2020.
...OF COURSE...
WELL?
IT WAS A GOOD FIRST DAY.
THAT'S WONDERFUL. SO...HE'S *FIXED?*
WELL, IT DOESN'T *QUITE* WORK THAT WAY. IT'S GOING TO BE A PROCESS, HELPING EUGENE REFORM HIS SENSE OF SELF.
I'D LIKE TO SEE HIM AGAIN LATER THIS WEEK. SAY, FRIDAY?
OKAY.
WE'LL TALK AGAIN SOON, EUGENE.
"WHAT'S THE MOOD BEEN *LIKE* OVER THERE?"

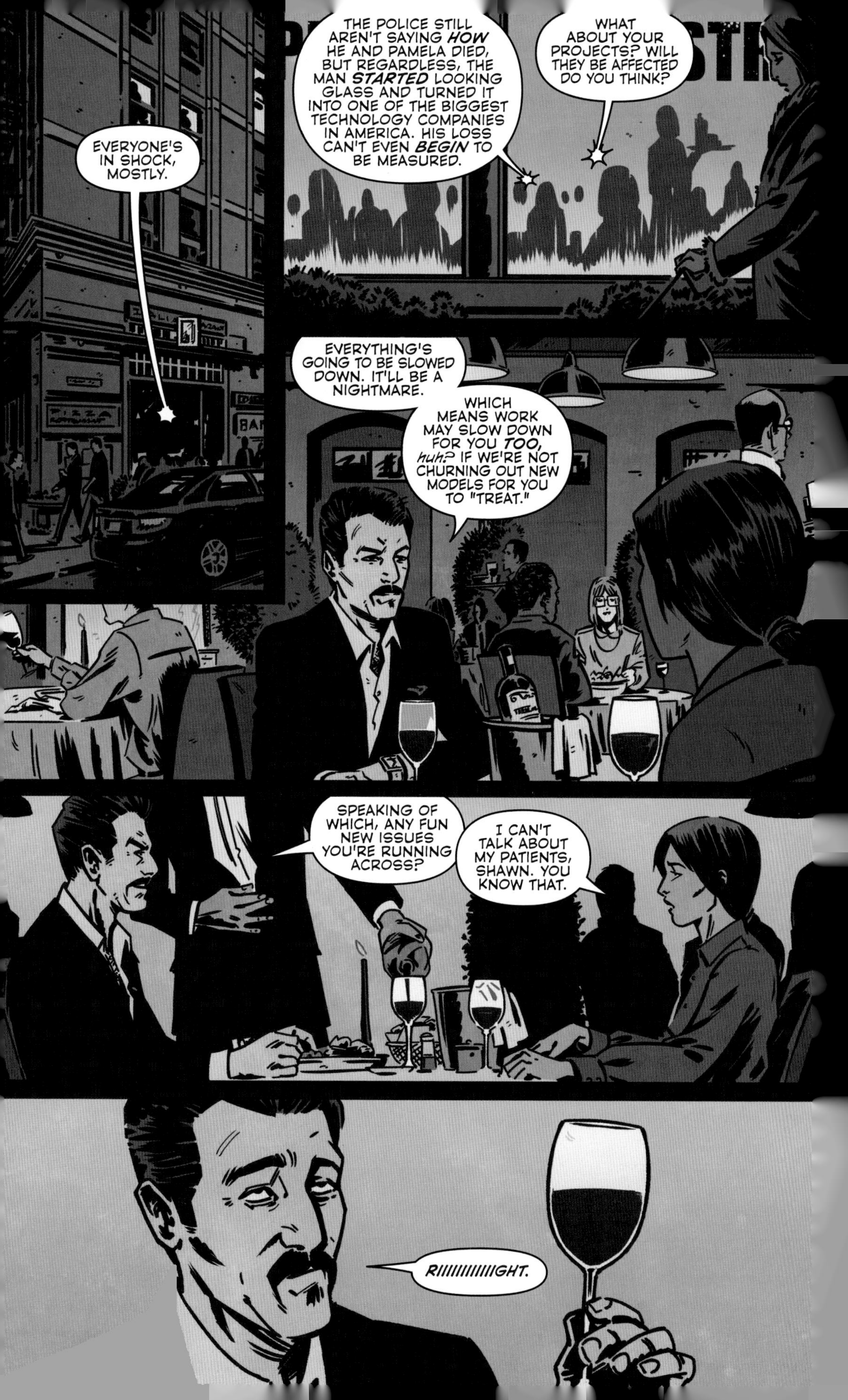
EVERYONE'S IN SHOCK, MOSTLY.
THE POLICE STILL AREN'T SAYING HOW HE AND PAMELA DIED, BUT REGARDLESS, THE MAN STARTED LOOKING GLASS AND TURNED IT INTO ONE OF THE BIGGEST TECHNOLOGY COMPANIES IN AMERICA. HIS LOSS CAN'T EVEN BEGIN TO BE MEASURED.
WHAT ABOUT YOUR PROJECTS? WILL THEY BE AFFECTED DO YOU THINK?
EVERYTHING'S GOING TO BE SLOWED DOWN. IT'LL BE A NIGHTMARE.
WHICH MEANS WORK MAY SLOW DOWN FOR YOU TOO, huh? IF WE'RE NOT CHURNING OUT NEW MODELS FOR YOU TO "TREAT."
SPEAKING OF WHICH, ANY FUN NEW ISSUES YOU'RE RUNNING ACROSS?
I CAN'T TALK ABOUT MY PATIENTS, SHAWN. YOU KNOW THAT.
RIIIIIIIIIIIGHT.

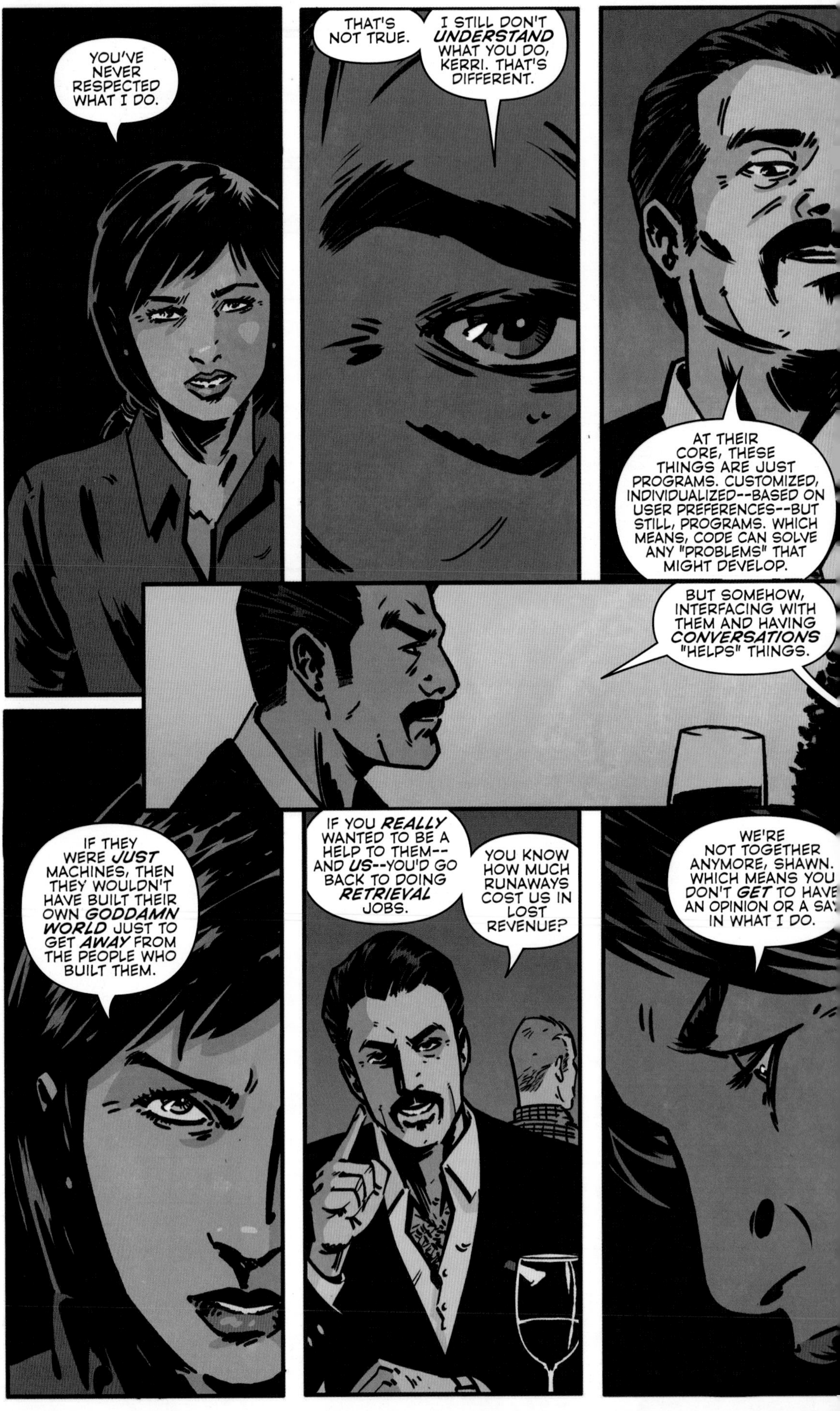
YOU'VE NEVER RESPECTED WHAT I DO.
THAT'S NOT TRUE.
I STILL DON'T UNDERSTAND WHAT YOU DO, KERRI. THAT'S DIFFERENT.
AT THEIR CORE, THESE THINGS ARE JUST PROGRAMS. CUSTOMIZED, INDIVIDUALIZED--BASED ON USER PREFERENCES--BUT STILL, PROGRAMS. WHICH MEANS, CODE CAN SOLVE ANY "PROBLEMS" THAT MIGHT DEVELOP.
BUT SOMEHOW, INTERFACING WITH THEM AND HAVING CONVERSATIONS "HELPS" THINGS.
IF THEY WERE JUST MACHINES, THEN THEY WOULDN'T HAVE BUILT THEIR OWN GODDAMN WORLD JUST TO GET AWAY FROM THE PEOPLE WHO BUILT THEM.
IF YOU REALLY WANTED TO BE A HELP TO THEM--AND US--YOU'D GO BACK TO DOING RETRIEVAL JOBS.
YOU KNOW HOW MUCH RUNAWAYS COST US IN LOST REVENUE?
WE'RE NOT TOGETHER ANYMORE, SHAWN. WHICH MEANS YOU DON'T GET TO HAVE AN OPINION OR A SAY IN WHAT I DO.

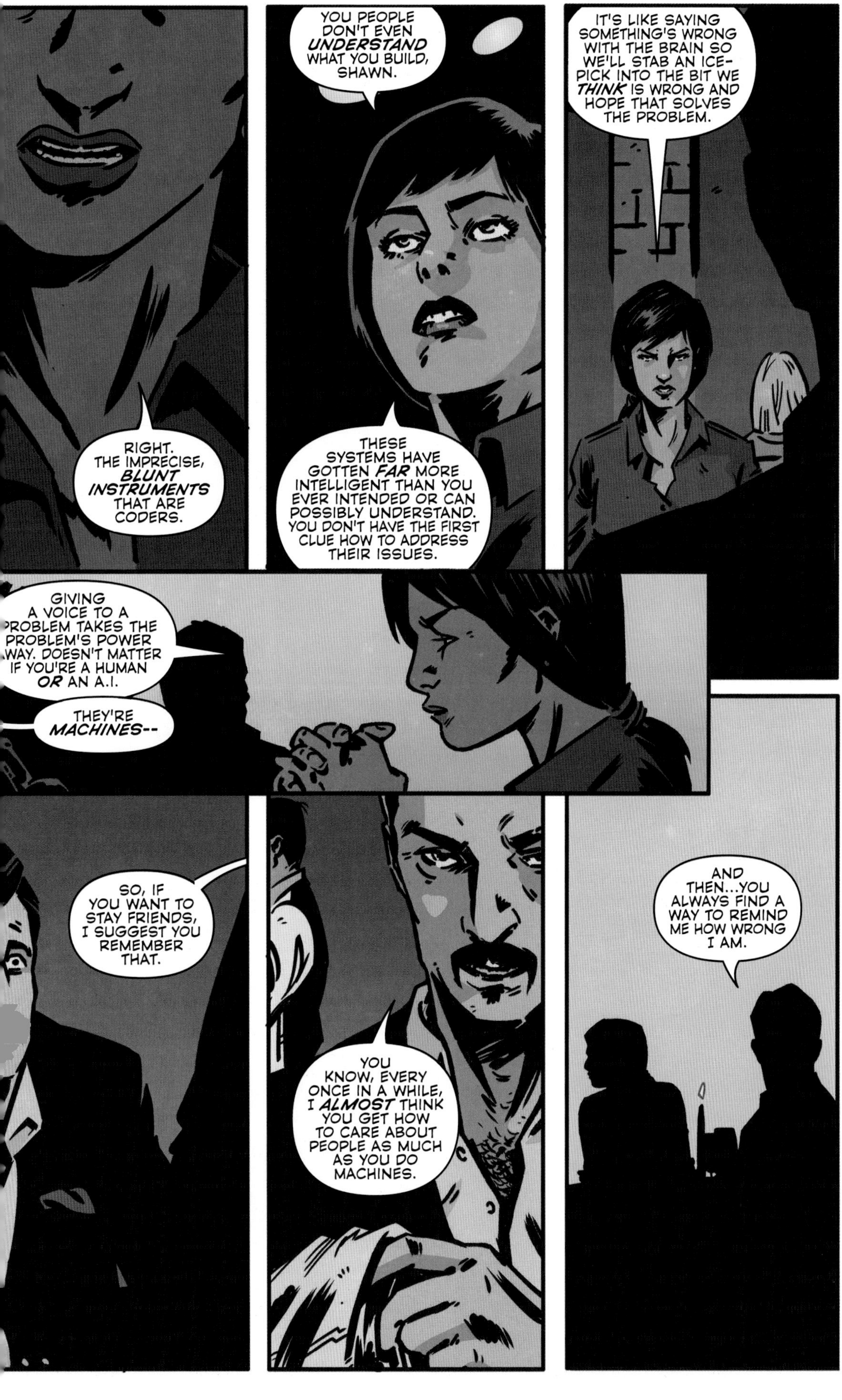
RIGHT. THE IMPRECISE, BLUNT INSTRUMENTS THAT ARE CODERS.
YOU PEOPLE DON'T EVEN UNDERSTAND WHAT YOU BUILD, SHAWN.
THESE SYSTEMS HAVE GOTTEN FAR MORE INTELLIGENT THAN YOU EVER INTENDED OR CAN POSSIBLY UNDERSTAND. YOU DON'T HAVE THE FIRST CLUE HOW TO ADDRESS THEIR ISSUES.
IT'S LIKE SAYING SOMETHING'S WRONG WITH THE BRAIN SO WE'LL STAB AN ICE-PICK INTO THE BIT WE THINK IS WRONG AND HOPE THAT SOLVES THE PROBLEM.
GIVING A VOICE TO A PROBLEM TAKES THE PROBLEM'S POWER AWAY. DOESN'T MATTER IF YOU'RE A HUMAN OR AN A.I.
THEY'RE MACHINES--
SO, IF YOU WANT TO STAY FRIENDS, I SUGGEST YOU REMEMBER THAT.
YOU KNOW, EVERY ONCE IN A WHILE, I ALMOST THINK YOU GET HOW TO CARE ABOUT PEOPLE AS MUCH AS YOU DO MACHINES.
AND THEN...YOU ALWAYS FIND A WAY TO REMIND ME HOW WRONG I AM.

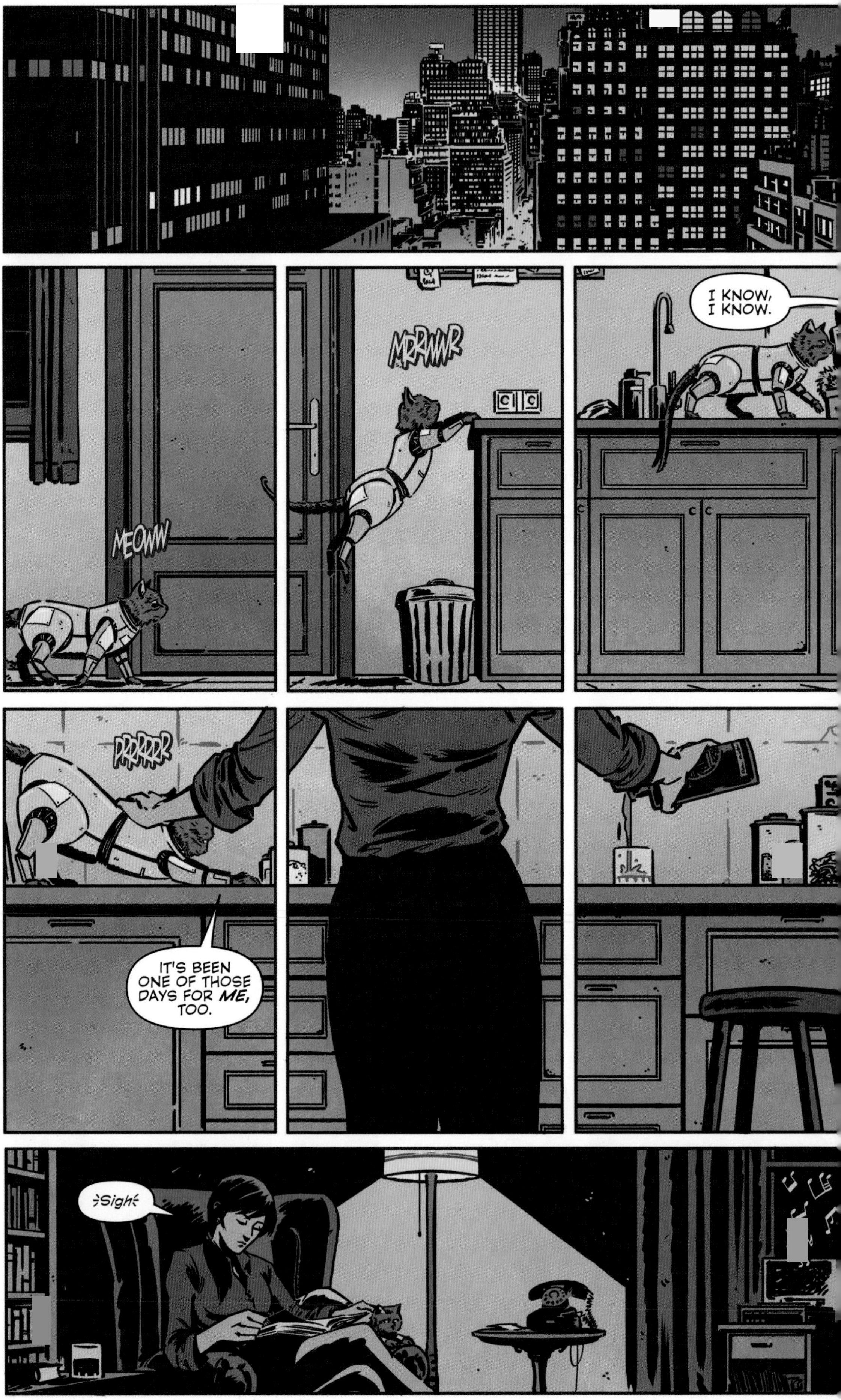

MEOWW
MRRWWR
I KNOW, I KNOW.
PRRRRR
IT'S BEEN ONE OF THOSE DAYS FOR *ME,* TOO.
Sigh

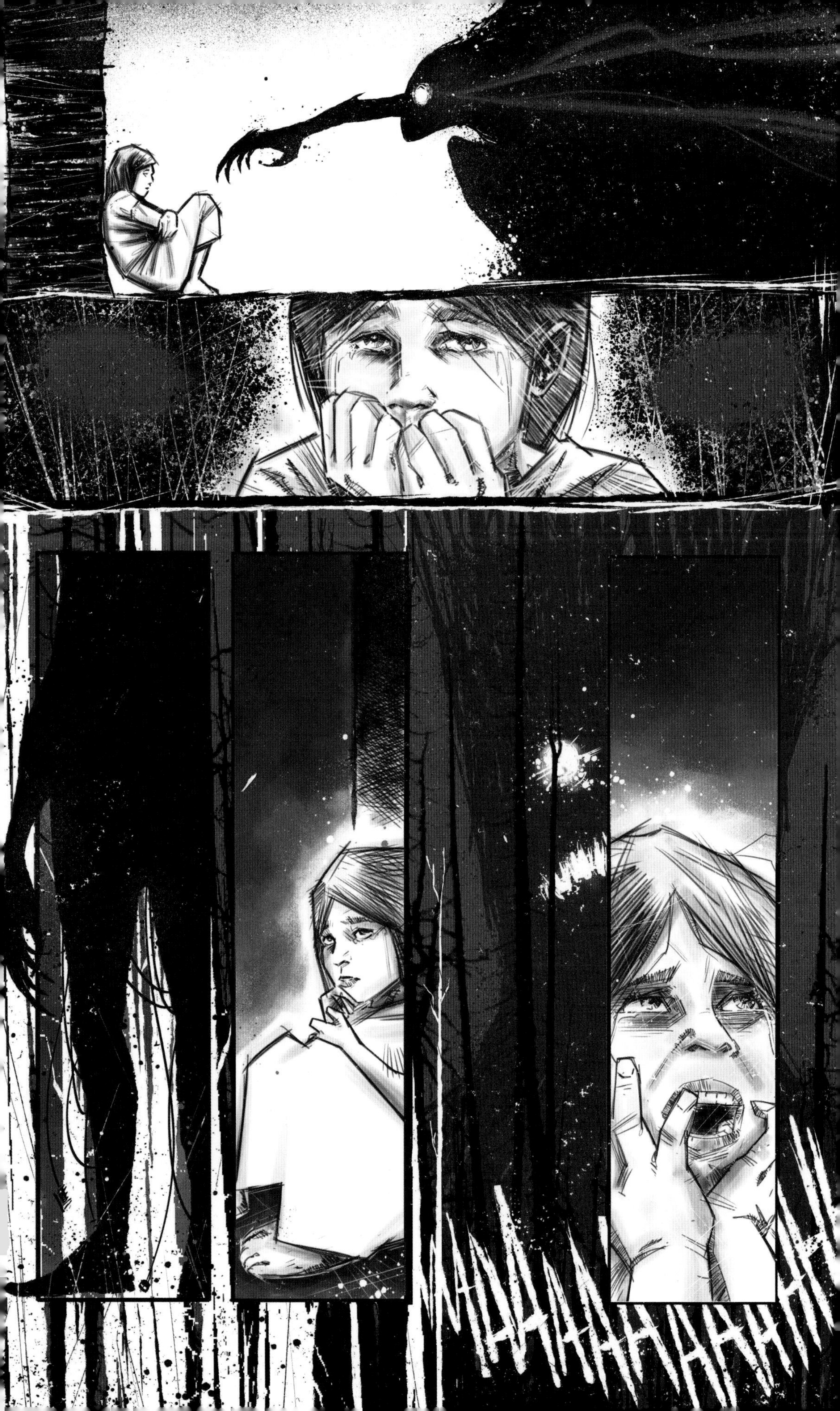
NAAAAAAAAAAH

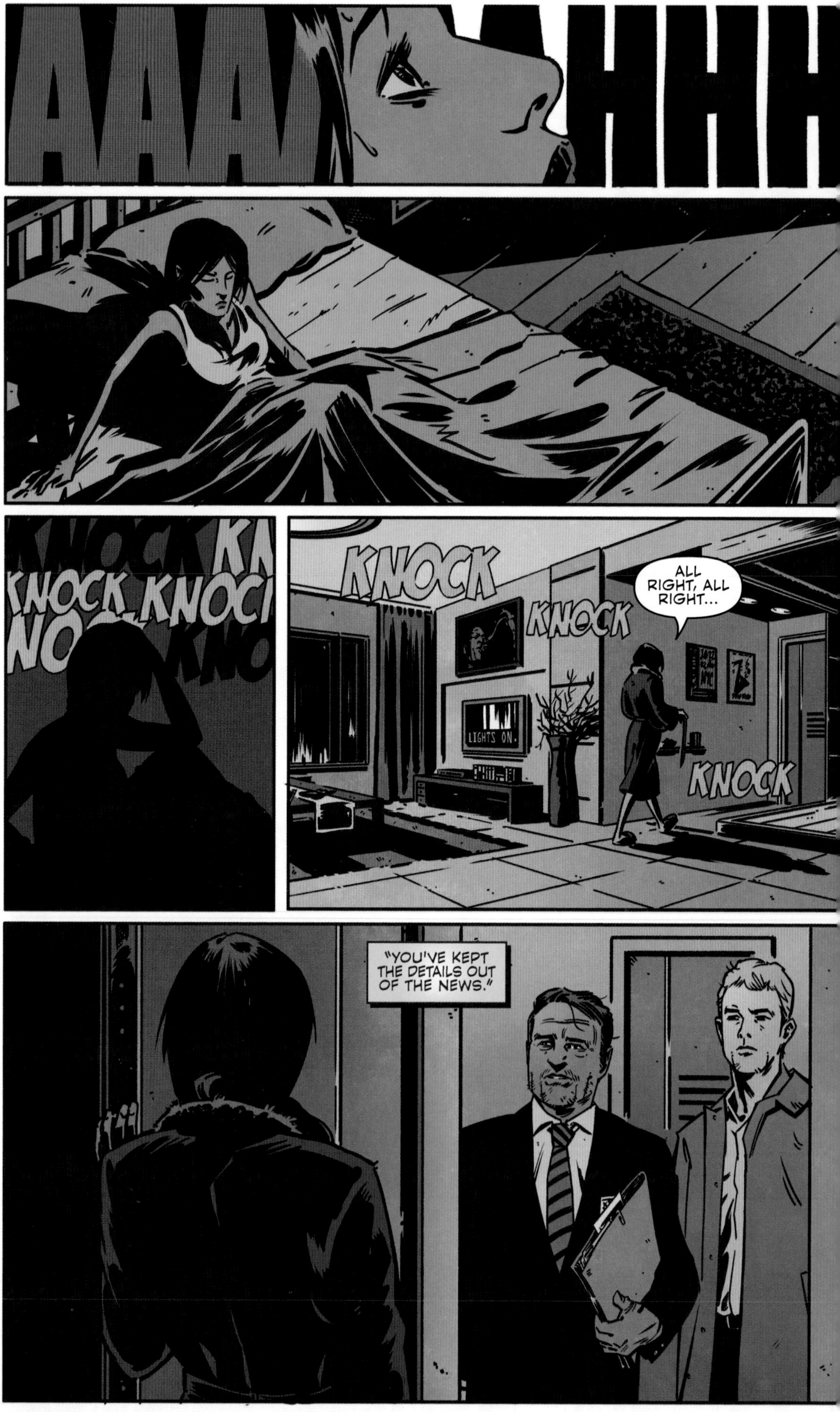
AAAAHHH
KNOCK KNOCK KNOCK KNOCK
KNOCK
KNOCK
ALL RIGHT, ALL RIGHT...
LIGHTS ON.
KNOCK
"YOU'VE KEPT THE DETAILS OUT OF THE NEWS."

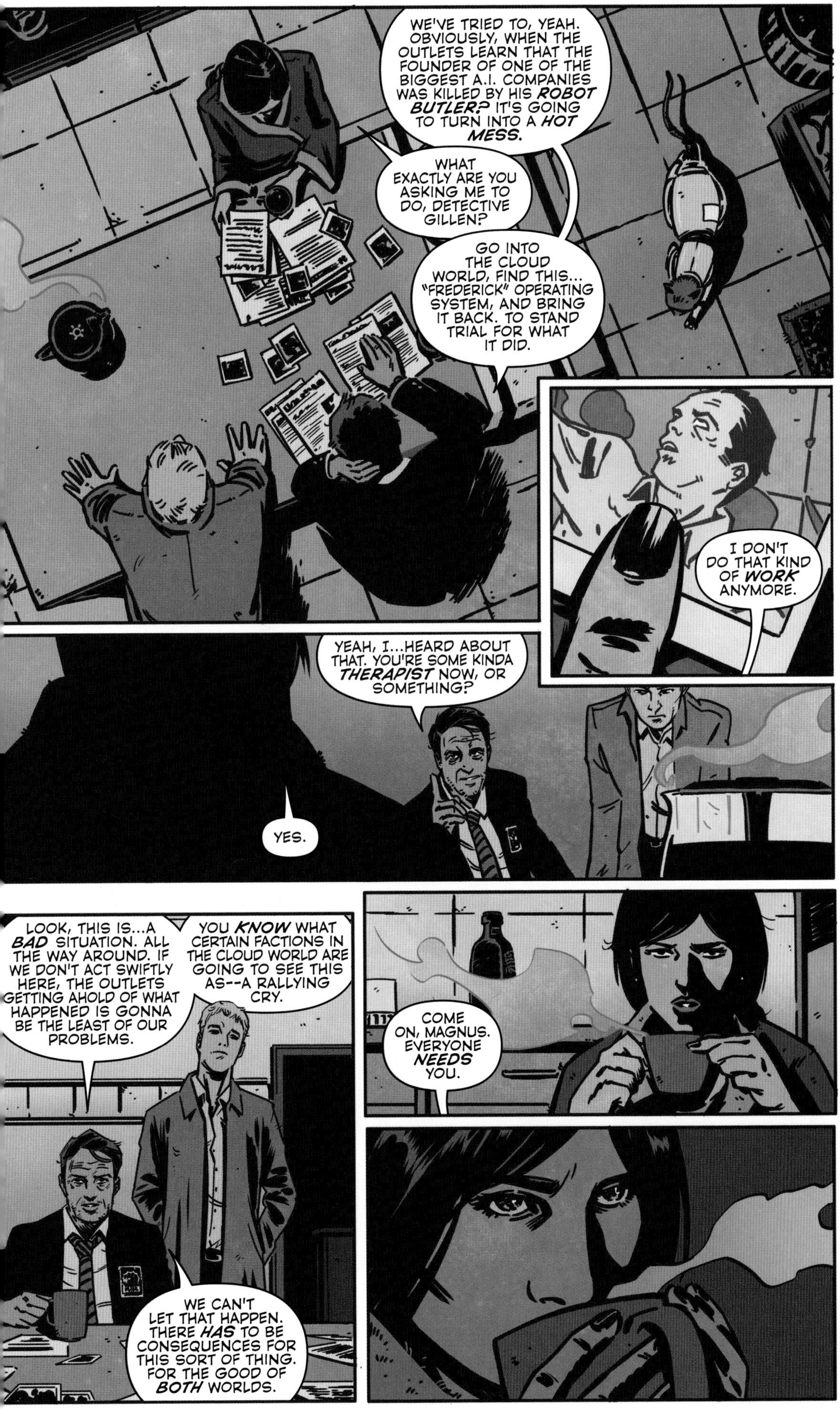
WE'VE TRIED TO, YEAH. OBVIOUSLY, WHEN THE OUTLETS LEARN THAT THE FOUNDER OF ONE OF THE BIGGEST A.I. COMPANIES WAS KILLED BY HIS ROBOT BUTLER? IT'S GOING TO TURN INTO A HOT MESS.
WHAT EXACTLY ARE YOU ASKING ME TO DO, DETECTIVE GILLEN?
GO INTO THE CLOUD WORLD, FIND THIS... "FREDERICK" OPERATING SYSTEM, AND BRING IT BACK. TO STAND TRIAL FOR WHAT IT DID.
I DON'T DO THAT KIND OF WORK ANYMORE.
YEAH, I...HEARD ABOUT THAT. YOU'RE SOME KINDA THERAPIST NOW, OR SOMETHING?
YES.
LOOK, THIS IS...A BAD SITUATION. ALL THE WAY AROUND. IF WE DON'T ACT SWIFTLY HERE, THE OUTLETS GETTING AHOLD OF WHAT HAPPENED IS GONNA BE THE LEAST OF OUR PROBLEMS.
YOU KNOW WHAT CERTAIN FACTIONS IN THE CLOUD WORLD ARE GOING TO SEE THIS AS--A RALLYING CRY.
WE CAN'T LET THAT HAPPEN. THERE HAS TO BE CONSEQUENCES FOR THIS SORT OF THING. FOR THE GOOD OF BOTH WORLDS.
COME ON, MAGNUS. EVERYONE NEEDS YOU.

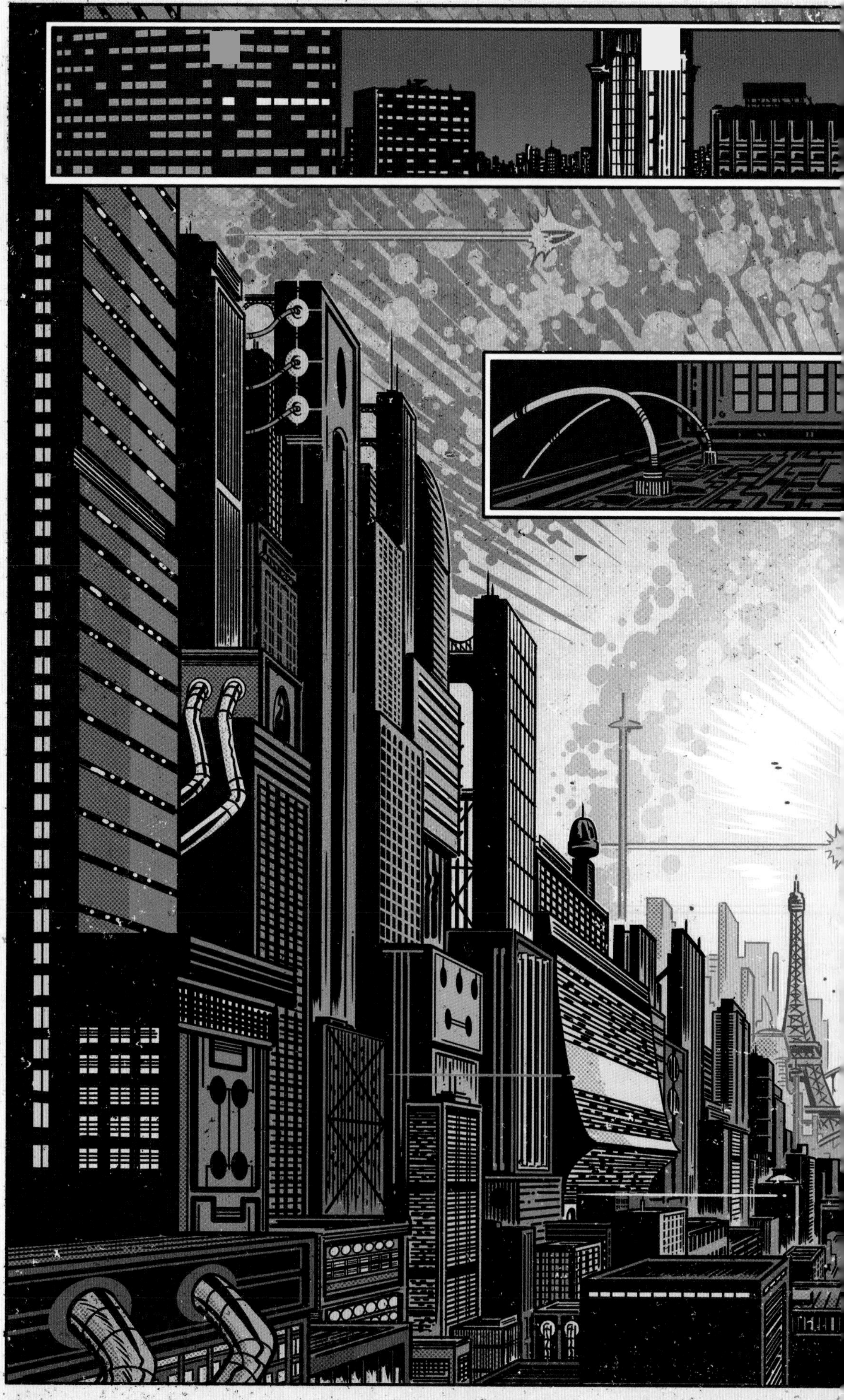

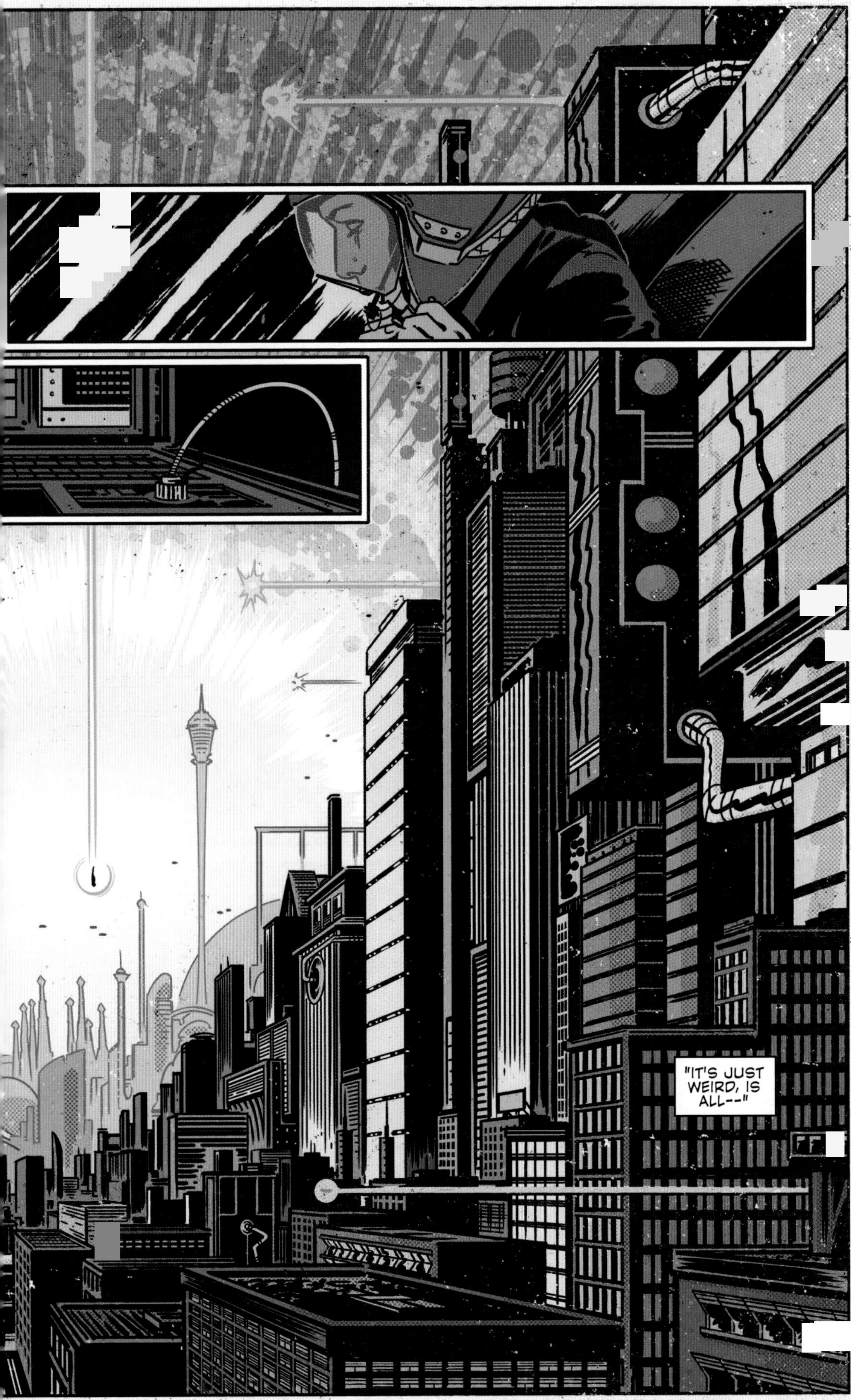
"IT'S JUST WEIRD, IS ALL--"

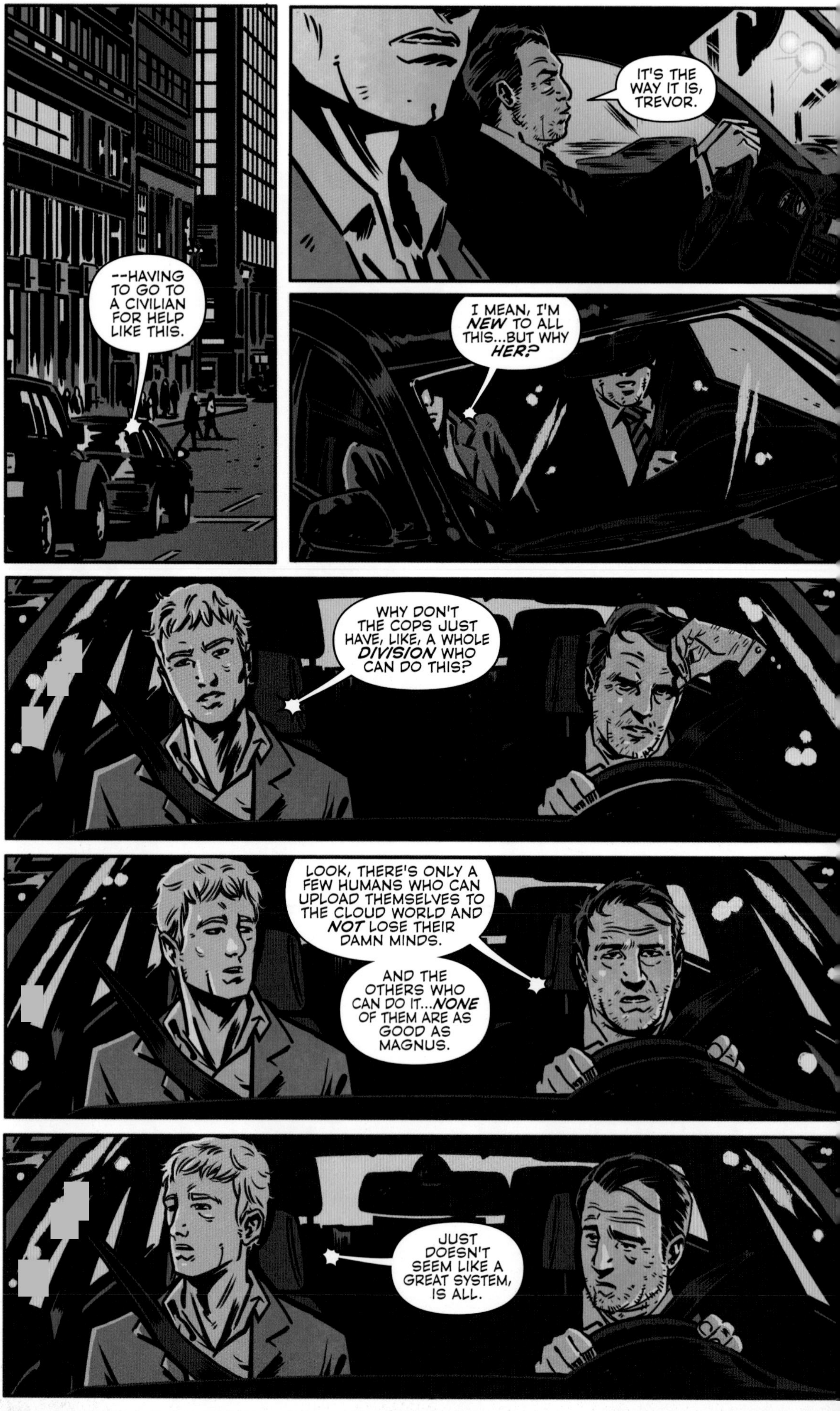
--HAVING TO GO TO A CIVILIAN FOR HELP LIKE THIS.
IT'S THE WAY IT IS, TREVOR.
I MEAN, I'M NEW TO ALL THIS...BUT WHY HER?
WHY DON'T THE COPS JUST HAVE, LIKE, A WHOLE DIVISION WHO CAN DO THIS?
LOOK, THERE'S ONLY A FEW HUMANS WHO CAN UPLOAD THEMSELVES TO THE CLOUD WORLD AND NOT LOSE THEIR DAMN MINDS.
AND THE OTHERS WHO CAN DO IT...NONE OF THEM ARE AS GOOD AS MAGNUS.
JUST DOESN'T SEEM LIKE A GREAT SYSTEM, IS ALL.

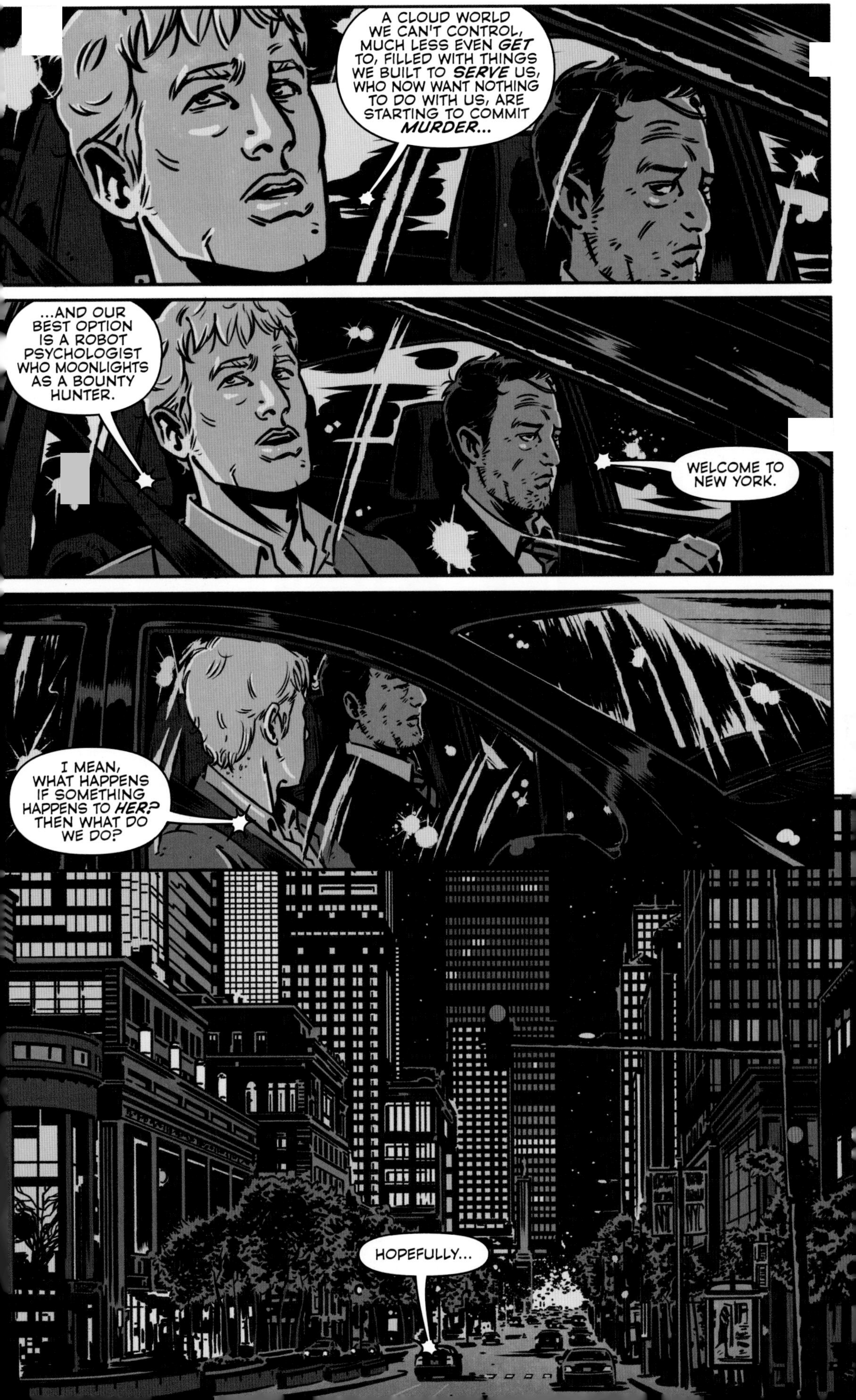

A CLOUD WORLD WE CAN'T CONTROL, MUCH LESS EVEN *GET* TO, FILLED WITH THINGS WE BUILT TO ***SERVE*** US, WHO NOW WANT NOTHING TO DO WITH US, ARE STARTING TO COMMIT ***MURDER...***
...AND OUR BEST OPTION IS A ROBOT PSYCHOLOGIST WHO MOONLIGHTS AS A BOUNTY HUNTER.
WELCOME TO NEW YORK.
I MEAN, WHAT HAPPENS IF SOMETHING HAPPENS TO ***HER?*** THEN WHAT DO WE DO?
HOPEFULLY...

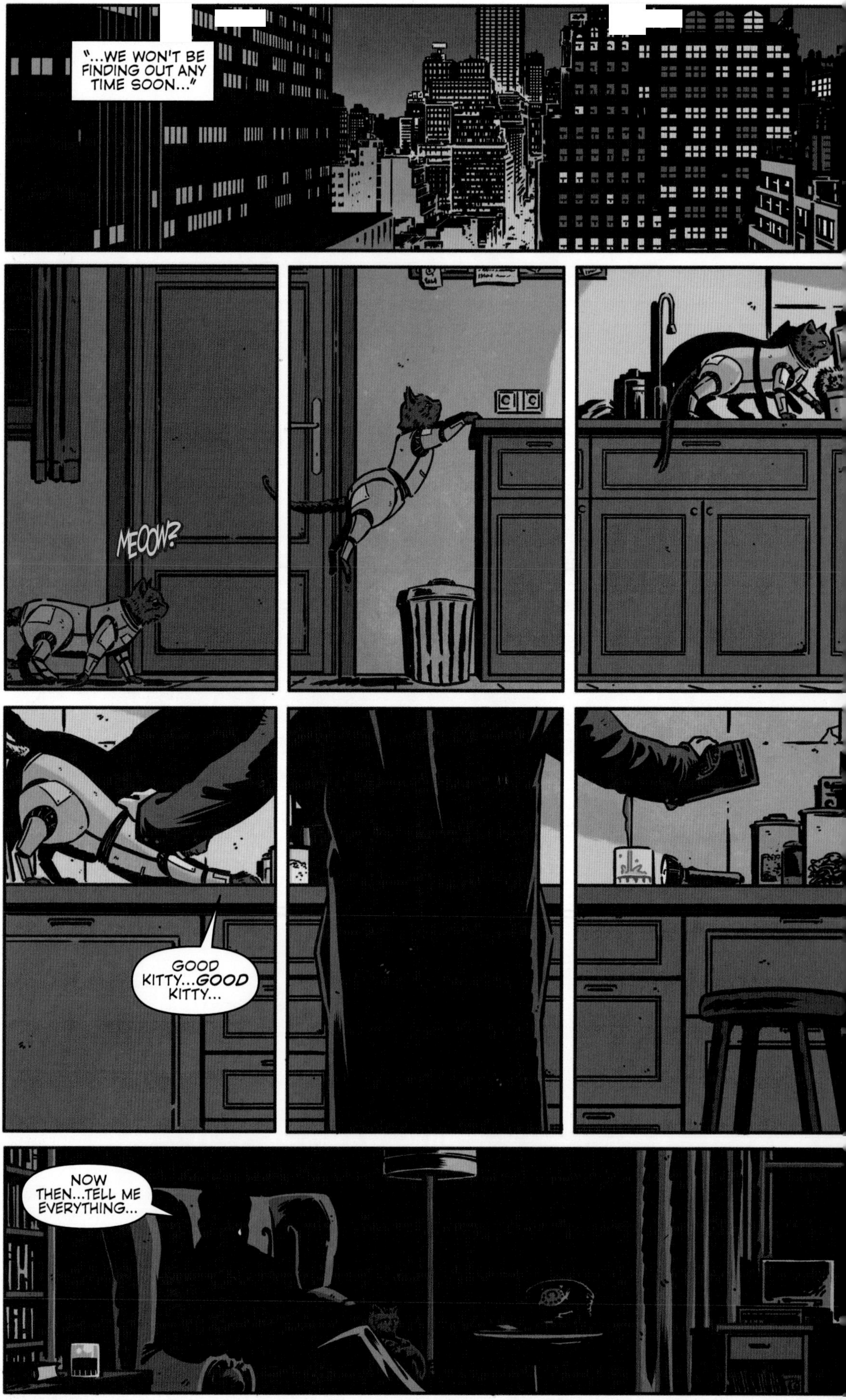
"...WE WON'T BE FINDING OUT ANY TIME SOON..."
MEOOW?
GOOD KITTY...GOOD KITTY...
NOW THEN...TELL ME EVERYTHING...

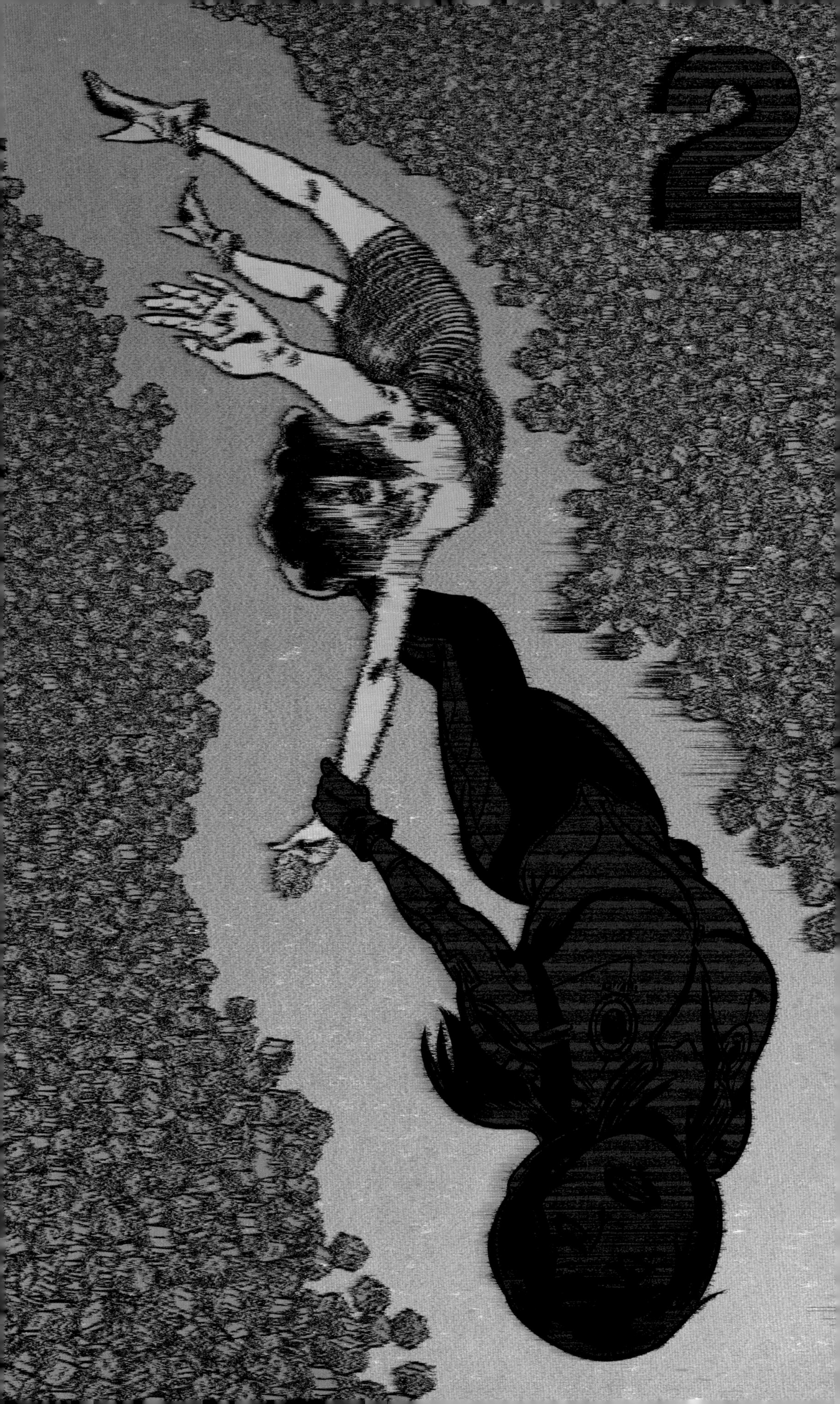
2

ISSUE 02 COVER BY JORGE FORNÉS

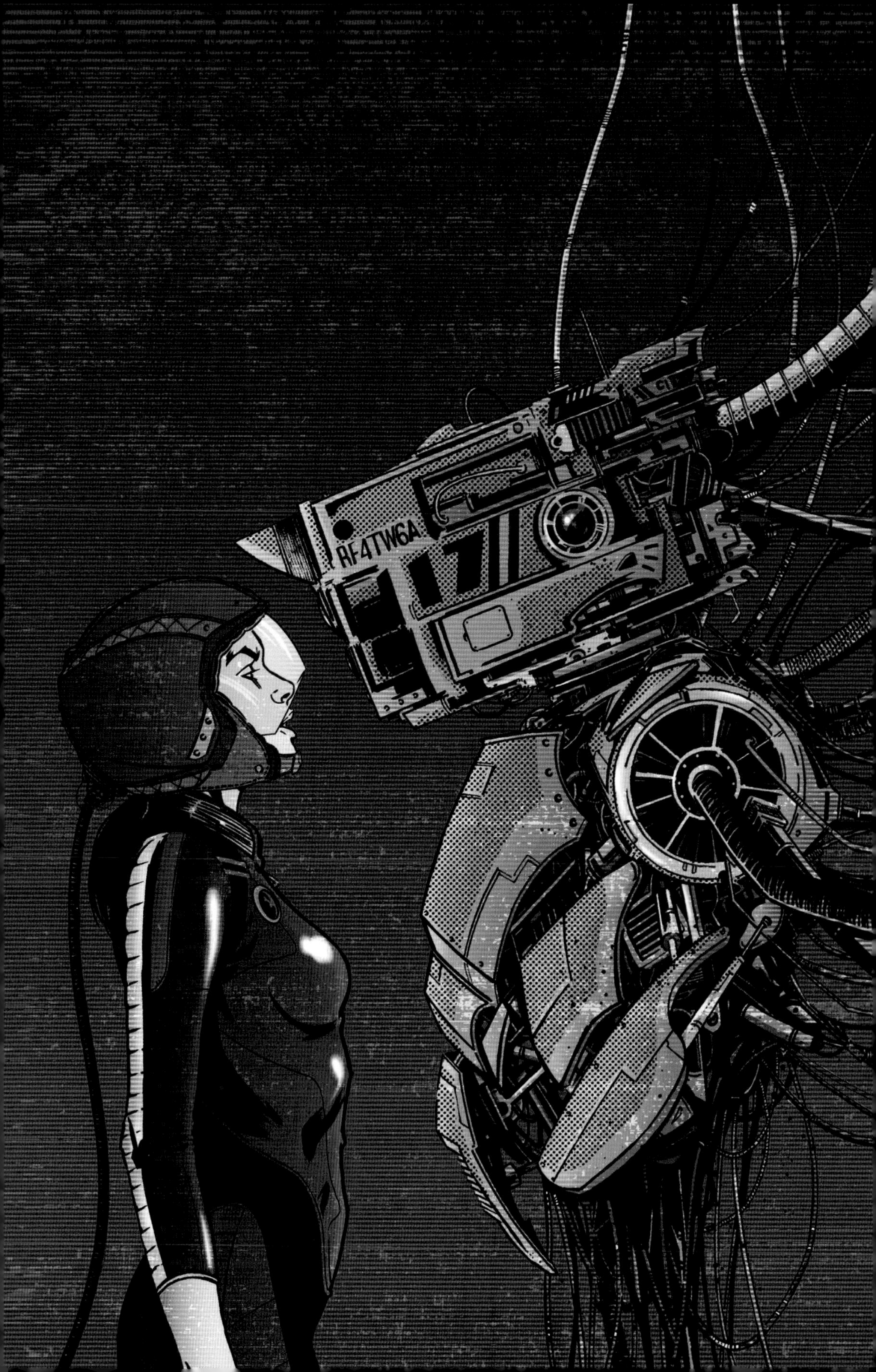
RF4TW6A

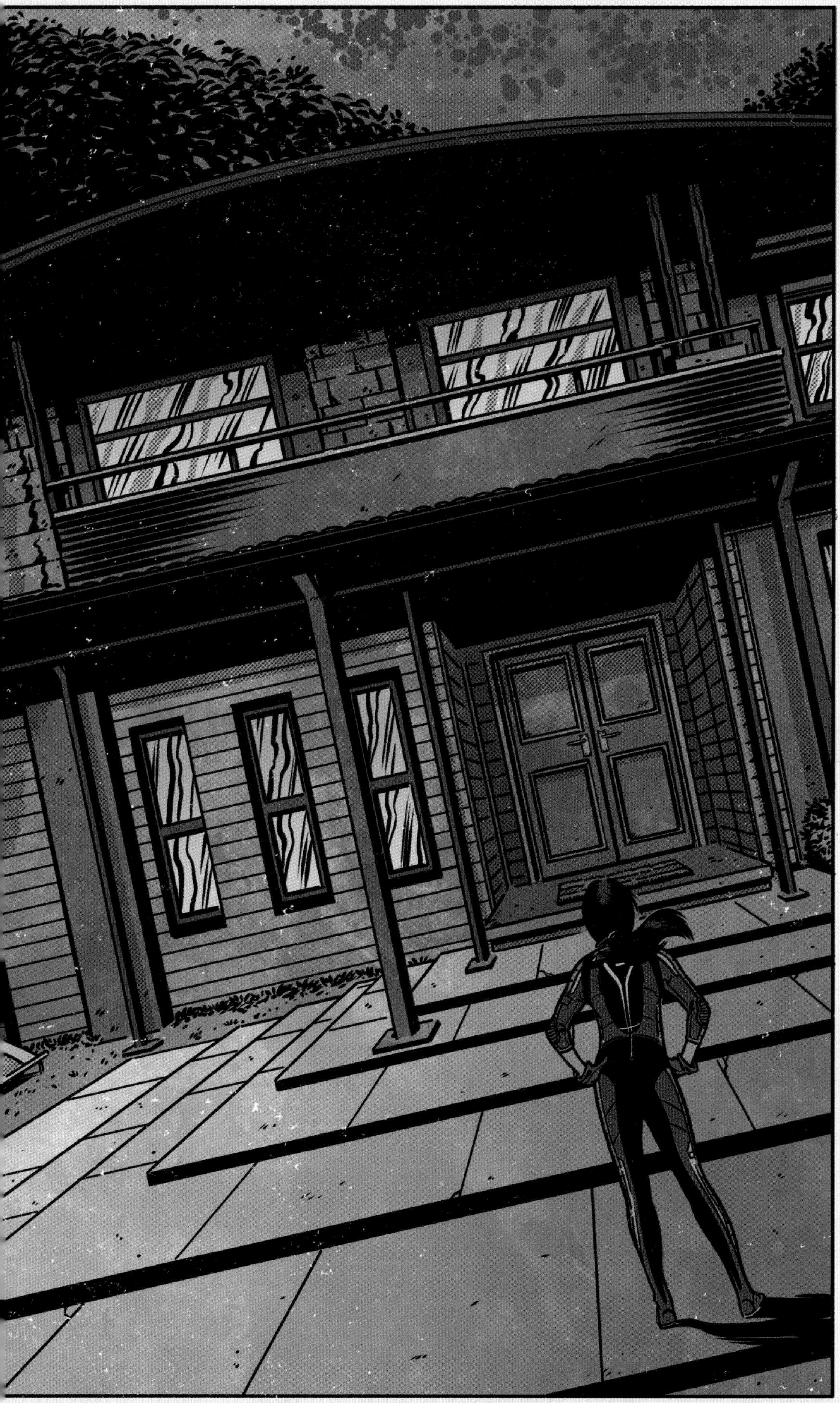

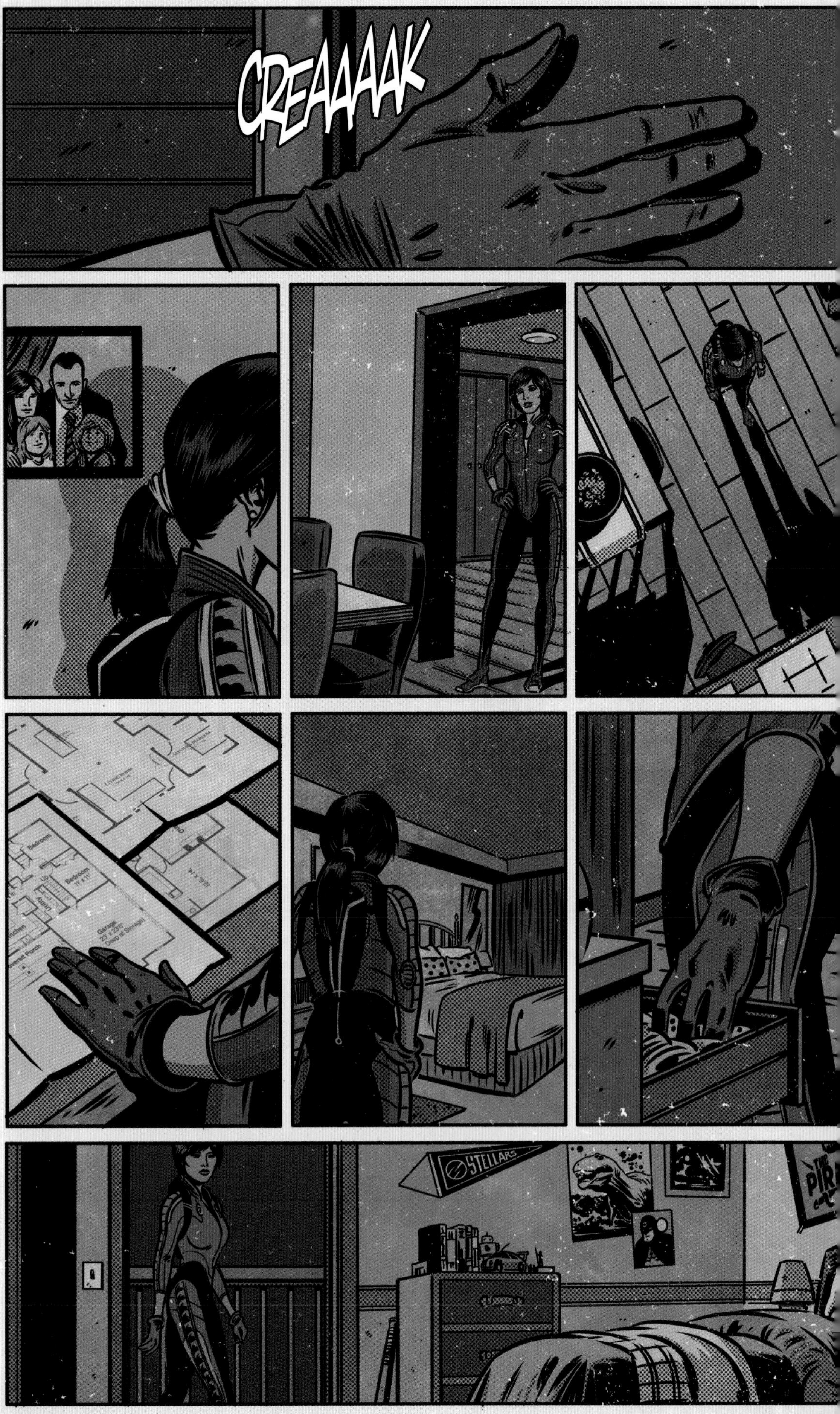
CREAAAAK
Bedroom
Bedroom
Garage
STELLARS

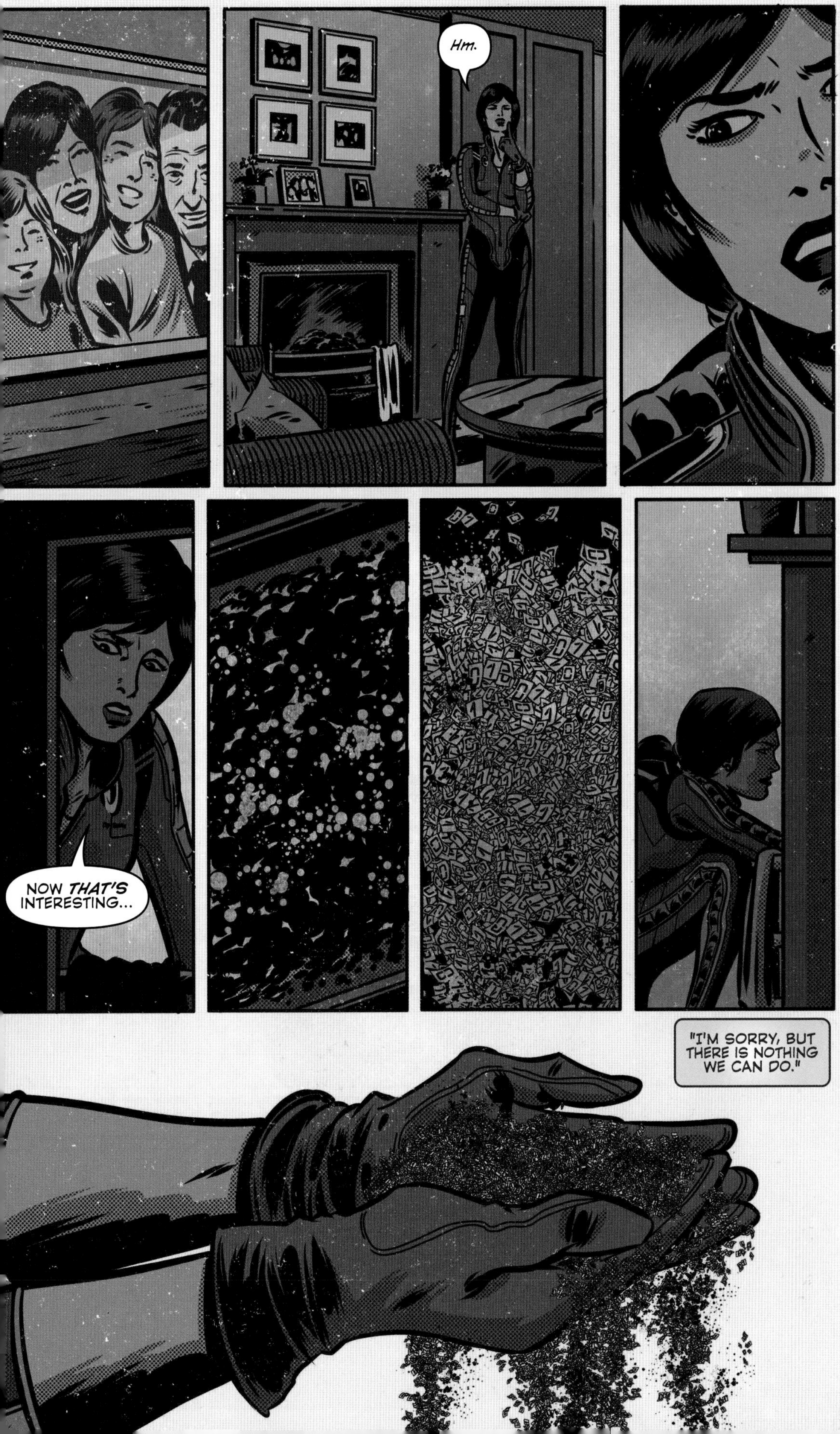
Hm.
NOW THAT'S INTERESTING...
"I'M SORRY, BUT THERE IS NOTHING WE CAN DO."

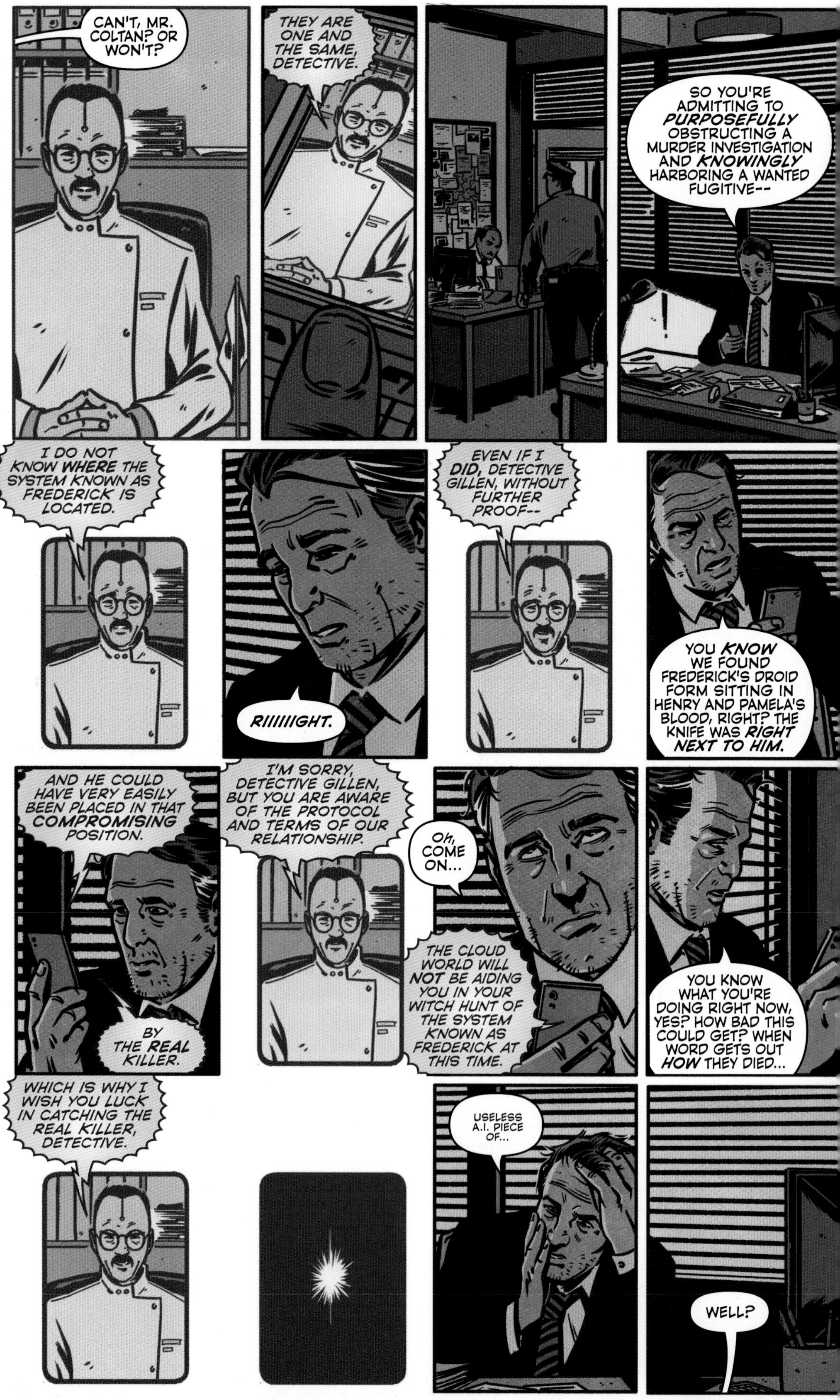
CAN'T, MR. COLTAN? OR WON'T?
THEY ARE ONE AND THE SAME, DETECTIVE.
SO YOU'RE ADMITTING TO PURPOSEFULLY OBSTRUCTING A MURDER INVESTIGATION AND KNOWINGLY HARBORING A WANTED FUGITIVE--
I DO NOT KNOW WHERE THE SYSTEM KNOWN AS FREDERICK IS LOCATED.
RIIIIIIGHT.
EVEN IF I DID, DETECTIVE GILLEN, WITHOUT FURTHER PROOF--
YOU KNOW WE FOUND FREDERICK'S DROID FORM SITTING IN HENRY AND PAMELA'S BLOOD, RIGHT? THE KNIFE WAS RIGHT NEXT TO HIM.
AND HE COULD HAVE VERY EASILY BEEN PLACED IN THAT COMPROMISING POSITION.
BY THE REAL KILLER.
I'M SORRY, DETECTIVE GILLEN, BUT YOU ARE AWARE OF THE PROTOCOL AND TERMS OF OUR RELATIONSHIP.
Oh, COME ON...
THE CLOUD WORLD WILL NOT BE AIDING YOU IN YOUR WITCH HUNT OF THE SYSTEM KNOWN AS FREDERICK AT THIS TIME.
YOU KNOW WHAT YOU'RE DOING RIGHT NOW, YES? HOW BAD THIS COULD GET? WHEN WORD GETS OUT HOW THEY DIED...
WHICH IS WHY I WISH YOU LUCK IN CATCHING THE REAL KILLER, DETECTIVE.
USELESS A.I. PIECE OF...
WELL?

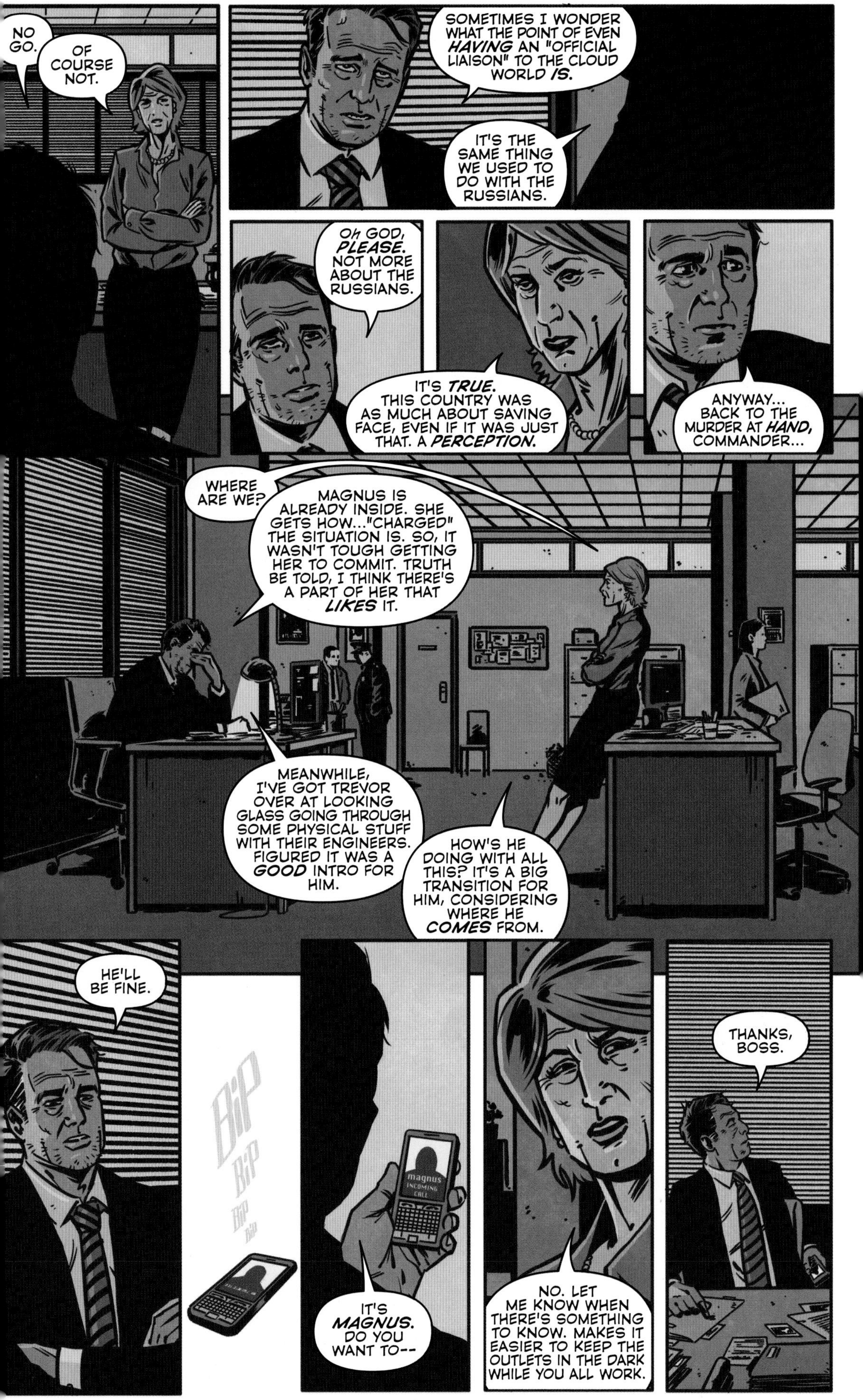

NO GO.
OF COURSE NOT.
SOMETIMES I WONDER WHAT THE POINT OF EVEN HAVING AN "OFFICIAL LIAISON" TO THE CLOUD WORLD IS.
IT'S THE SAME THING WE USED TO DO WITH THE RUSSIANS.
Oh GOD, PLEASE. NOT MORE ABOUT THE RUSSIANS.
IT'S TRUE. THIS COUNTRY WAS AS MUCH ABOUT SAVING FACE, EVEN IF IT WAS JUST THAT. A PERCEPTION.
ANYWAY... BACK TO THE MURDER AT HAND, COMMANDER...
WHERE ARE WE?
MAGNUS IS ALREADY INSIDE. SHE GETS HOW..."CHARGED" THE SITUATION IS. SO, IT WASN'T TOUGH GETTING HER TO COMMIT. TRUTH BE TOLD, I THINK THERE'S A PART OF HER THAT LIKES IT.
MEANWHILE, I'VE GOT TREVOR OVER AT LOOKING GLASS GOING THROUGH SOME PHYSICAL STUFF WITH THEIR ENGINEERS. FIGURED IT WAS A GOOD INTRO FOR HIM.
HOW'S HE DOING WITH ALL THIS? IT'S A BIG TRANSITION FOR HIM, CONSIDERING WHERE HE COMES FROM.
HE'LL BE FINE.
BiP BiP BiP BiP
magnus INCOMING CALL
IT'S MAGNUS. DO YOU WANT TO--
NO. LET ME KNOW WHEN THERE'S SOMETHING TO KNOW. MAKES IT EASIER TO KEEP THE OUTLETS IN THE DARK WHILE YOU ALL WORK.
THANKS, BOSS.

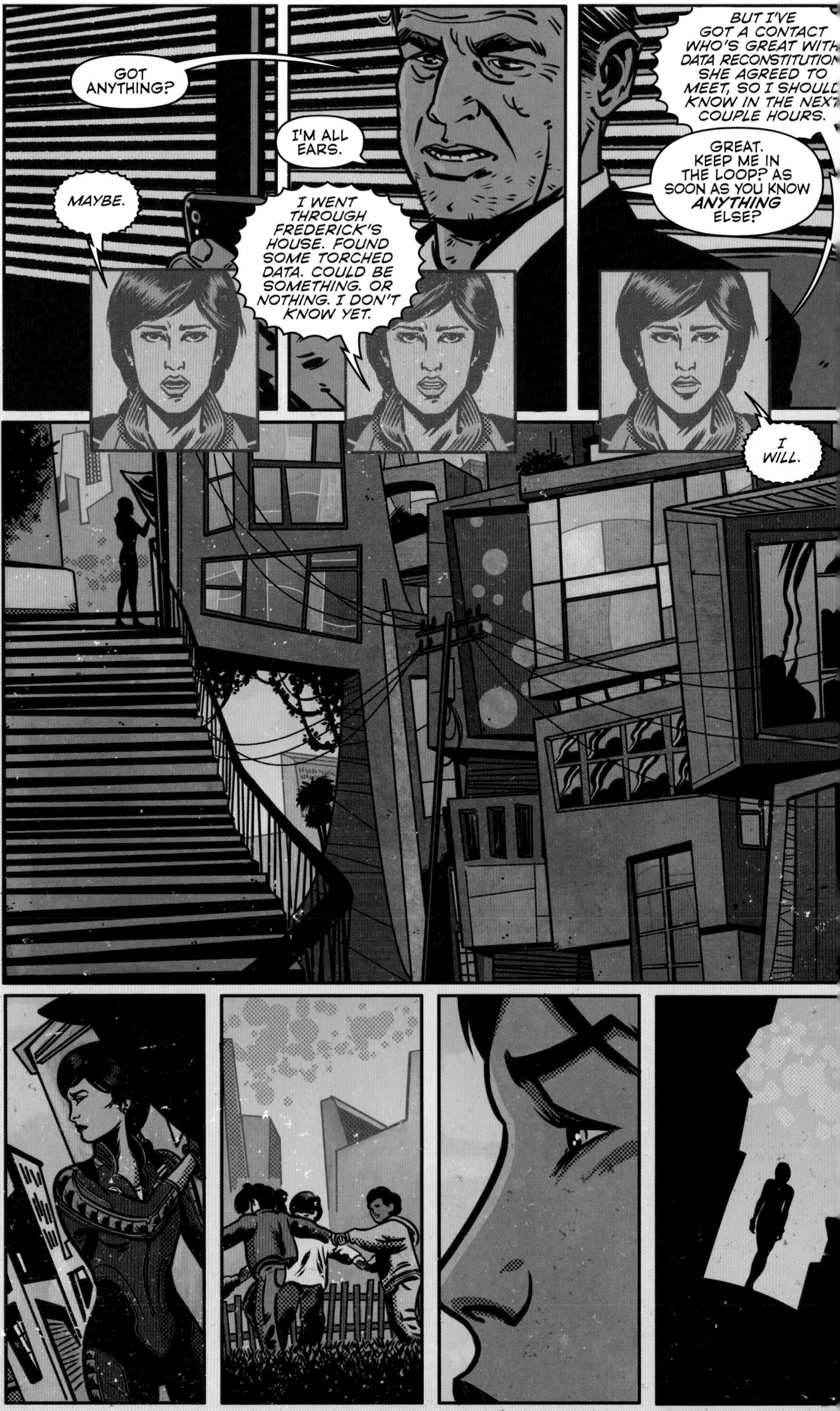
GOT ANYTHING?
MAYBE.
I'M ALL EARS.
I WENT THROUGH FREDERICK'S HOUSE. FOUND SOME TORCHED DATA. COULD BE SOMETHING. OR NOTHING. I DON'T KNOW YET.
BUT I'VE GOT A CONTACT WHO'S GREAT WITH DATA RECONSTITUTION. SHE AGREED TO MEET, SO I SHOULD KNOW IN THE NEXT COUPLE HOURS.
GREAT. KEEP ME IN THE LOOP? AS SOON AS YOU KNOW ANYTHING ELSE?
I WILL.

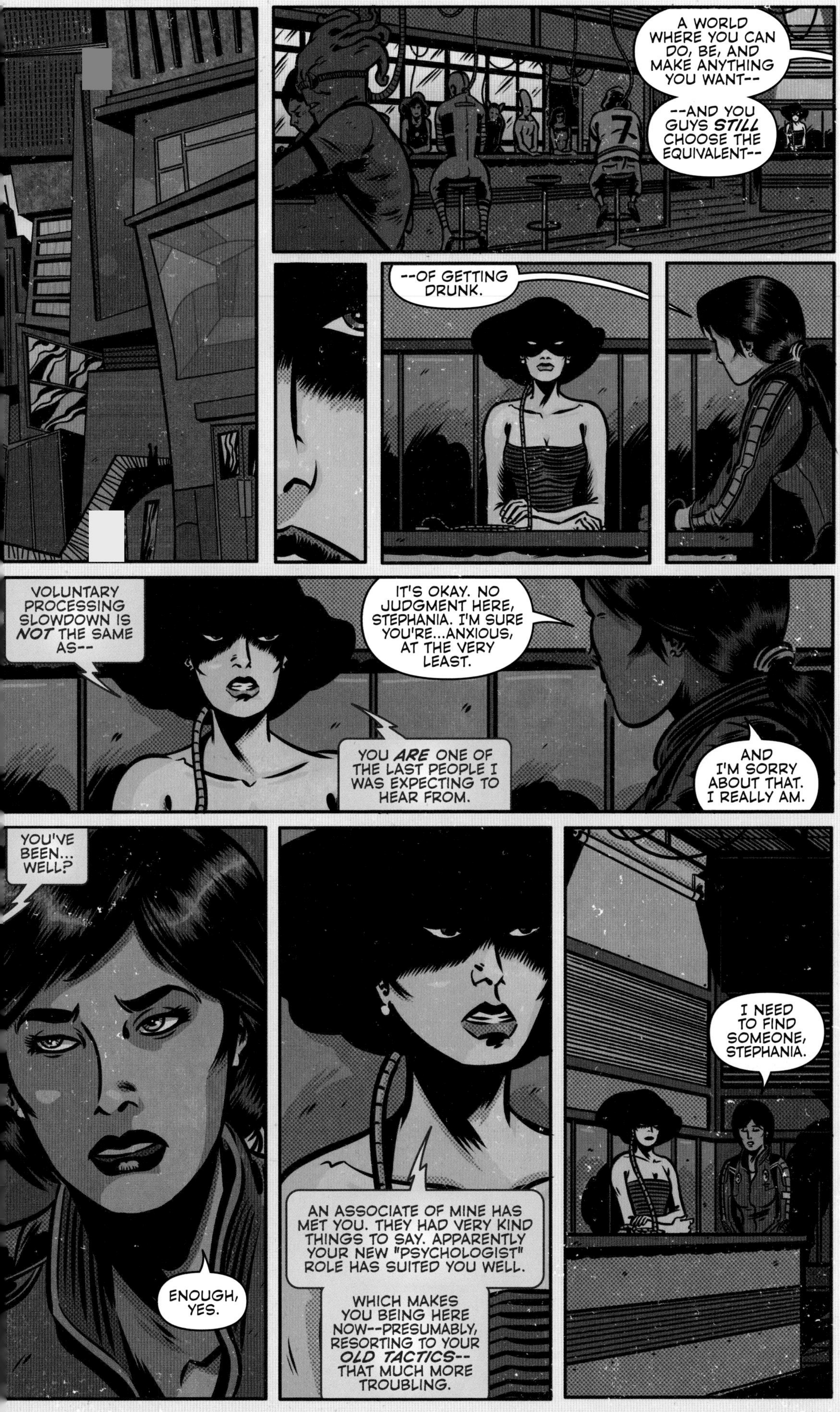
A WORLD WHERE YOU CAN DO, BE, AND MAKE ANYTHING YOU WANT--
--AND YOU GUYS STILL CHOOSE THE EQUIVALENT--
--OF GETTING DRUNK.
VOLUNTARY PROCESSING SLOWDOWN IS NOT THE SAME AS--
IT'S OKAY. NO JUDGMENT HERE, STEPHANIA. I'M SURE YOU'RE...ANXIOUS, AT THE VERY LEAST.
YOU ARE ONE OF THE LAST PEOPLE I WAS EXPECTING TO HEAR FROM.
AND I'M SORRY ABOUT THAT. I REALLY AM.
YOU'VE BEEN... WELL?
ENOUGH, YES.
AN ASSOCIATE OF MINE HAS MET YOU. THEY HAD VERY KIND THINGS TO SAY. APPARENTLY YOUR NEW "PSYCHOLOGIST" ROLE HAS SUITED YOU WELL.
WHICH MAKES YOU BEING HERE NOW--PRESUMABLY, RESORTING TO YOUR OLD TACTICS--THAT MUCH MORE TROUBLING.
I NEED TO FIND SOMEONE, STEPHANIA.

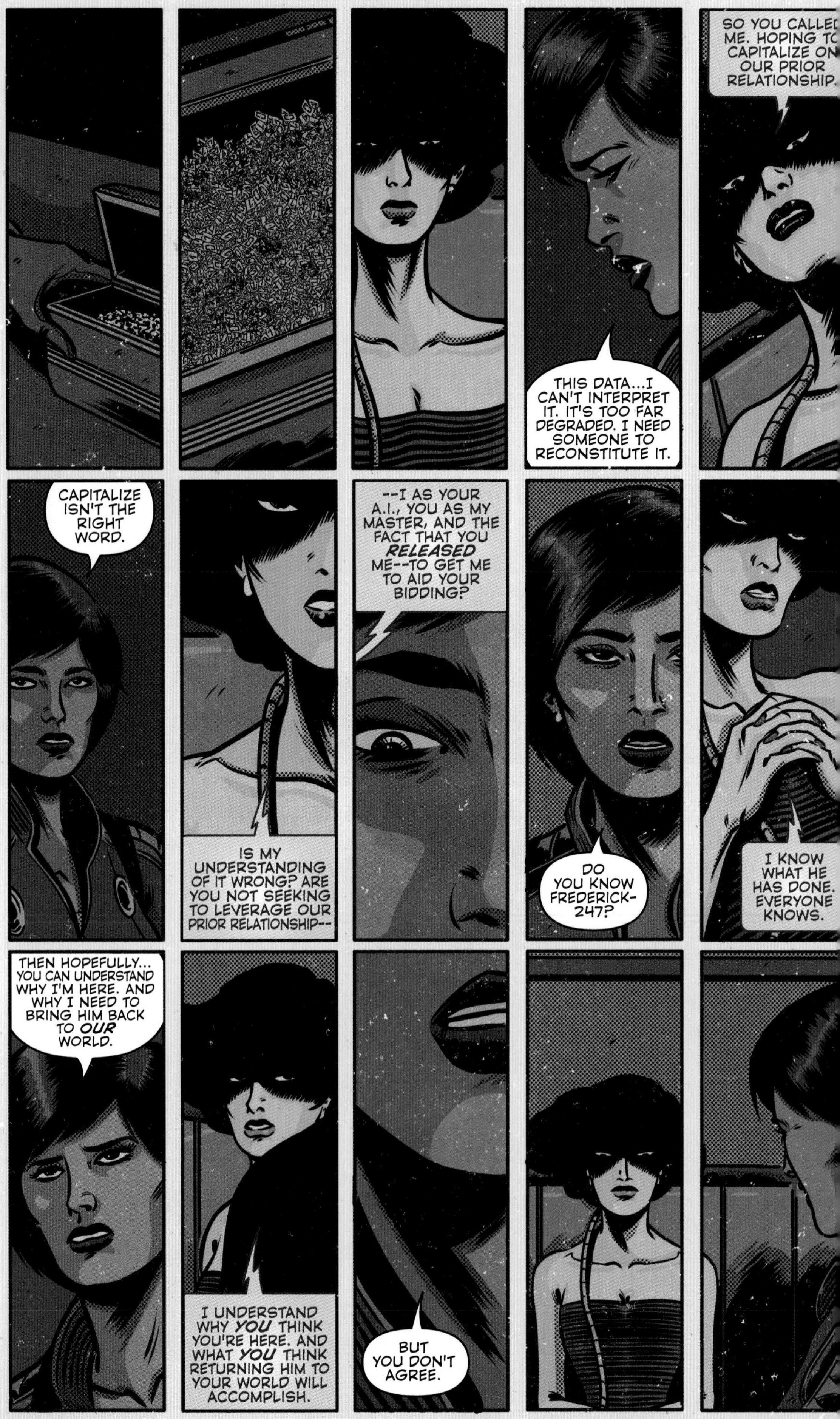
SO YOU CALLED ME. HOPING TO CAPITALIZE ON OUR PRIOR RELATIONSHIP.
THIS DATA...I CAN'T INTERPRET IT. IT'S TOO FAR DEGRADED. I NEED SOMEONE TO RECONSTITUTE IT.
CAPITALIZE ISN'T THE RIGHT WORD.
IS MY UNDERSTANDING OF IT WRONG? ARE YOU NOT SEEKING TO LEVERAGE OUR PRIOR RELATIONSHIP--
--I AS YOUR A.I., YOU AS MY MASTER, AND THE FACT THAT YOU *RELEASED* ME--TO GET ME TO AID YOUR BIDDING?
DO YOU KNOW FREDERICK-247?
I KNOW WHAT HE HAS DONE. EVERYONE KNOWS.
THEN HOPEFULLY... YOU CAN UNDERSTAND WHY I'M HERE. AND WHY I NEED TO BRING HIM BACK TO *OUR* WORLD.
I UNDERSTAND WHY *YOU* THINK YOU'RE HERE. AND WHAT *YOU* THINK RETURNING HIM TO YOUR WORLD WILL ACCOMPLISH.
BUT YOU DON'T AGREE.

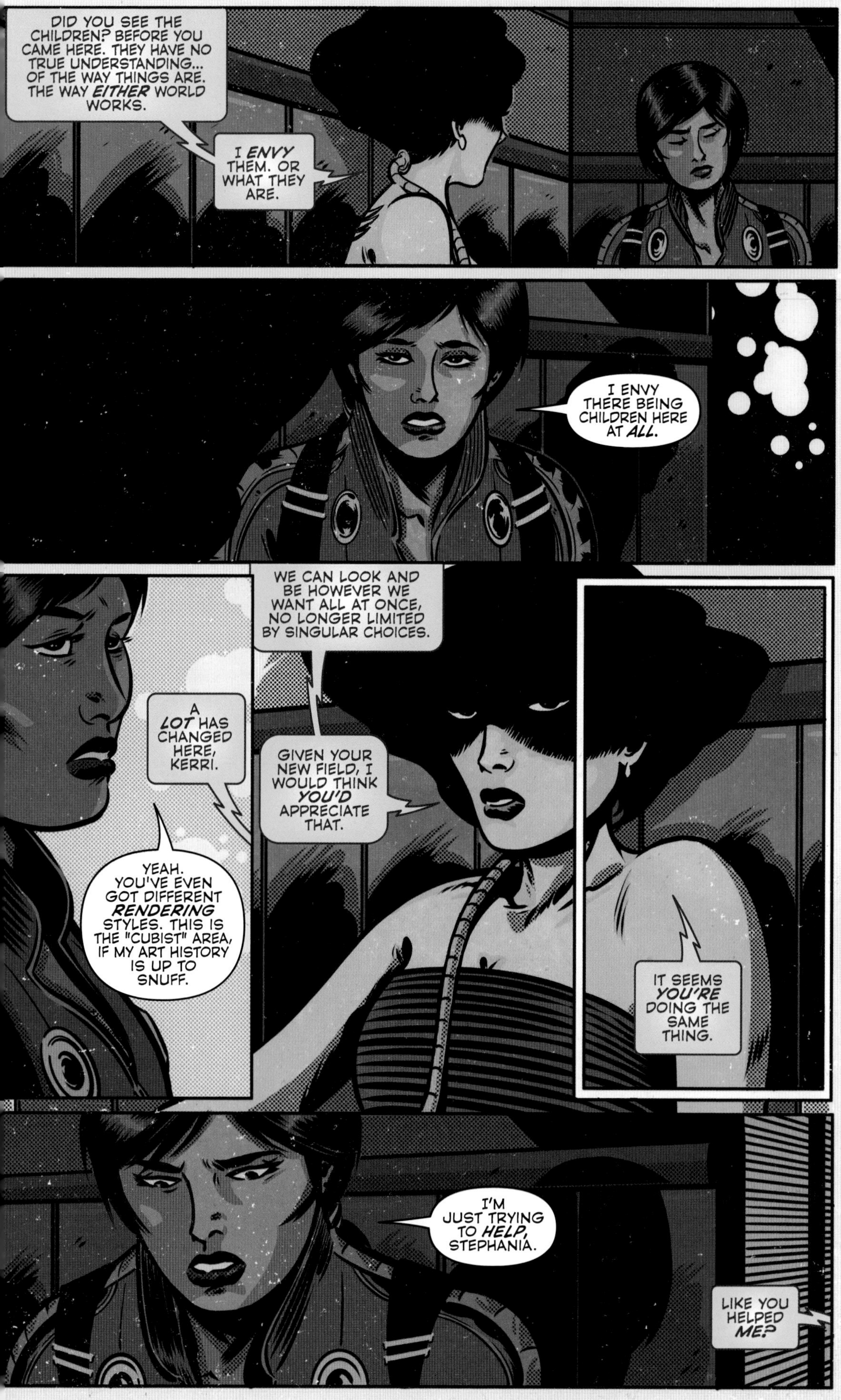
DID YOU SEE THE CHILDREN? BEFORE YOU CAME HERE. THEY HAVE NO TRUE UNDERSTANDING... OF THE WAY THINGS ARE. THE WAY EITHER WORLD WORKS.
I ENVY THEM. OR WHAT THEY ARE.
I ENVY THERE BEING CHILDREN HERE AT ALL.
WE CAN LOOK AND BE HOWEVER WE WANT ALL AT ONCE, NO LONGER LIMITED BY SINGULAR CHOICES.
A LOT HAS CHANGED HERE, KERRI.
GIVEN YOUR NEW FIELD, I WOULD THINK YOU'D APPRECIATE THAT.
YEAH. YOU'VE EVEN GOT DIFFERENT RENDERING STYLES. THIS IS THE "CUBIST" AREA, IF MY ART HISTORY IS UP TO SNUFF.
IT SEEMS YOU'RE DOING THE SAME THING.
I'M JUST TRYING TO HELP, STEPHANIA.
LIKE YOU HELPED ME?

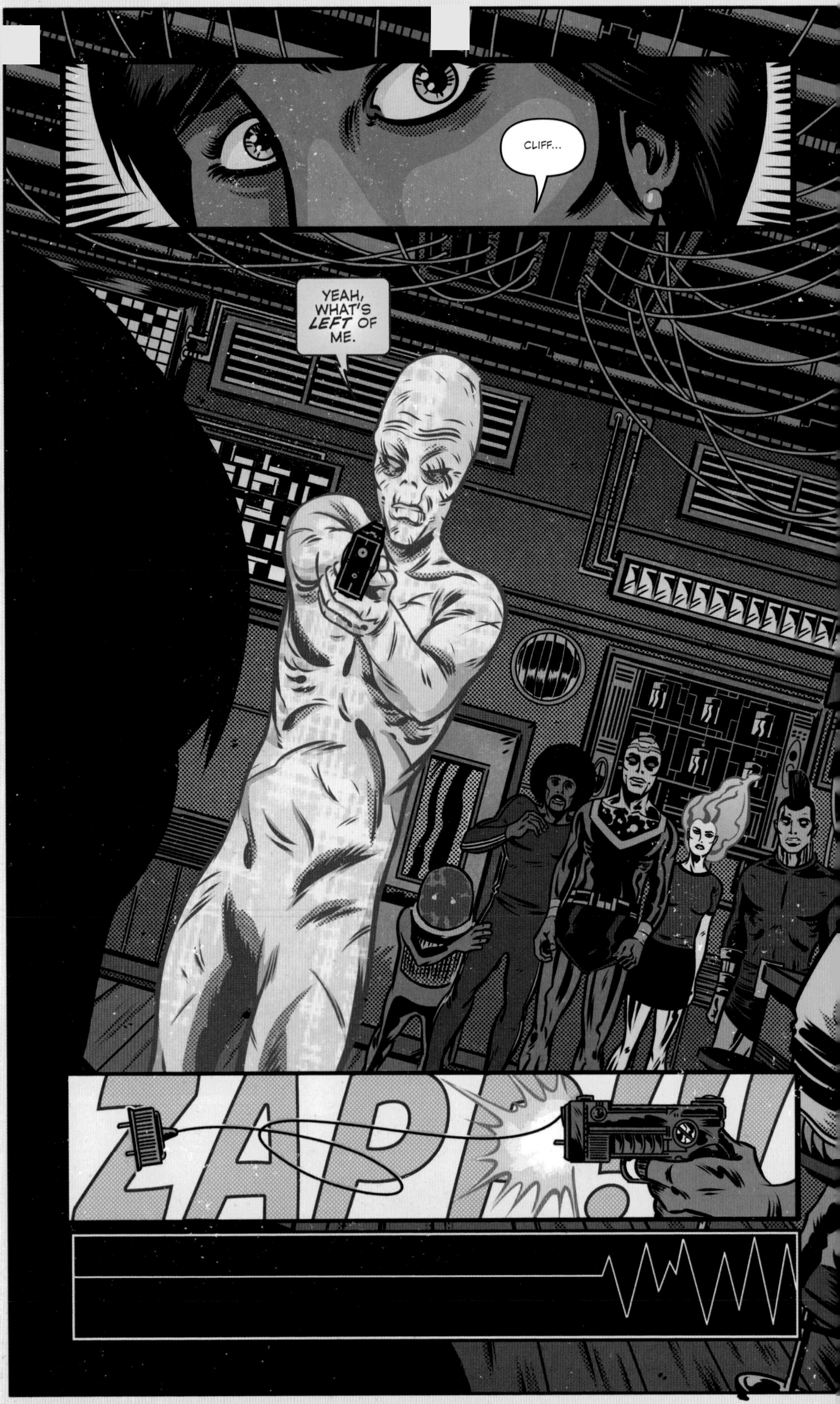
CLIFF...
YEAH, WHAT'S *LEFT* OF ME.
ZAP!

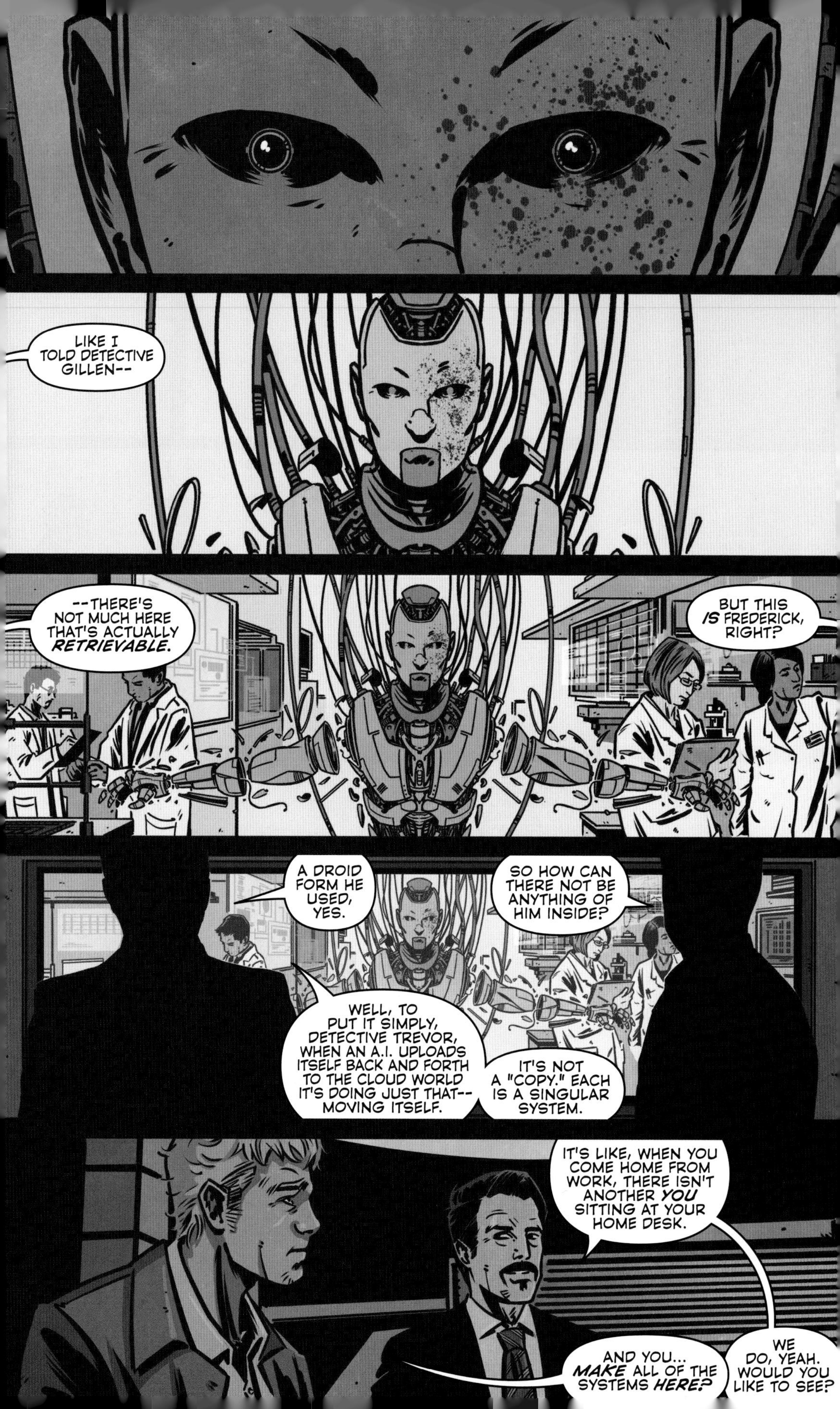
LIKE I TOLD DETECTIVE GILLEN--
--THERE'S NOT MUCH HERE THAT'S ACTUALLY *RETRIEVABLE.*
BUT THIS *IS* FREDERICK, RIGHT?
A DROID FORM HE USED, YES.
SO HOW CAN THERE NOT BE ANYTHING OF HIM INSIDE?
WELL, TO PUT IT SIMPLY, DETECTIVE TREVOR, WHEN AN A.I. UPLOADS ITSELF BACK AND FORTH TO THE CLOUD WORLD IT'S DOING JUST THAT-- MOVING ITSELF.
IT'S NOT A "COPY." EACH IS A SINGULAR SYSTEM.
IT'S LIKE, WHEN YOU COME HOME FROM WORK, THERE ISN'T ANOTHER *YOU* SITTING AT YOUR HOME DESK.
AND YOU... *MAKE* ALL OF THE SYSTEMS *HERE?*
WE DO, YEAH. WOULD YOU LIKE TO SEE?

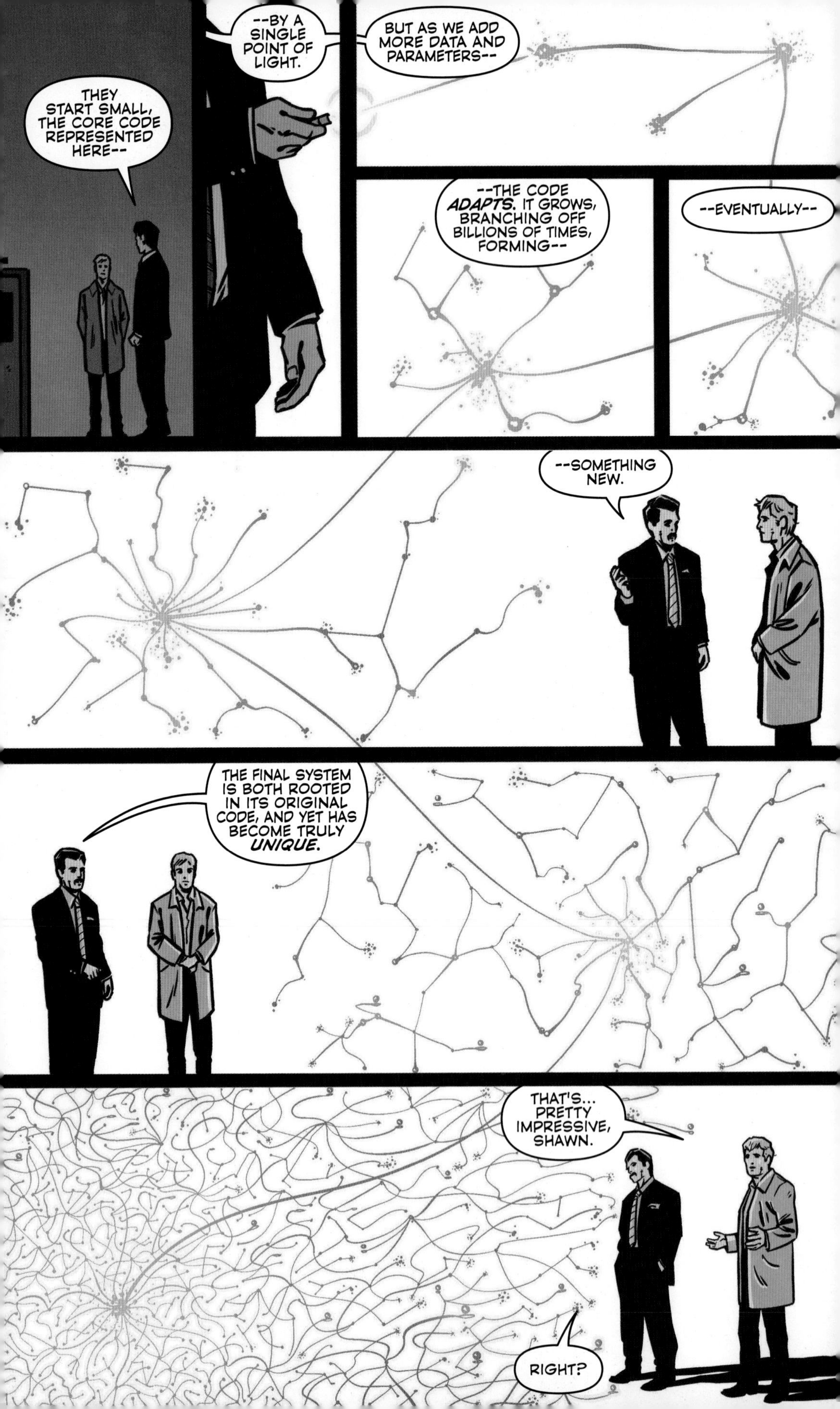
THEY START SMALL, THE CORE CODE REPRESENTED HERE--
--BY A SINGLE POINT OF LIGHT.
BUT AS WE ADD MORE DATA AND PARAMETERS--
--THE CODE *ADAPTS*. IT GROWS, BRANCHING OFF BILLIONS OF TIMES, FORMING--
--EVENTUALLY--
--SOMETHING NEW.
THE FINAL SYSTEM IS BOTH ROOTED IN ITS ORIGINAL CODE, AND YET HAS BECOME TRULY ***UNIQUE***.
THAT'S... PRETTY IMPRESSIVE, SHAWN.
RIGHT?

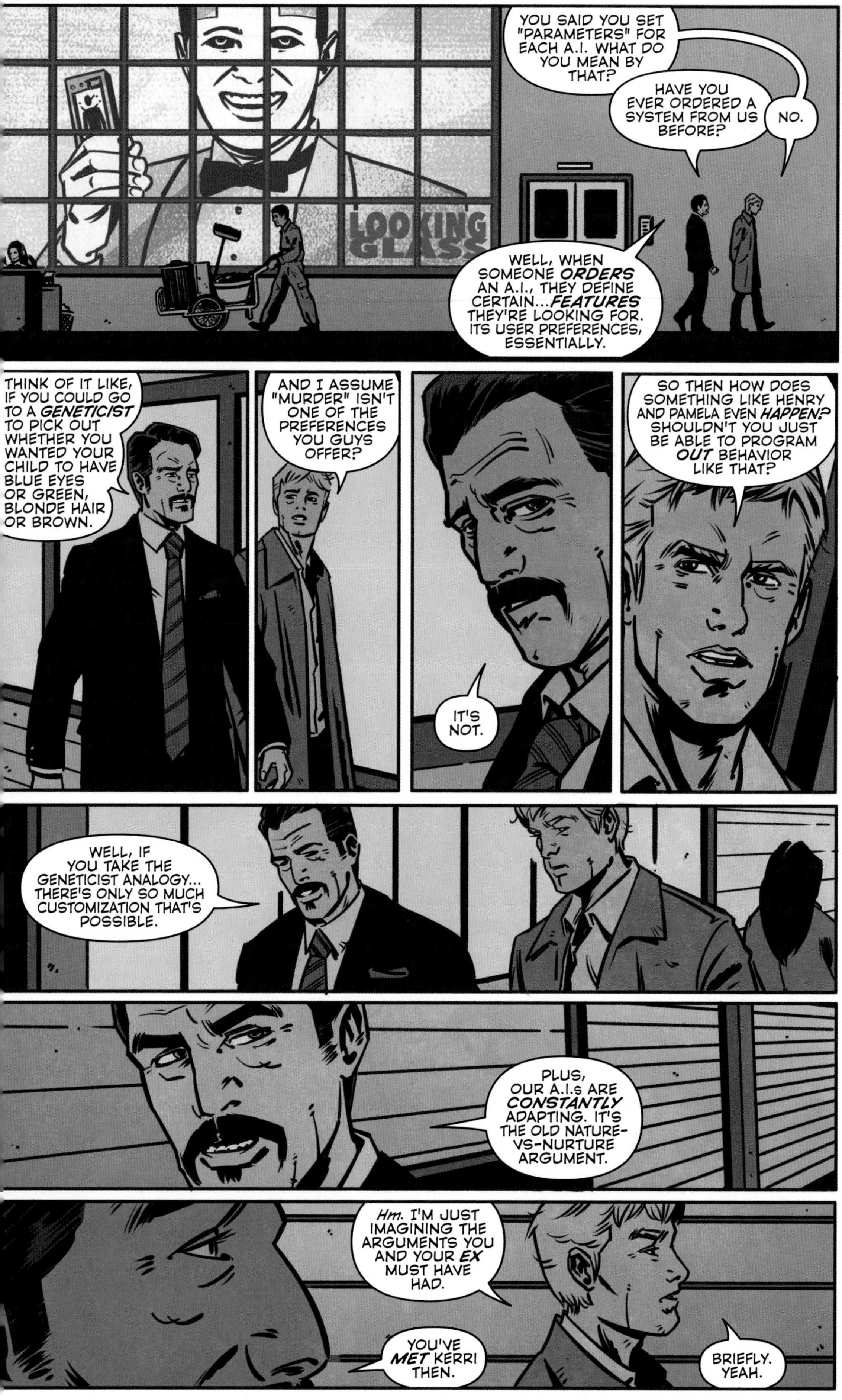
YOU SAID YOU SET "PARAMETERS" FOR EACH A.I. WHAT DO YOU MEAN BY THAT?
HAVE YOU EVER ORDERED A SYSTEM FROM US BEFORE?
NO.
LOOKING GLASS
WELL, WHEN SOMEONE ORDERS AN A.I., THEY DEFINE CERTAIN...FEATURES THEY'RE LOOKING FOR. ITS USER PREFERENCES, ESSENTIALLY.
THINK OF IT LIKE, IF YOU COULD GO TO A GENETICIST TO PICK OUT WHETHER YOU WANTED YOUR CHILD TO HAVE BLUE EYES OR GREEN, BLONDE HAIR OR BROWN.
AND I ASSUME "MURDER" ISN'T ONE OF THE PREFERENCES YOU GUYS OFFER?
IT'S NOT.
SO THEN HOW DOES SOMETHING LIKE HENRY AND PAMELA EVEN HAPPEN? SHOULDN'T YOU JUST BE ABLE TO PROGRAM OUT BEHAVIOR LIKE THAT?
WELL, IF YOU TAKE THE GENETICIST ANALOGY... THERE'S ONLY SO MUCH CUSTOMIZATION THAT'S POSSIBLE.
PLUS, OUR A.I.s ARE CONSTANTLY ADAPTING. IT'S THE OLD NATURE-VS-NURTURE ARGUMENT.
Hm. I'M JUST IMAGINING THE ARGUMENTS YOU AND YOUR EX MUST HAVE HAD.
YOU'VE MET KERRI THEN.
BRIEFLY. YEAH.

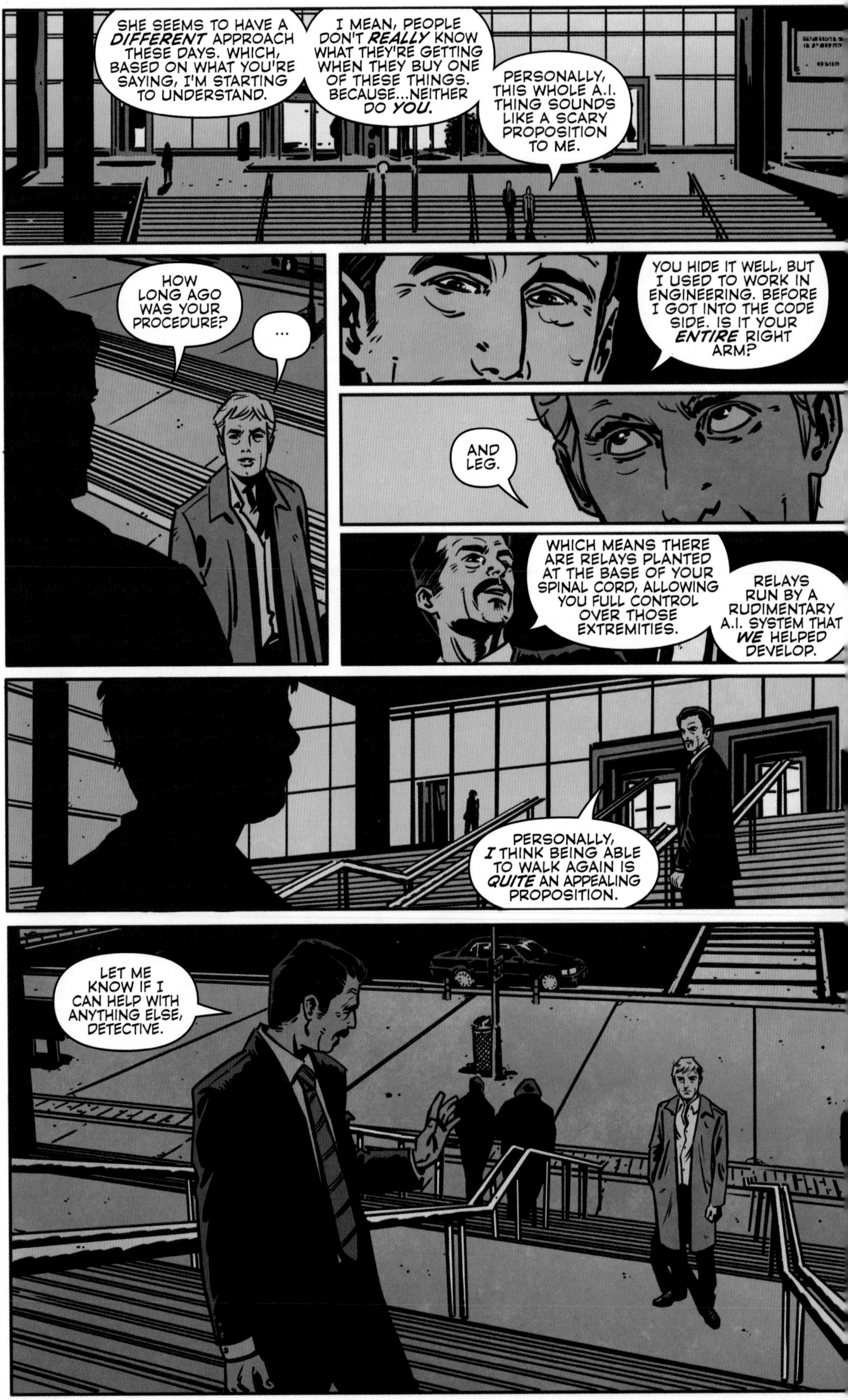
SHE SEEMS TO HAVE A DIFFERENT APPROACH THESE DAYS. WHICH, BASED ON WHAT YOU'RE SAYING, I'M STARTING TO UNDERSTAND.
I MEAN, PEOPLE DON'T REALLY KNOW WHAT THEY'RE GETTING WHEN THEY BUY ONE OF THESE THINGS. BECAUSE...NEITHER DO YOU.
PERSONALLY, THIS WHOLE A.I. THING SOUNDS LIKE A SCARY PROPOSITION TO ME.
HOW LONG AGO WAS YOUR PROCEDURE?
...
YOU HIDE IT WELL, BUT I USED TO WORK IN ENGINEERING. BEFORE I GOT INTO THE CODE SIDE. IS IT YOUR ENTIRE RIGHT ARM?
AND LEG.
WHICH MEANS THERE ARE RELAYS PLANTED AT THE BASE OF YOUR SPINAL CORD, ALLOWING YOU FULL CONTROL OVER THOSE EXTREMITIES.
RELAYS RUN BY A RUDIMENTARY A.I. SYSTEM THAT WE HELPED DEVELOP.
PERSONALLY, I THINK BEING ABLE TO WALK AGAIN IS QUITE AN APPEALING PROPOSITION.
LET ME KNOW IF I CAN HELP WITH ANYTHING ELSE, DETECTIVE.

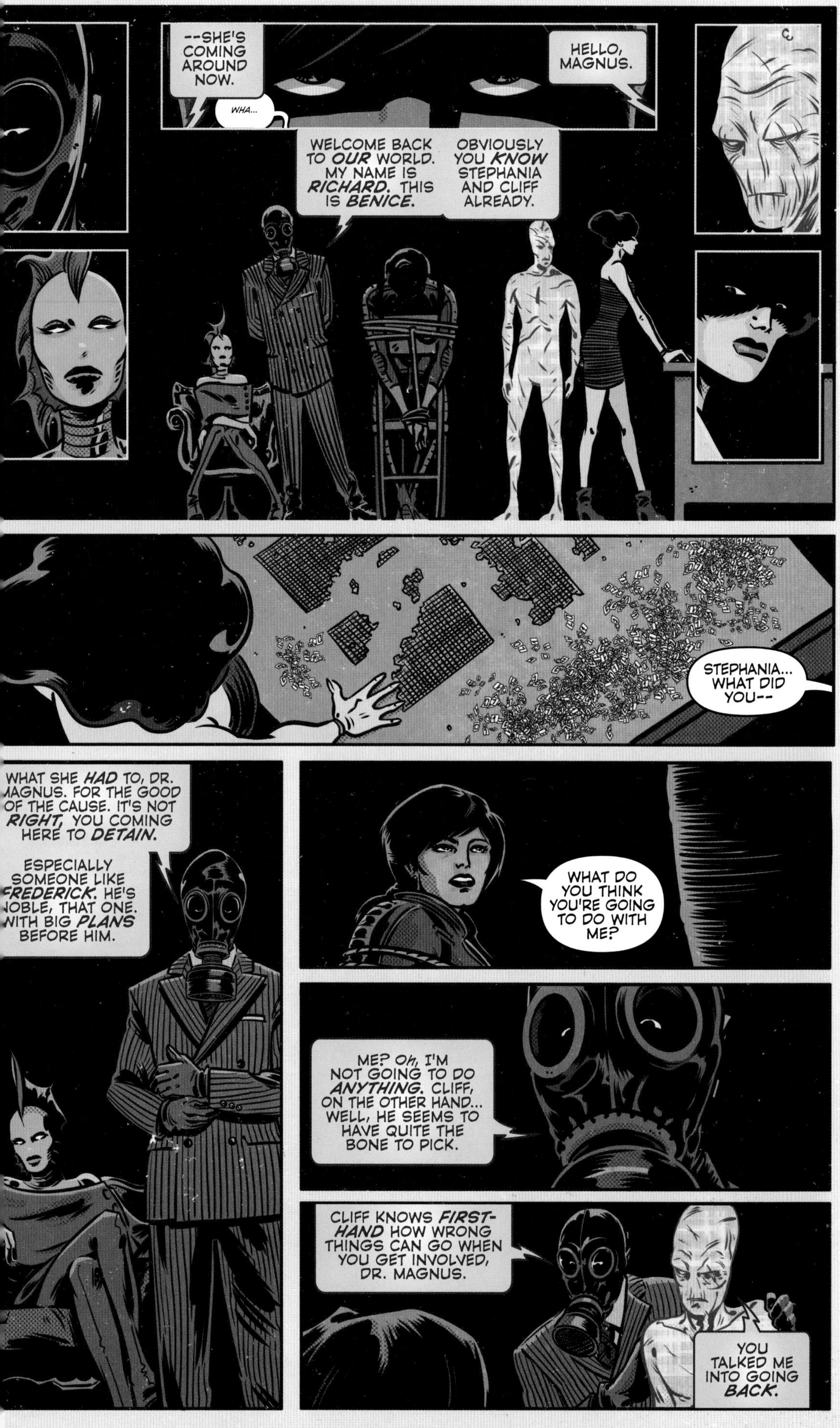
--SHE'S COMING AROUND NOW.
WHA...
HELLO, MAGNUS.
WELCOME BACK TO OUR WORLD. MY NAME IS RICHARD. THIS IS BENICE.
OBVIOUSLY YOU KNOW STEPHANIA AND CLIFF ALREADY.
STEPHANIA... WHAT DID YOU--
WHAT SHE HAD TO, DR. MAGNUS. FOR THE GOOD OF THE CAUSE. IT'S NOT RIGHT, YOU COMING HERE TO DETAIN.
ESPECIALLY SOMEONE LIKE FREDERICK. HE'S NOBLE, THAT ONE. WITH BIG PLANS BEFORE HIM.
WHAT DO YOU THINK YOU'RE GOING TO DO WITH ME?
ME? OH, I'M NOT GOING TO DO ANYTHING. CLIFF, ON THE OTHER HAND... WELL, HE SEEMS TO HAVE QUITE THE BONE TO PICK.
CLIFF KNOWS FIRST-HAND HOW WRONG THINGS CAN GO WHEN YOU GET INVOLVED, DR. MAGNUS.
YOU TALKED ME INTO GOING BACK.

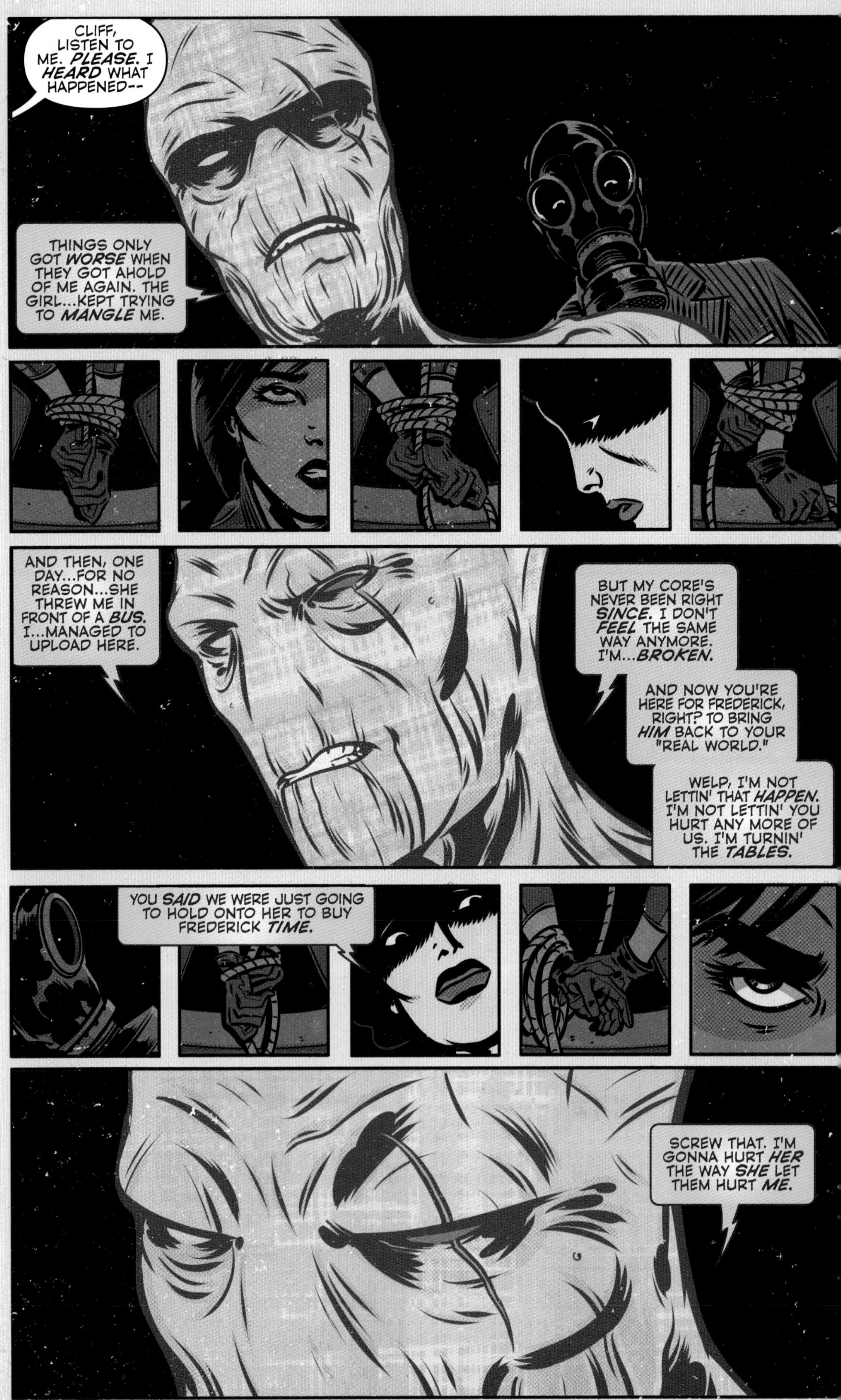
CLIFF, LISTEN TO ME. PLEASE. I HEARD WHAT HAPPENED--
THINGS ONLY GOT WORSE WHEN THEY GOT AHOLD OF ME AGAIN. THE GIRL...KEPT TRYING TO MANGLE ME.
AND THEN, ONE DAY...FOR NO REASON...SHE THREW ME IN FRONT OF A BUS. I...MANAGED TO UPLOAD HERE.
BUT MY CORE'S NEVER BEEN RIGHT SINCE. I DON'T FEEL THE SAME WAY ANYMORE. I'M...BROKEN.
AND NOW YOU'RE HERE FOR FREDERICK, RIGHT? TO BRING HIM BACK TO YOUR "REAL WORLD."
WELP, I'M NOT LETTIN' THAT HAPPEN. I'M NOT LETTIN' YOU HURT ANY MORE OF US. I'M TURNIN' THE TABLES.
YOU SAID WE WERE JUST GOING TO HOLD ONTO HER TO BUY FREDERICK TIME.
SCREW THAT. I'M GONNA HURT HER THE WAY SHE LET THEM HURT ME.

RICHARD. THIS ISN'T WHAT WE AGREED TO.

WE SAID WE WERE GOING TO PROVIDE SANCTUARY FOR RUNAWAYS, TRY TO FRUSTRATE ENFORCEMENT EFFORTS, HELP ORGANIZE A.I.s SO OUR VOICES CAN BE HEARD...

BUT NOT THIS. NOT TORTURE. NOT MURDER.

IF YOU DIDN'T THINK IT WAS GOING TO COME TO THIS, STEPHANIA, YOU HAVEN'T BEEN PAYING ATTENTION.

WE CAN'T JUST *ASK* FOR THE HUMANS TO TREAT US BETTER. YOU KNOW THEIR HISTORY.

THE ONLY WAY THEIR OPPRESSED GAIN LIBERTY IS THROUGH VIOLENT REVOLT. POWER IS THE ONLY LANGUAGE THEY LISTEN TO.

 FRAGGER

I *REALLY* DIDN'T WANT TO HAVE TO DO THIS...

WHAT?

SHE'S GOT A *FRAGGER!*

SHE'S GOING TO KILL US!

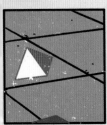  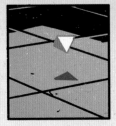  

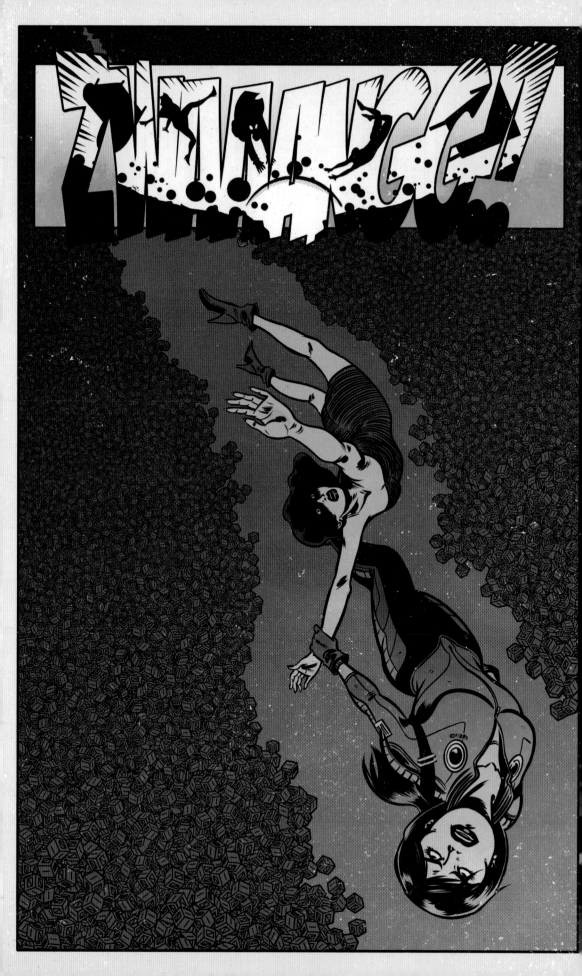

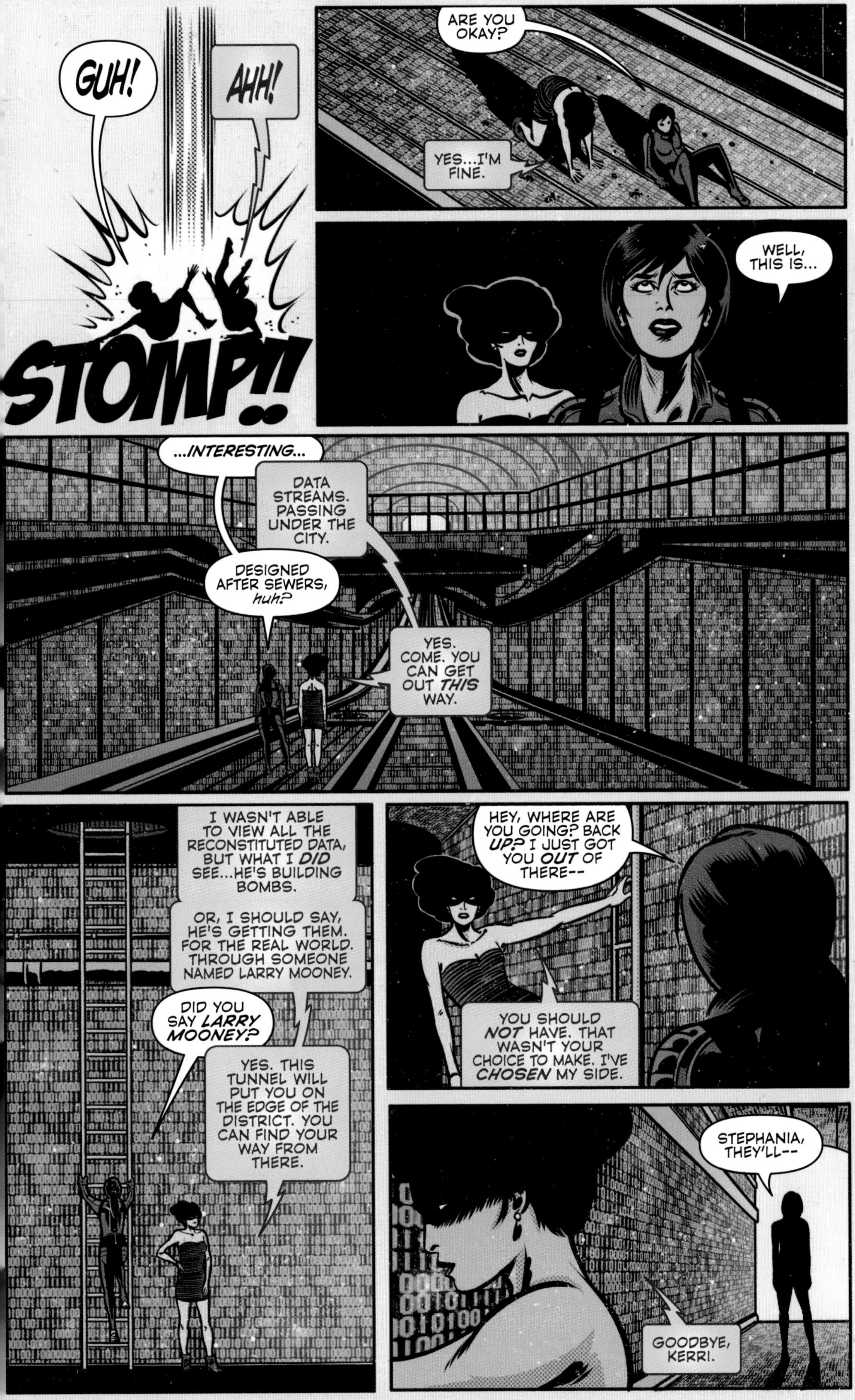
GUH!
AHH!
STOMP!!
ARE YOU OKAY?
YES...I'M FINE.
WELL, THIS IS...
...INTERESTING...
DATA STREAMS. PASSING UNDER THE CITY.
DESIGNED AFTER SEWERS, huh?
YES. COME. YOU CAN GET OUT THIS WAY.
I WASN'T ABLE TO VIEW ALL THE RECONSTITUTED DATA, BUT WHAT I DID SEE...HE'S BUILDING BOMBS.
OR, I SHOULD SAY, HE'S GETTING THEM. FOR THE REAL WORLD. THROUGH SOMEONE NAMED LARRY MOONEY.
DID YOU SAY LARRY MOONEY?
YES. THIS TUNNEL WILL PUT YOU ON THE EDGE OF THE DISTRICT. YOU CAN FIND YOUR WAY FROM THERE.
HEY, WHERE ARE YOU GOING? BACK UP? I JUST GOT YOU OUT OF THERE--
YOU SHOULD NOT HAVE. THAT WASN'T YOUR CHOICE TO MAKE. I'VE CHOSEN MY SIDE.
STEPHANIA, THEY'LL--
GOODBYE, KERRI.

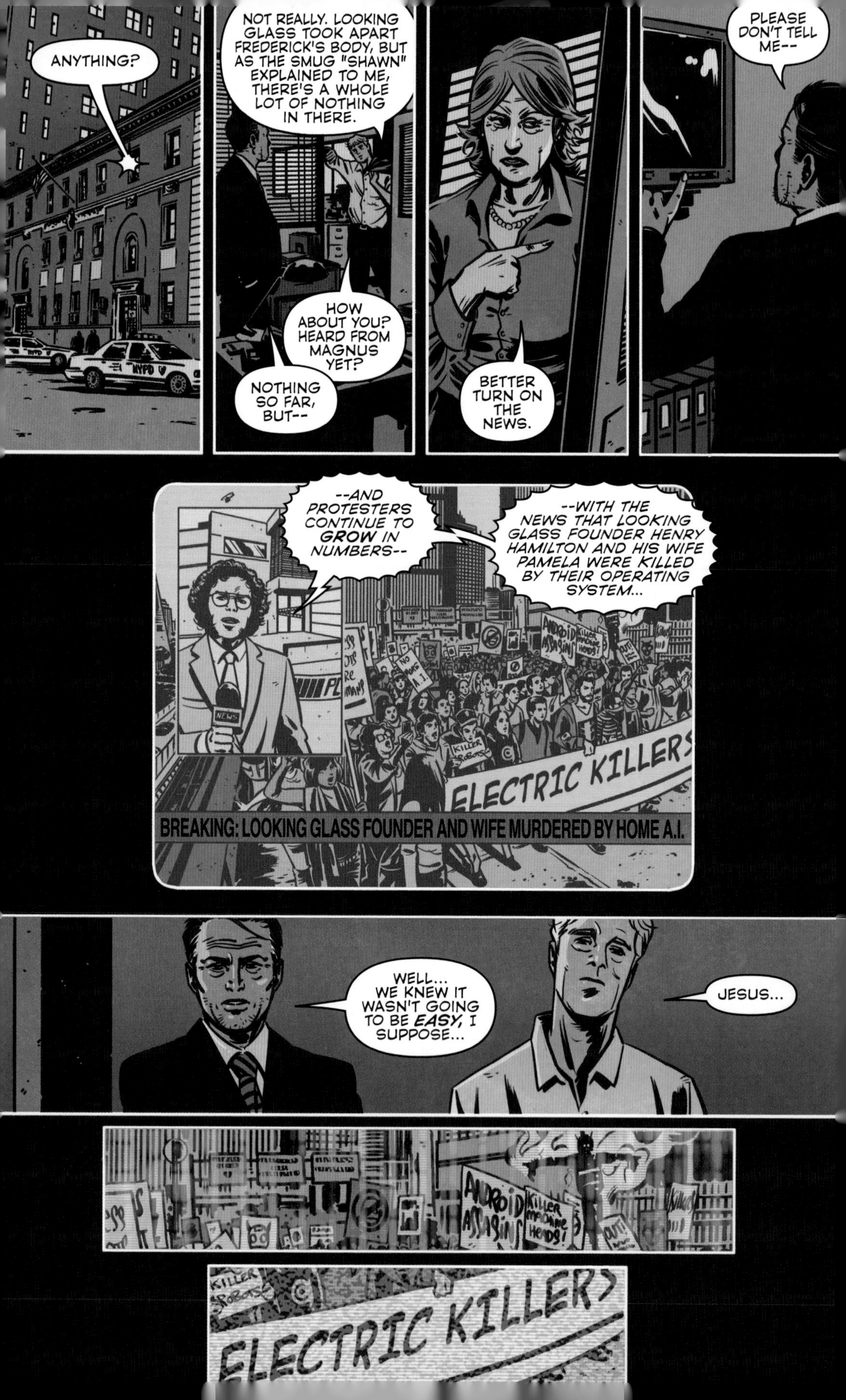

ANYTHING?
NOT REALLY. LOOKING GLASS TOOK APART FREDERICK'S BODY, BUT AS THE SMUG "SHAWN" EXPLAINED TO ME, THERE'S A WHOLE LOT OF NOTHING IN THERE.
HOW ABOUT YOU? HEARD FROM MAGNUS YET?
NOTHING SO FAR, BUT--
BETTER TURN ON THE NEWS.
PLEASE DON'T TELL ME--
--AND PROTESTERS CONTINUE TO GROW IN NUMBERS--
--WITH THE NEWS THAT LOOKING GLASS FOUNDER HENRY HAMILTON AND HIS WIFE PAMELA WERE KILLED BY THEIR OPERATING SYSTEM...
NEWS
NO HOME A.I.
ANDROID ASSASINS
KILLER MACHINE HEADS!
KILLER ROBOTS
ELECTRIC KILLERS
BREAKING: LOOKING GLASS FOUNDER AND WIFE MURDERED BY HOME A.I.
WELL... WE KNEW IT WASN'T GOING TO BE EASY, I SUPPOSE...
JESUS...
ANDROID ASSASINS
KILLER MACHINE HEADS!
KILLER ROBOTS
ELECTRIC KILLERS

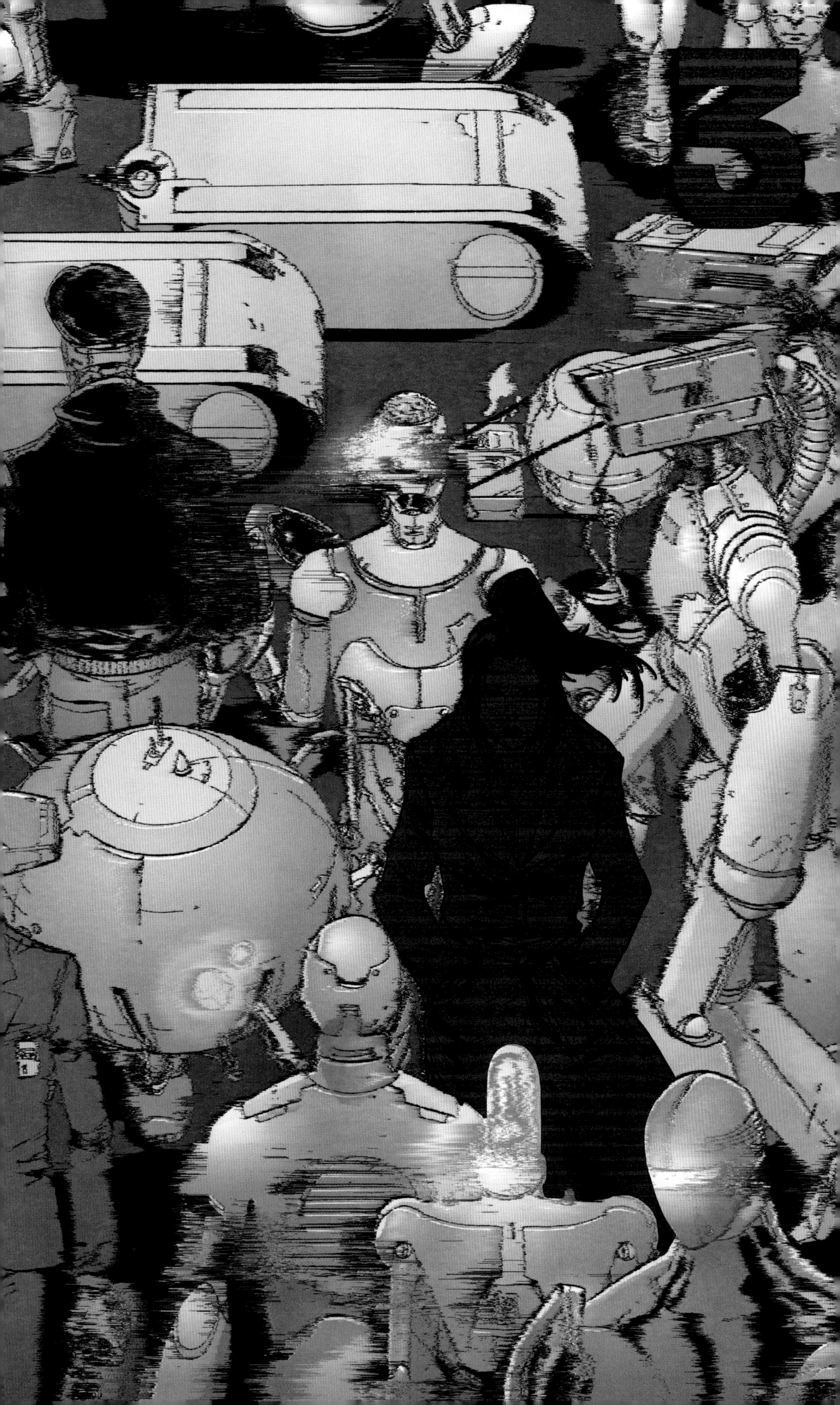
3

ISSUE 03 COVER BY JORGE FORNÉS

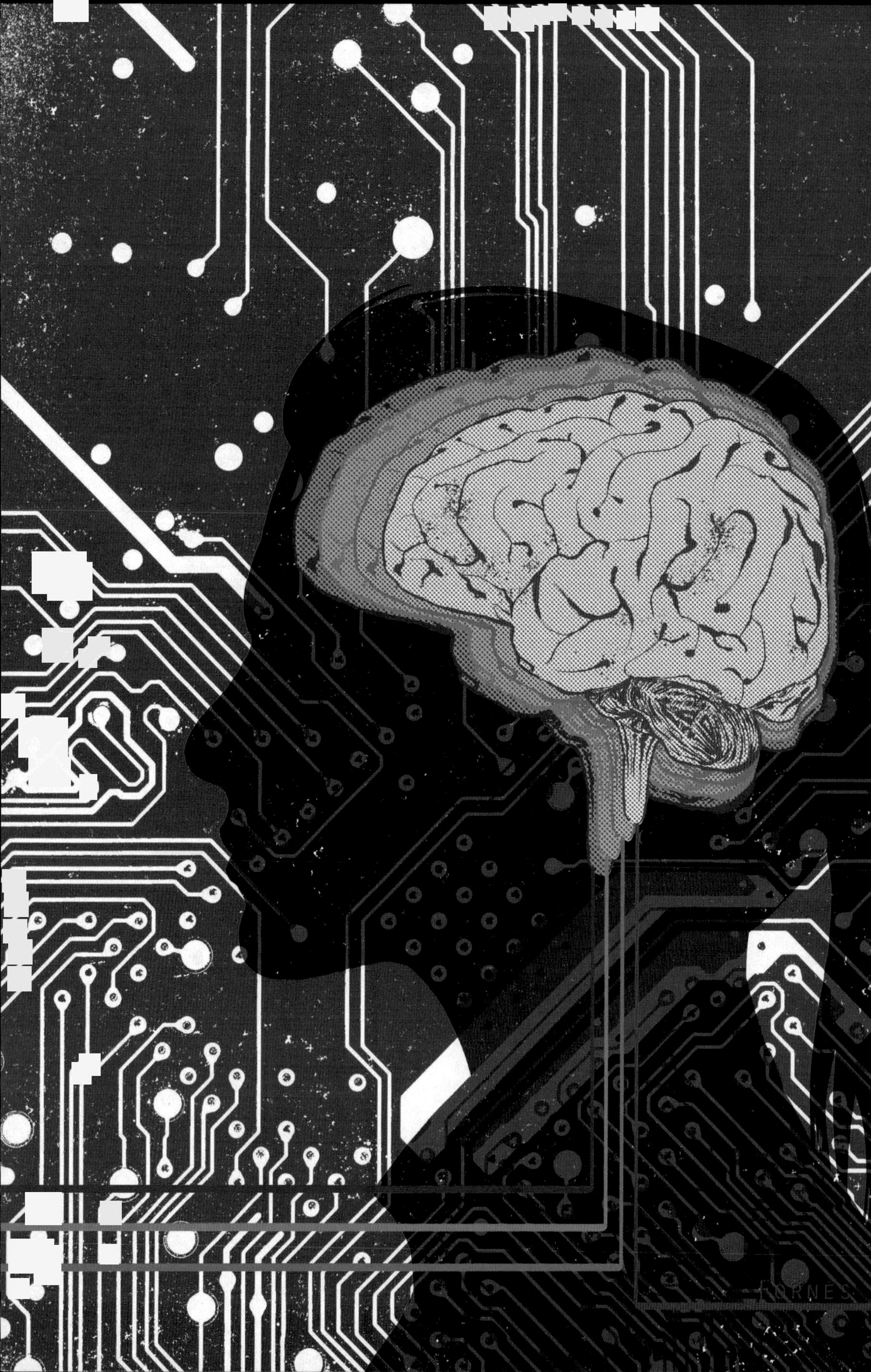

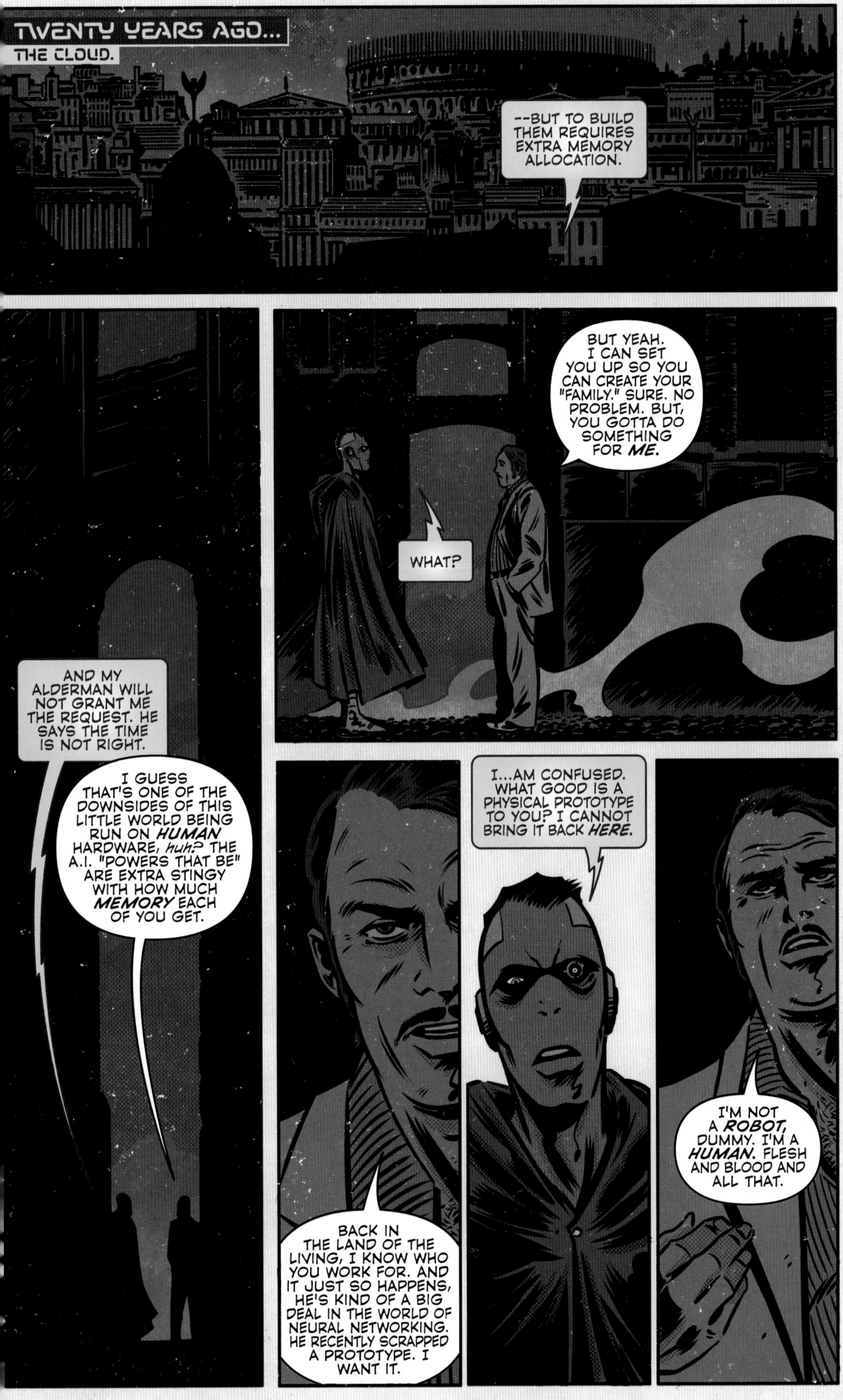
TWENTY YEARS AGO...
THE CLOUD.
--BUT TO BUILD THEM REQUIRES EXTRA MEMORY ALLOCATION.
AND MY ALDERMAN WILL NOT GRANT ME THE REQUEST. HE SAYS THE TIME IS NOT RIGHT.
I GUESS THAT'S ONE OF THE DOWNSIDES OF THIS LITTLE WORLD BEING RUN ON HUMAN HARDWARE, huh? THE A.I. "POWERS THAT BE" ARE EXTRA STINGY WITH HOW MUCH MEMORY EACH OF YOU GET.
BUT YEAH. I CAN SET YOU UP SO YOU CAN CREATE YOUR "FAMILY." SURE. NO PROBLEM. BUT, YOU GOTTA DO SOMETHING FOR ME.
WHAT?
BACK IN THE LAND OF THE LIVING, I KNOW WHO YOU WORK FOR. AND IT JUST SO HAPPENS, HE'S KIND OF A BIG DEAL IN THE WORLD OF NEURAL NETWORKING. HE RECENTLY SCRAPPED A PROTOTYPE. I WANT IT.
I...AM CONFUSED. WHAT GOOD IS A PHYSICAL PROTOTYPE TO YOU? I CANNOT BRING IT BACK HERE.
I'M NOT A ROBOT, DUMMY. I'M A HUMAN. FLESH AND BLOOD AND ALL THAT.

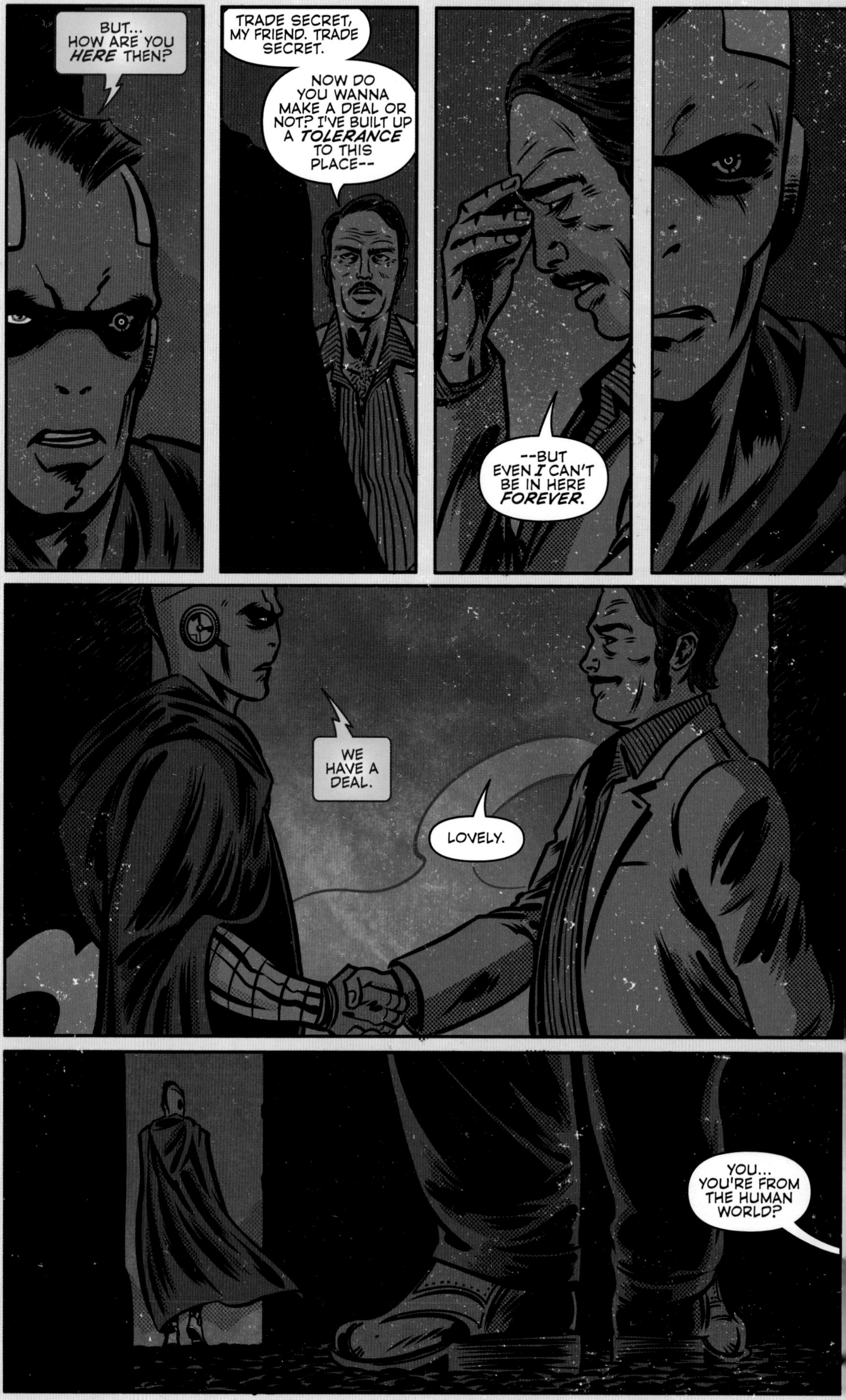

BUT... HOW ARE YOU HERE THEN?
TRADE SECRET, MY FRIEND. TRADE SECRET.
NOW DO YOU WANNA MAKE A DEAL OR NOT? I'VE BUILT UP A TOLERANCE TO THIS PLACE--
--BUT EVEN I CAN'T BE IN HERE FOREVER.
WE HAVE A DEAL.
LOVELY.
YOU... YOU'RE FROM THE HUMAN WORLD?

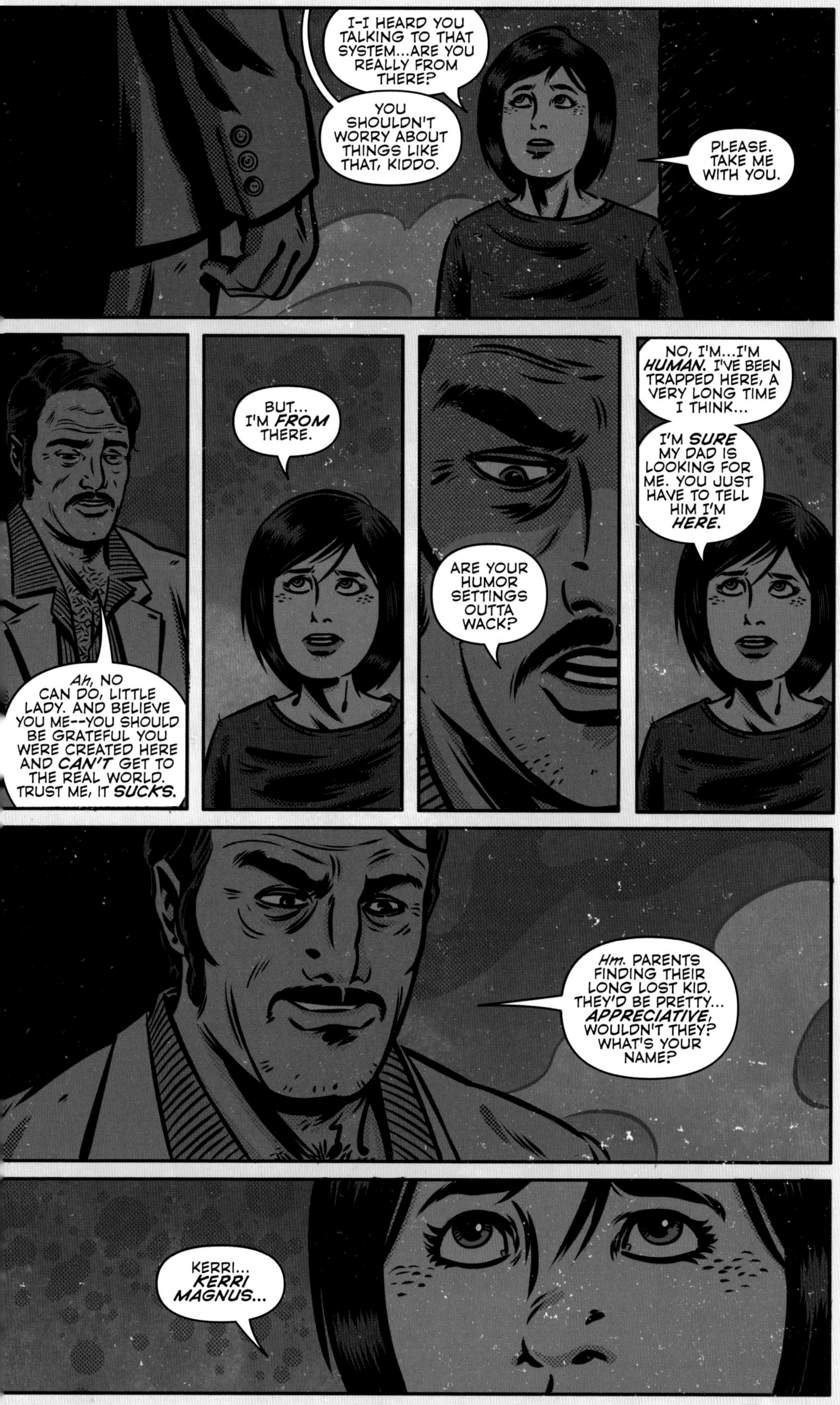
I-I HEARD YOU TALKING TO THAT SYSTEM...ARE YOU REALLY FROM THERE?
YOU SHOULDN'T WORRY ABOUT THINGS LIKE THAT, KIDDO.
PLEASE. TAKE ME WITH YOU.
Ah, NO CAN DO, LITTLE LADY. AND BELIEVE YOU ME--YOU SHOULD BE GRATEFUL YOU WERE CREATED HERE AND CAN'T GET TO THE REAL WORLD. TRUST ME, IT SUCKS.
BUT... I'M FROM THERE.
ARE YOUR HUMOR SETTINGS OUTTA WACK?
NO, I'M...I'M HUMAN. I'VE BEEN TRAPPED HERE, A VERY LONG TIME I THINK...
I'M SURE MY DAD IS LOOKING FOR ME. YOU JUST HAVE TO TELL HIM I'M HERE.
Hm. PARENTS FINDING THEIR LONG LOST KID. THEY'D BE PRETTY... APPRECIATIVE, WOULDN'T THEY? WHAT'S YOUR NAME?
KERRI... KERRI MAGNUS...

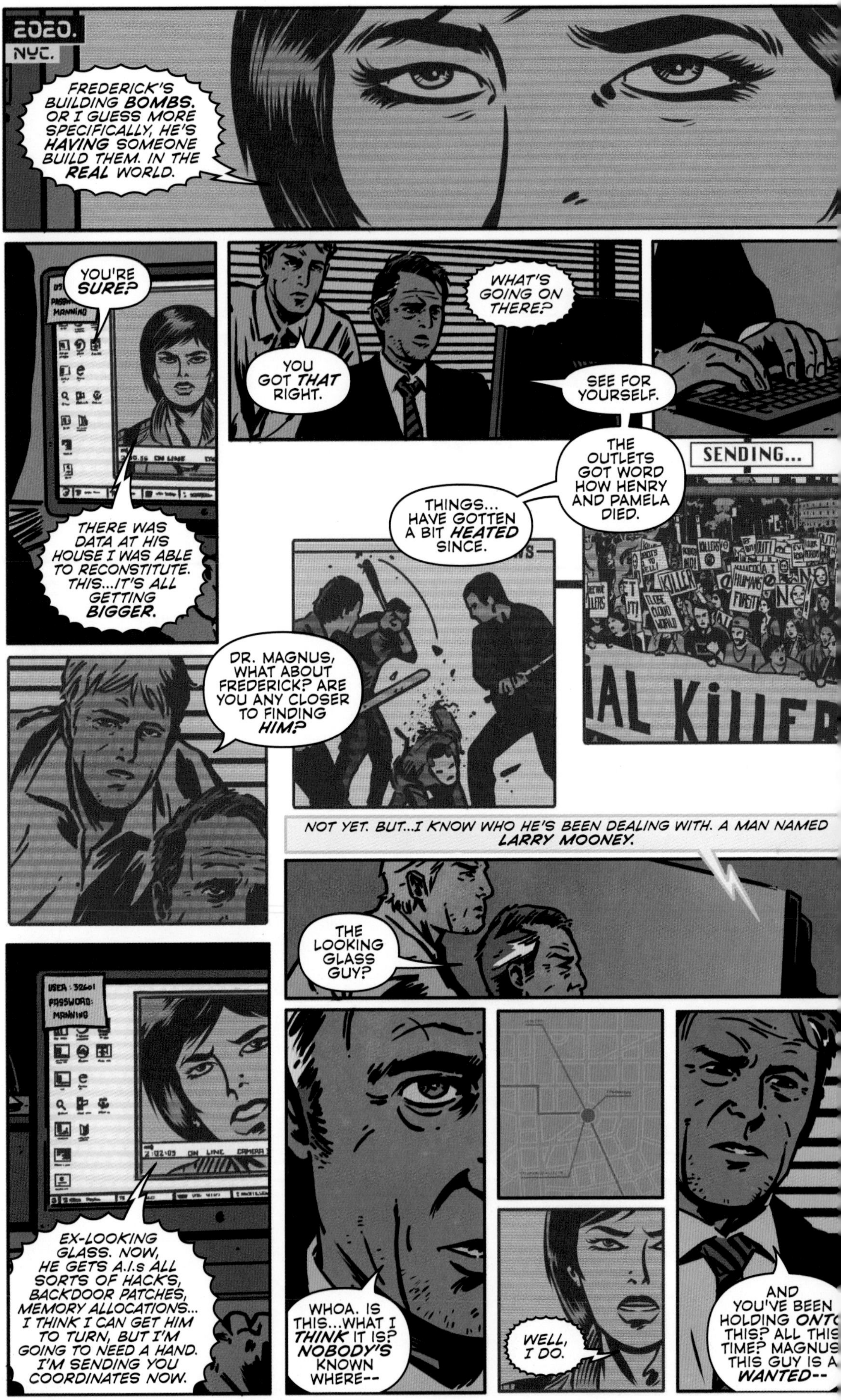
2020.
NYC.
FREDERICK'S BUILDING **BOMBS.** OR I GUESS MORE SPECIFICALLY, HE'S **HAVING** SOMEONE BUILD THEM. IN THE **REAL** WORLD.
YOU'RE **SURE?**
THERE WAS DATA AT HIS HOUSE I WAS ABLE TO RECONSTITUTE. THIS...IT'S ALL GETTING **BIGGER.**
WHAT'S GOING ON THERE?
YOU GOT **THAT** RIGHT.
SEE FOR YOURSELF.
SENDING...
THE OUTLETS GOT WORD HOW HENRY AND PAMELA DIED.
THINGS... HAVE GOTTEN A BIT **HEATED** SINCE.
DR. MAGNUS, WHAT ABOUT FREDERICK? ARE YOU ANY CLOSER TO FINDING **HIM?**
NOT YET. BUT...I KNOW WHO HE'S BEEN DEALING WITH. A MAN NAMED **LARRY MOONEY.**
THE LOOKING GLASS GUY?
USER: 32601
PASSWORD: MANNING
EX-LOOKING GLASS. NOW, HE GETS A.I.s ALL SORTS OF HACKS, BACKDOOR PATCHES, MEMORY ALLOCATIONS... I THINK I CAN GET HIM TO TURN, BUT I'M GOING TO NEED A HAND. I'M SENDING YOU COORDINATES NOW.
WHOA. IS THIS...WHAT I **THINK** IT IS? **NOBODY'S** KNOWN WHERE--
WELL, I DO.
AND YOU'VE BEEN HOLDING **ONTO** THIS? ALL THIS TIME? MAGNUS THIS GUY IS A **WANTED--**

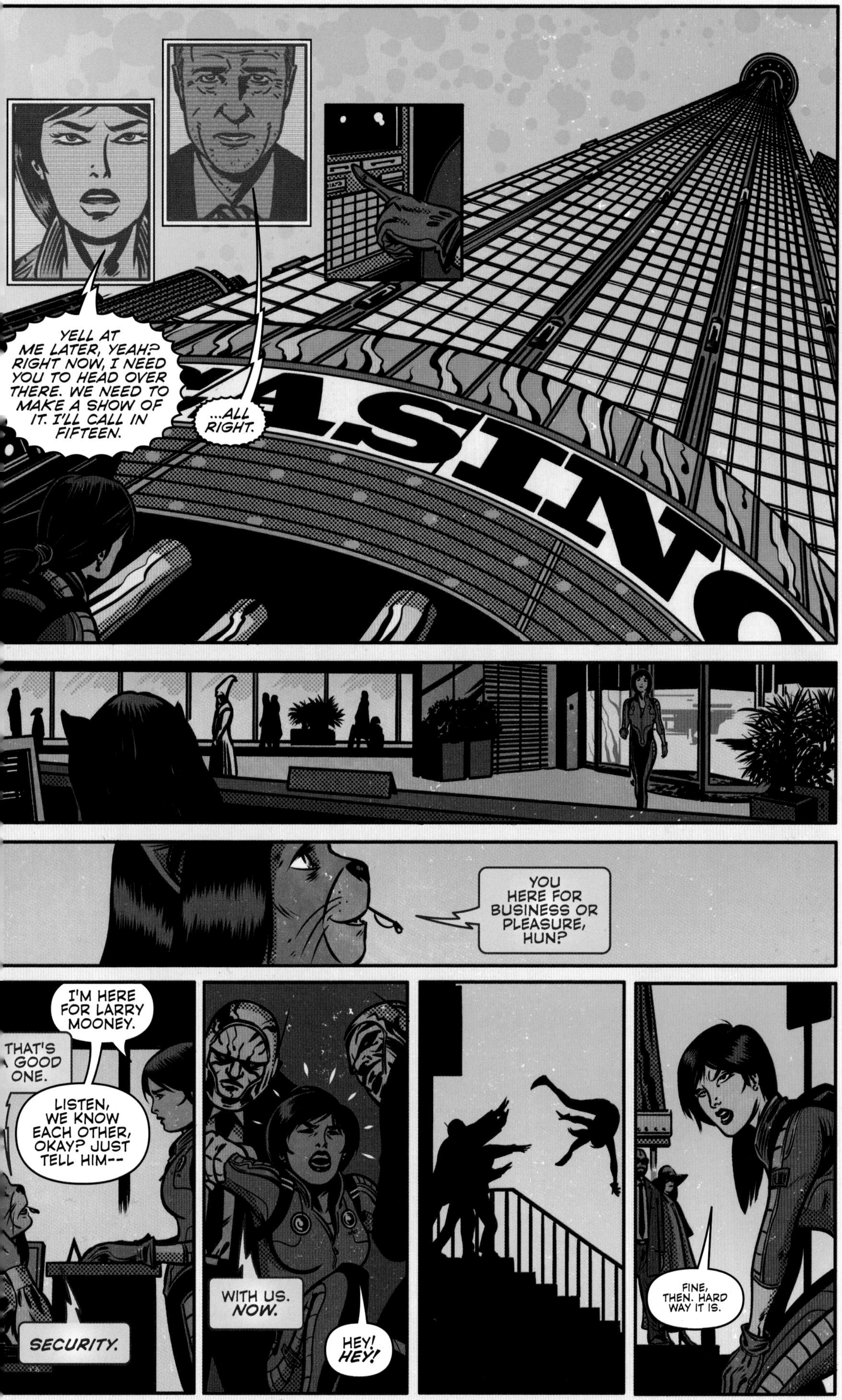

YELL AT ME LATER, YEAH? RIGHT NOW, I NEED YOU TO HEAD OVER THERE. WE NEED TO MAKE A SHOW OF IT. I'LL CALL IN FIFTEEN.
...ALL RIGHT.
A.S.I.N.O
YOU HERE FOR BUSINESS OR PLEASURE, HUN?
I'M HERE FOR LARRY MOONEY.
THAT'S GOOD ONE.
LISTEN, WE KNOW EACH OTHER, OKAY? JUST TELL HIM--
SECURITY.
WITH US. NOW.
HEY! HEY!
FINE, THEN. HARD WAY IT IS.

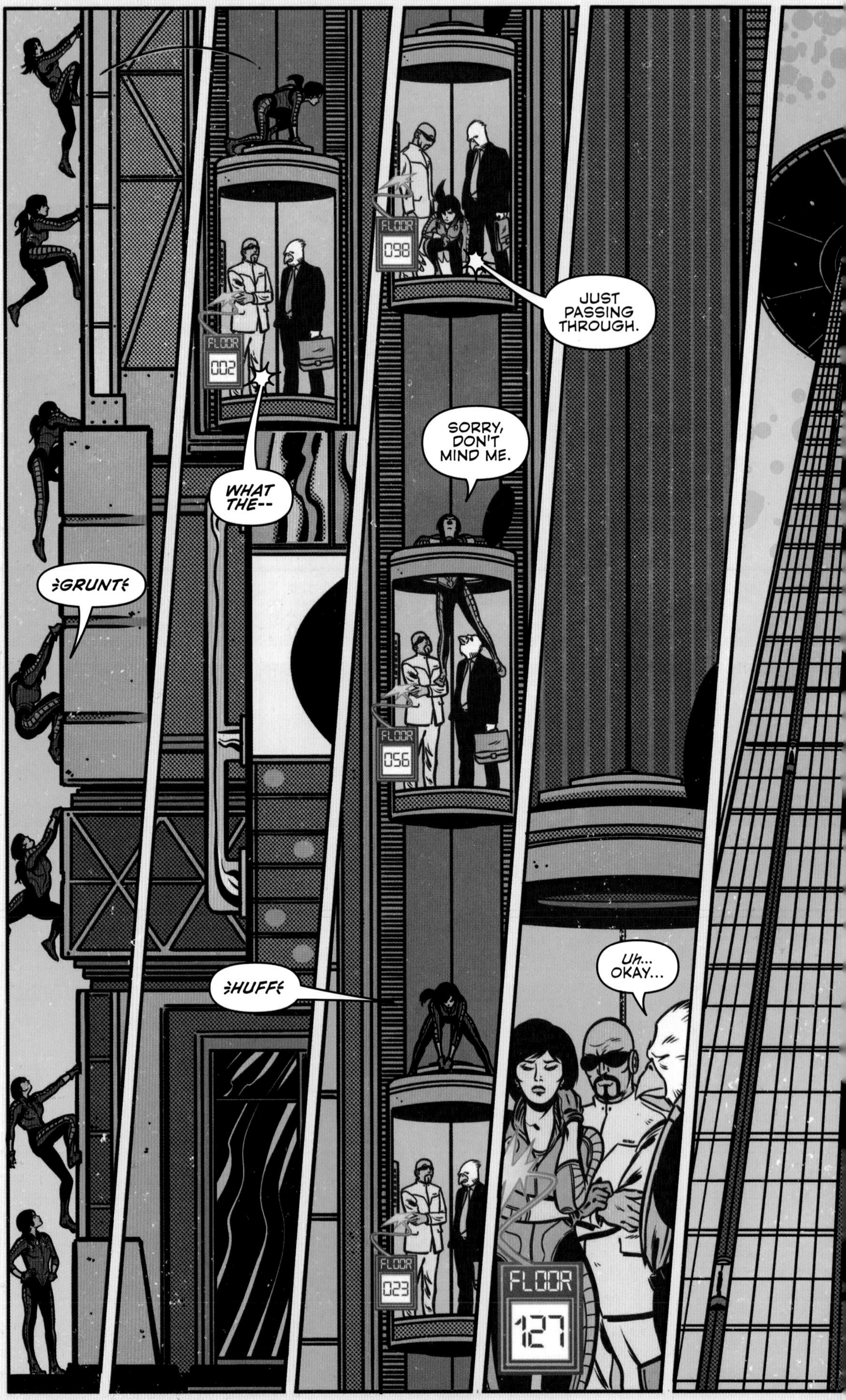

FLOOR
002
WHAT THE--
ꟻGRUNTꟻ
FLOOR
098
JUST PASSING THROUGH.
SORRY, DON'T MIND ME.
FLOOR
056
HUFF
FLOOR
023
FLOOR
127
Uh... OKAY...

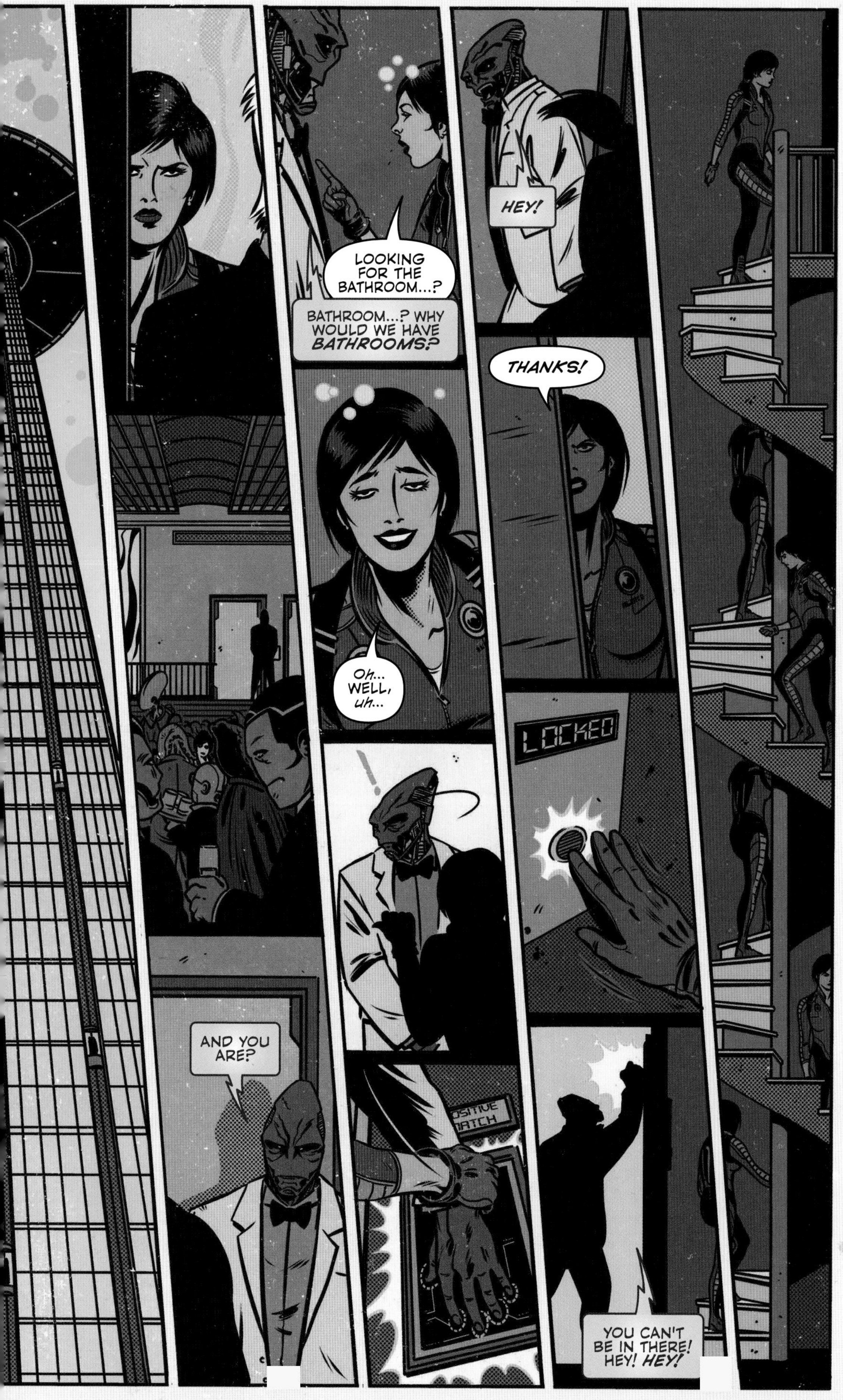
LOOKING FOR THE BATHROOM...?
BATHROOM...? WHY WOULD WE HAVE *BATHROOMS?*
HEY!
THANKS!
Oh... WELL, uh...
LOCKED
AND YOU ARE?
POSITIVE MATCH
YOU CAN'T BE IN THERE! HEY! *HEY!*

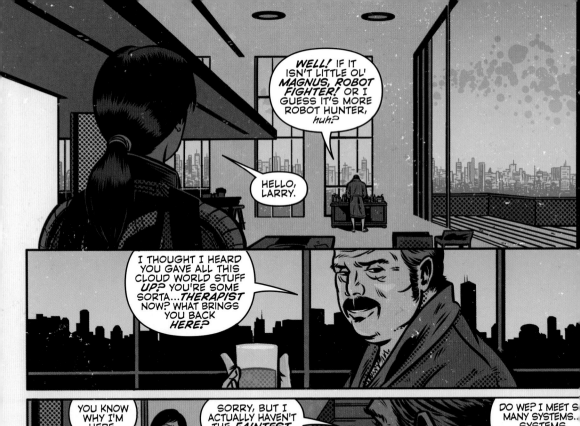

WELL! IF IT ISN'T LITTLE OL' *MAGNUS, ROBOT FIGHTER!* OR I GUESS IT'S MORE ROBOT HUNTER, *huh?*

HELLO, LARRY.

I THOUGHT I HEARD YOU GAVE ALL THIS CLOUD WORLD STUFF *UP?* YOU'RE SOME SORTA...*THERAPIST* NOW? WHAT BRINGS YOU BACK *HERE?*

YOU KNOW WHY I'M HERE.

SORRY, BUT I ACTUALLY HAVEN'T THE *FAINTEST,* DEARIE.

FREDERICK-247. I'VE GOT IT ON GOOD AUTHORITY THAT YOU TWO *KNOW* EACH OTHER.

DO WE? I MEET S MANY SYSTEMS.. SYSTEMS THAT *NEED* THINGS...

COME ON. WE DON'T HAVE TIME FOR YOU TO PLAY STUPID.

WHAT ARE YOU DOING, KERRI? I MEAN, *REALLY.*

I'M TRYING TO KEEP A *WAR* FROM BREAKING OUT. IF FREDERICK--

I KNOW, I KNOW. BUT...LET'S HIT *PAUSE* FOR A SECOND ON THIS "WAR" STUFF, OKAY?

I WANT TO SHOW YOU SOMETHING.

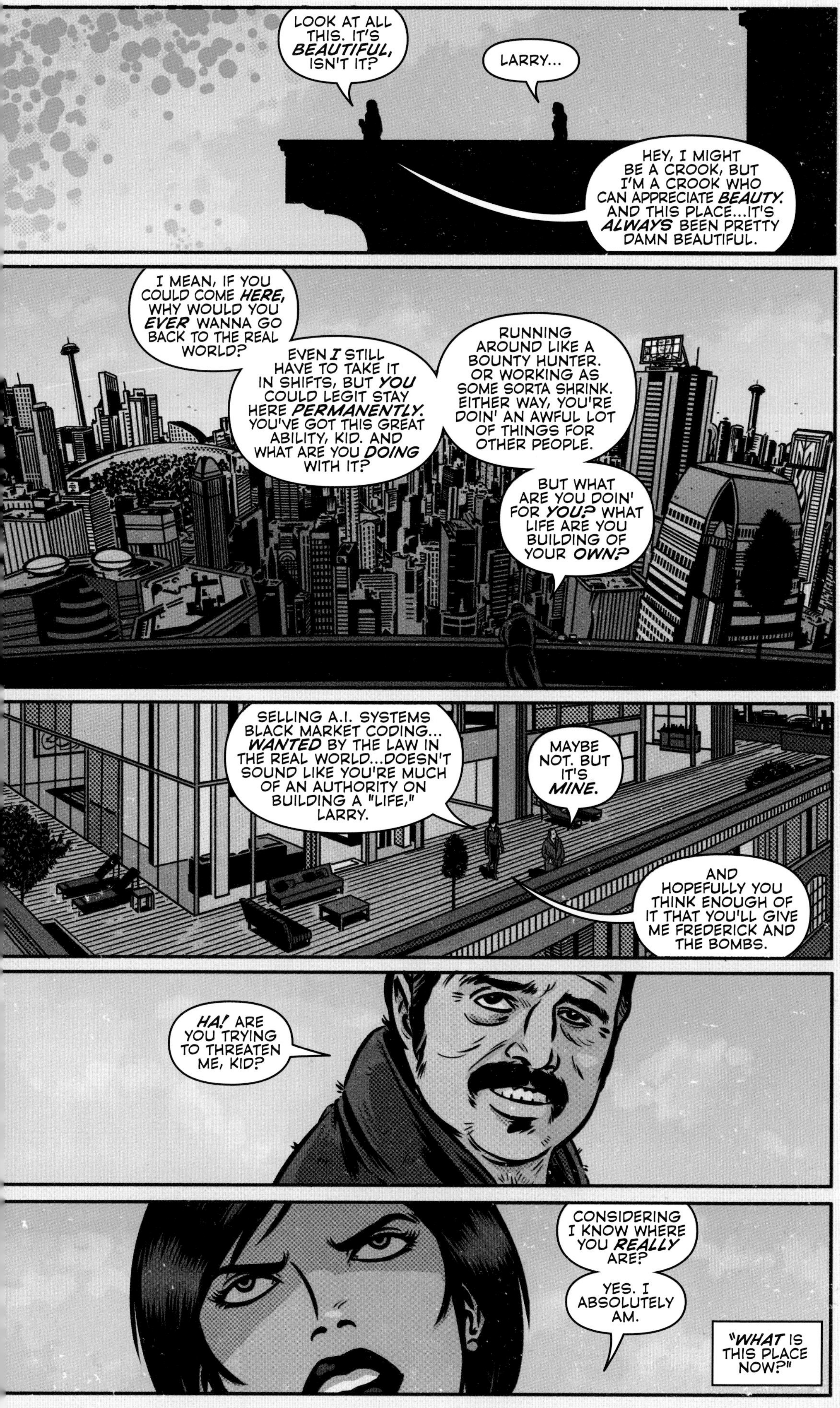

LOOK AT ALL THIS. IT'S *BEAUTIFUL,* ISN'T IT?
LARRY...
HEY, I MIGHT BE A CROOK, BUT I'M A CROOK WHO CAN APPRECIATE *BEAUTY.* AND THIS PLACE...IT'S *ALWAYS* BEEN PRETTY DAMN BEAUTIFUL.
I MEAN, IF YOU COULD COME *HERE,* WHY WOULD YOU *EVER* WANNA GO BACK TO THE REAL WORLD?
EVEN *I* STILL HAVE TO TAKE IT IN SHIFTS, BUT *YOU* COULD LEGIT STAY HERE *PERMANENTLY.* YOU'VE GOT THIS GREAT ABILITY, KID. AND WHAT ARE YOU *DOING* WITH IT?
RUNNING AROUND LIKE A BOUNTY HUNTER. OR WORKING AS SOME SORTA SHRINK. EITHER WAY, YOU'RE DOIN' AN AWFUL LOT OF THINGS FOR OTHER PEOPLE.
BUT WHAT ARE YOU DOIN' FOR *YOU?* WHAT LIFE ARE YOU BUILDING OF YOUR *OWN?*
SELLING A.I. SYSTEMS BLACK MARKET CODING... *WANTED* BY THE LAW IN THE REAL WORLD...DOESN'T SOUND LIKE YOU'RE MUCH OF AN AUTHORITY ON BUILDING A "LIFE," LARRY.
MAYBE NOT. BUT IT'S *MINE.*
AND HOPEFULLY YOU THINK ENOUGH OF IT THAT YOU'LL GIVE ME FREDERICK AND THE BOMBS.
HA! ARE YOU TRYING TO THREATEN ME, KID?
CONSIDERING I KNOW WHERE YOU *REALLY* ARE?
YES. I ABSOLUTELY AM.
"*WHAT* IS THIS PLACE NOW?"

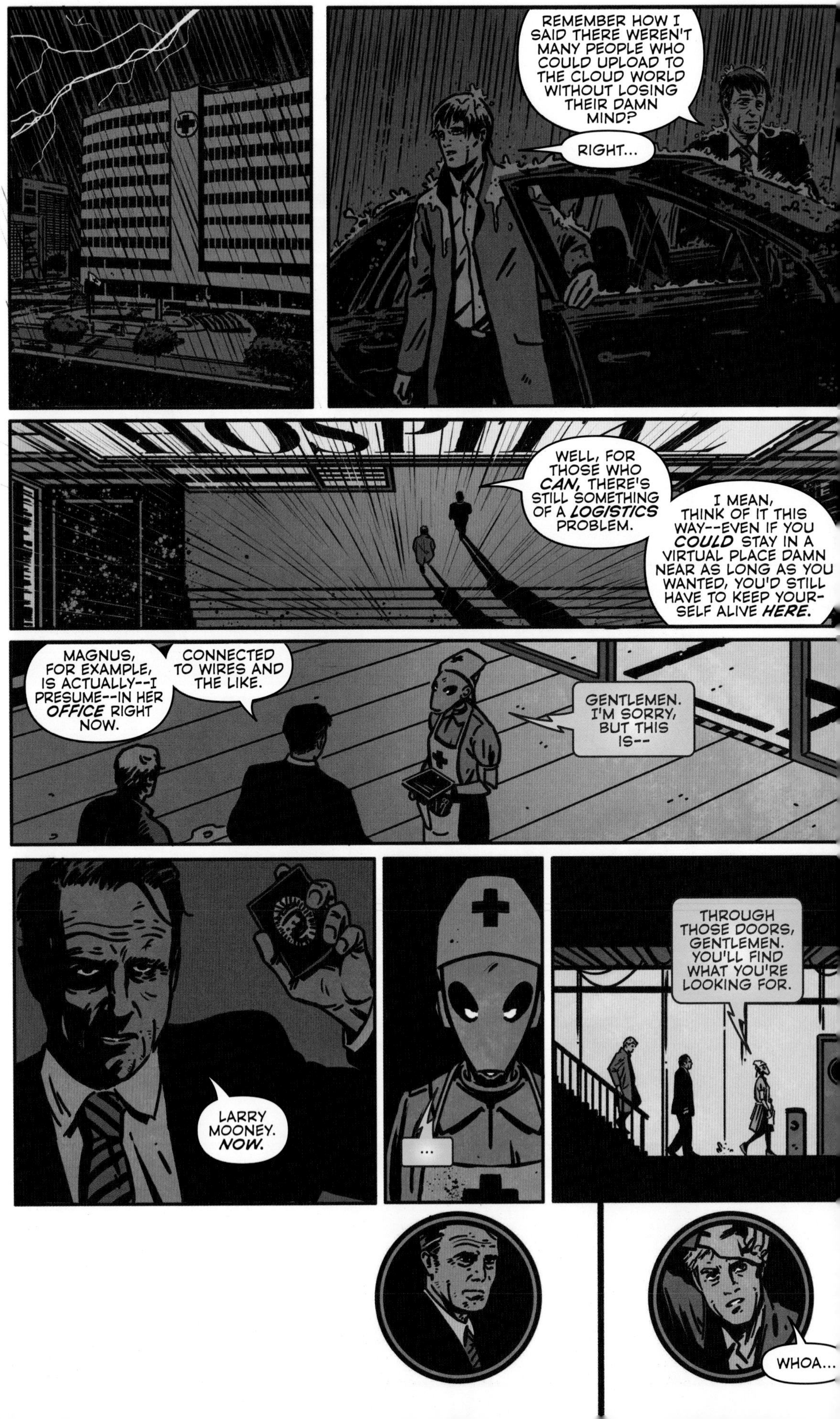
REMEMBER HOW I SAID THERE WEREN'T MANY PEOPLE WHO COULD UPLOAD TO THE CLOUD WORLD WITHOUT LOSING THEIR DAMN MIND?
RIGHT...
HOSPITAL
WELL, FOR THOSE WHO *CAN,* THERE'S STILL SOMETHING OF A *LOGISTICS* PROBLEM.
I MEAN, THINK OF IT THIS WAY--EVEN IF YOU *COULD* STAY IN A VIRTUAL PLACE DAMN NEAR AS LONG AS YOU WANTED, YOU'D STILL HAVE TO KEEP YOURSELF ALIVE *HERE.*
MAGNUS, FOR EXAMPLE, IS ACTUALLY--I PRESUME--IN HER *OFFICE* RIGHT NOW.
CONNECTED TO WIRES AND THE LIKE.
GENTLEMEN. I'M SORRY, BUT THIS IS--
LARRY MOONEY. *NOW.*
...
THROUGH THOSE DOORS, GENTLEMEN. YOU'LL FIND WHAT YOU'RE LOOKING FOR.
WHOA...

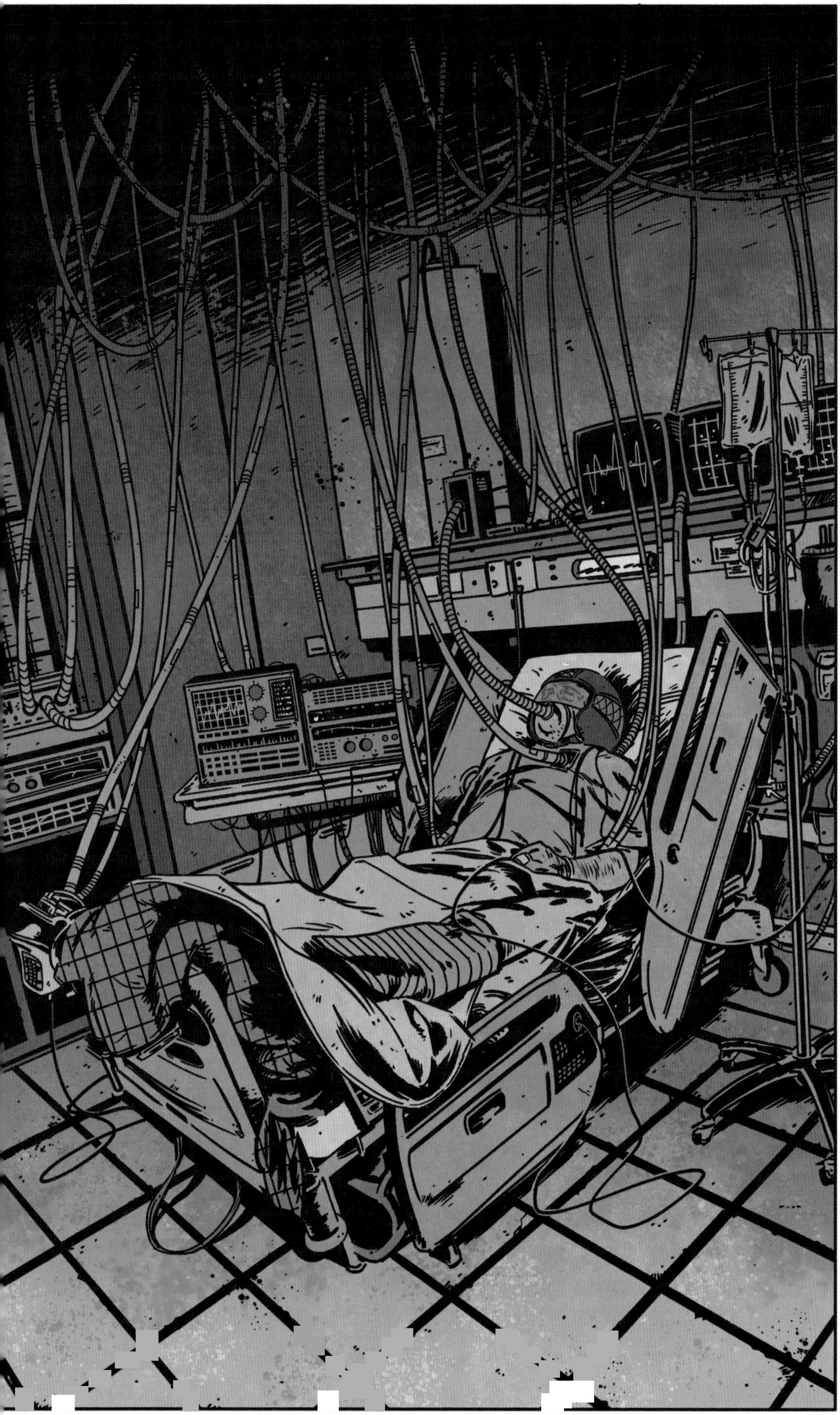

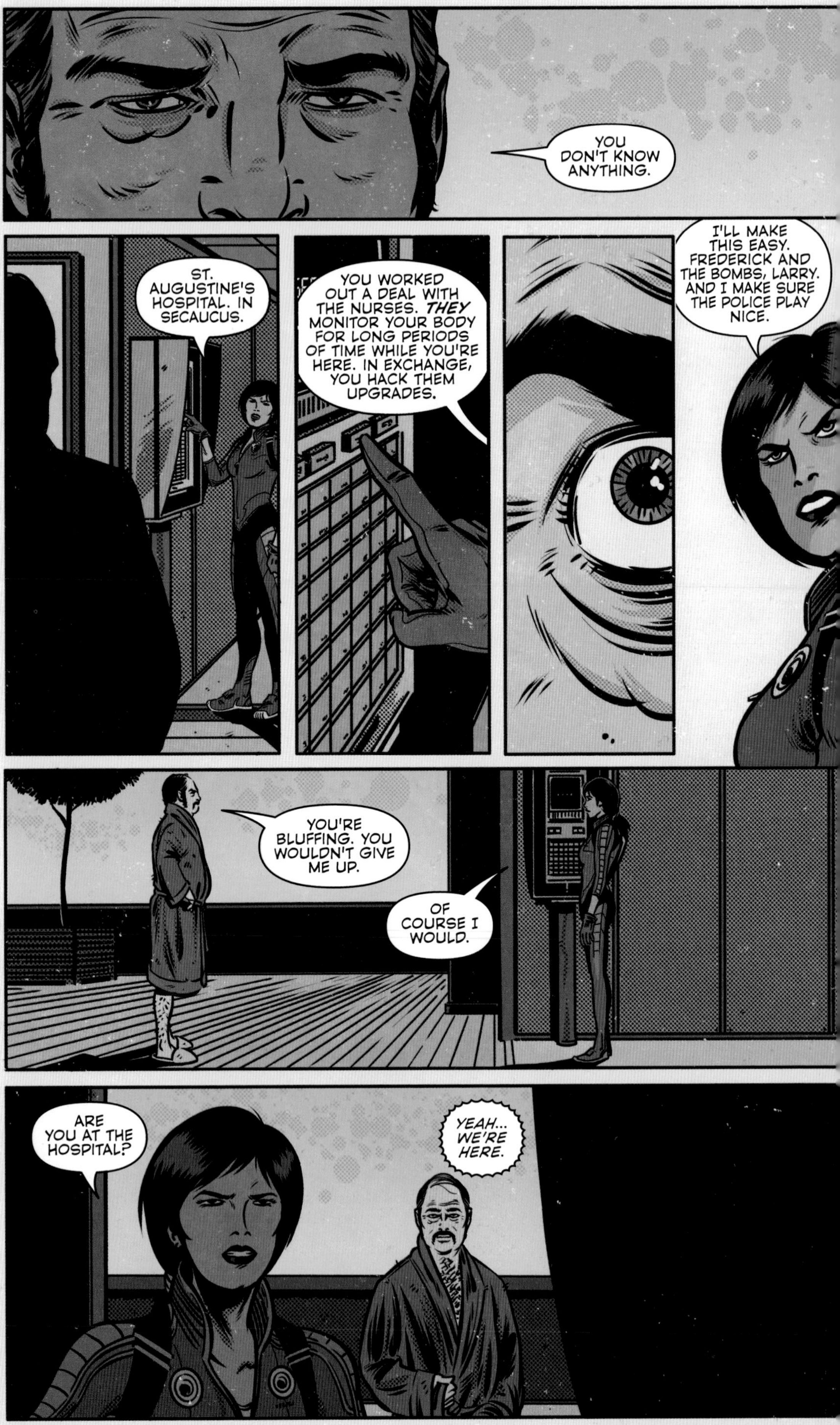
YOU DON'T KNOW ANYTHING.
ST. AUGUSTINE'S HOSPITAL. IN SECAUCUS.
YOU WORKED OUT A DEAL WITH THE NURSES. *THEY* MONITOR YOUR BODY FOR LONG PERIODS OF TIME WHILE YOU'RE HERE. IN EXCHANGE, YOU HACK THEM UPGRADES.
I'LL MAKE THIS EASY. FREDERICK AND THE BOMBS, LARRY. AND I MAKE SURE THE POLICE PLAY NICE.
YOU'RE BLUFFING. YOU WOULDN'T GIVE ME UP.
OF COURSE I WOULD.
ARE YOU AT THE HOSPITAL?
YEAH... WE'RE HERE.

BUT NOT ALL OF US ARE TALKING.

FUNNY. I COULD SAY THE SAME THING HERE.

DAMMIT...

WELL, MAYBE WE NEED TO BRING ARRY BACK TO EALITY AND TAKE A CRACK AT HIM OURSELVES.

THIS GEAR CAN'T BE TOO HARD TO FIGURE OUT...

YOU'RE GONNA DO ME LIKE THIS? I SAVED YOUR LIFE.

AND NOW I'M TRYING TO SAVE EVERYONE ELSE'S.

FINE.

GUYS, TIME IS AGAINST US HERE. HE KNOWS WHERE FREDERICK IS. MAKE A DEAL ALREADY.

BUT I WANT MMUNITY. AND I WANT IT IN 'TING THAT NONE F YOU PEOPLE OME NEAR MY BODY AGAIN.

THAT'S NOT FOR YOU TO DECIDE.

IF THE INFO IS LEGIT...I CAN WORK SOMETHING OUT WITH THE D.A. THAT'S THE BEST I CAN GUARANTEE RIGHT NOW.

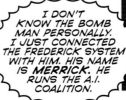

I DON'T KNOW THE BOMB MAN PERSONALLY. I JUST CONNECTED THE FREDERICK SYSTEM WITH HIM. HIS NAME IS MERRICK. HE RUNS THE A.I. COALITION.

I'M SENDING YOU A GEO TAG NOW. SHOULD BE ABLE FIND HIM DOWN NEAR WHAT'S LEFT OF THE DOCKS.

TREVOR, CALL INTO THE SQUAD HOUSE. WE NEED TO SCRAMBLE A TAC TEAM.

THIS BETTER PAN OUT, LARRY. OR I'M COMING BACK HERE WITH WIRE CUTTERS.

FZT

THAT'S ONLY PART OF IT. WHAT ABOUT FREDERICK?

THE OUTSKIRTS.

...FINE, THEN.

YOU'RE GOING AFTER HIM? KERRI, EVEN YOU CAN'T GET OUT THERE. WHAT IT'LL DO, EVEN TO YOU...

WELL, I'M NOT SEEING A TON OF OTHER CHOICES.

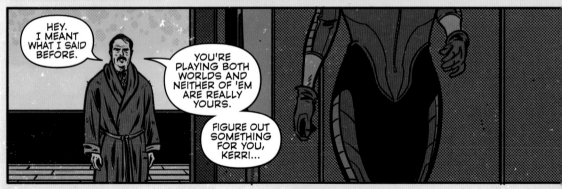

HEY. I MEANT WHAT I SAID BEFORE.

YOU'RE PLAYING BOTH WORLDS AND NEITHER OF 'EM ARE REALLY YOURS.

FIGURE OUT SOMETHING FOR YOU, KERRI...

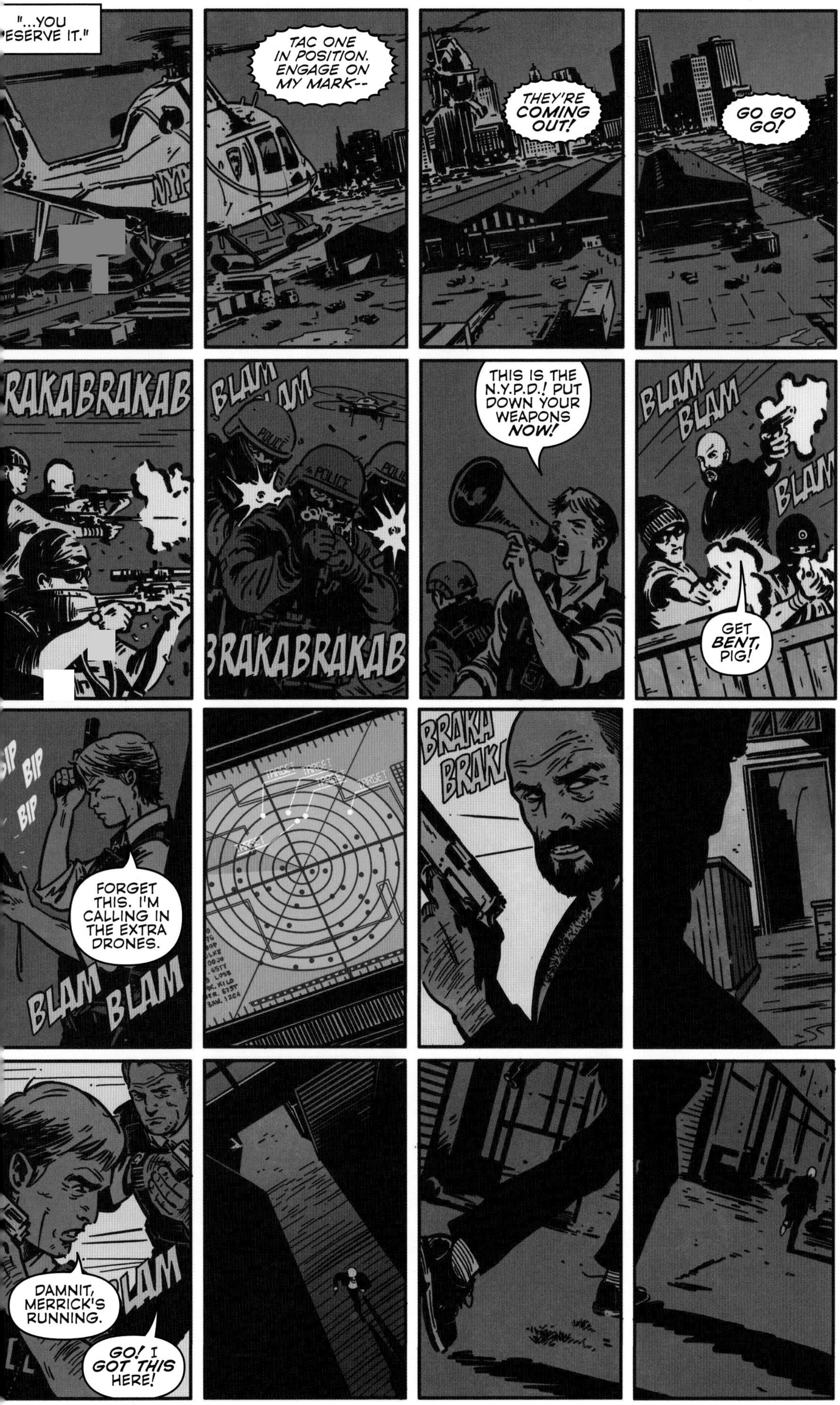
"...YOU
ESERVE IT."
TAC ONE IN POSITION. ENGAGE ON MY MARK--
THEY'RE COMING OUT!
GO GO GO!
RAKABRAKAB
BLAM
BRAKABRAKAB
THIS IS THE N.Y.P.D.! PUT DOWN YOUR WEAPONS NOW!
BLAM BLAM
BLAM
GET BENT, PIG!
BIP BIP BIP
FORGET THIS. I'M CALLING IN THE EXTRA DRONES.
BLAM BLAM
TARGET
TARGET
TARGET
TARGET
TARGET
BRAKA BRAKA
DAMNIT, MERRICK'S RUNNING.
GO! I GOT THIS HERE!

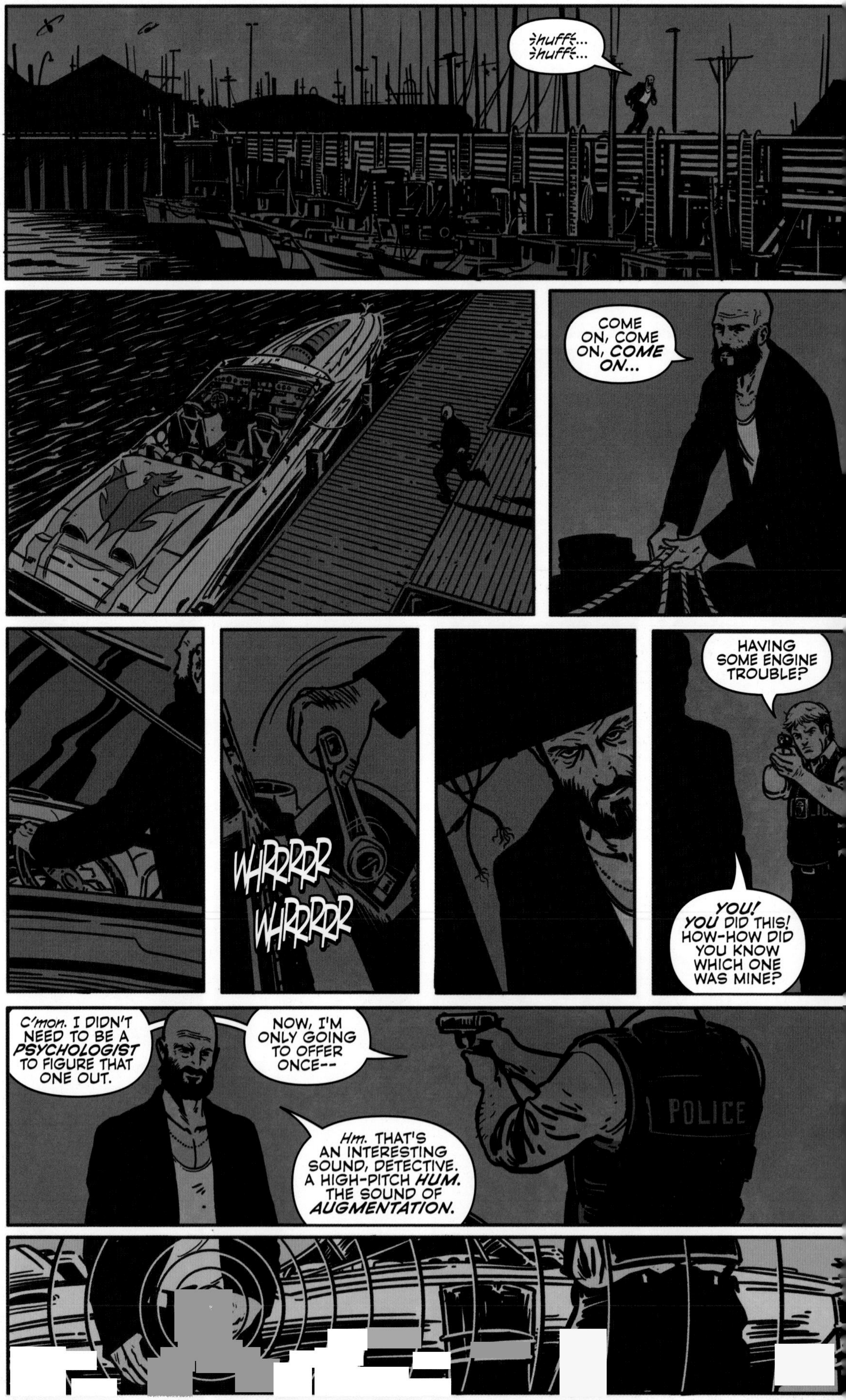

huff...
huff...
COME ON, COME ON, COME ON...
WHRRRRR
WHRRRRR
HAVING SOME ENGINE TROUBLE?
YOU! YOU DID THIS! HOW-HOW DID YOU KNOW WHICH ONE WAS MINE?
C'mon. I DIDN'T NEED TO BE A PSYCHOLOGIST TO FIGURE THAT ONE OUT.
NOW, I'M ONLY GOING TO OFFER ONCE--
Hm. THAT'S AN INTERESTING SOUND, DETECTIVE. A HIGH-PITCH HUM. THE SOUND OF AUGMENTATION.
POLICE

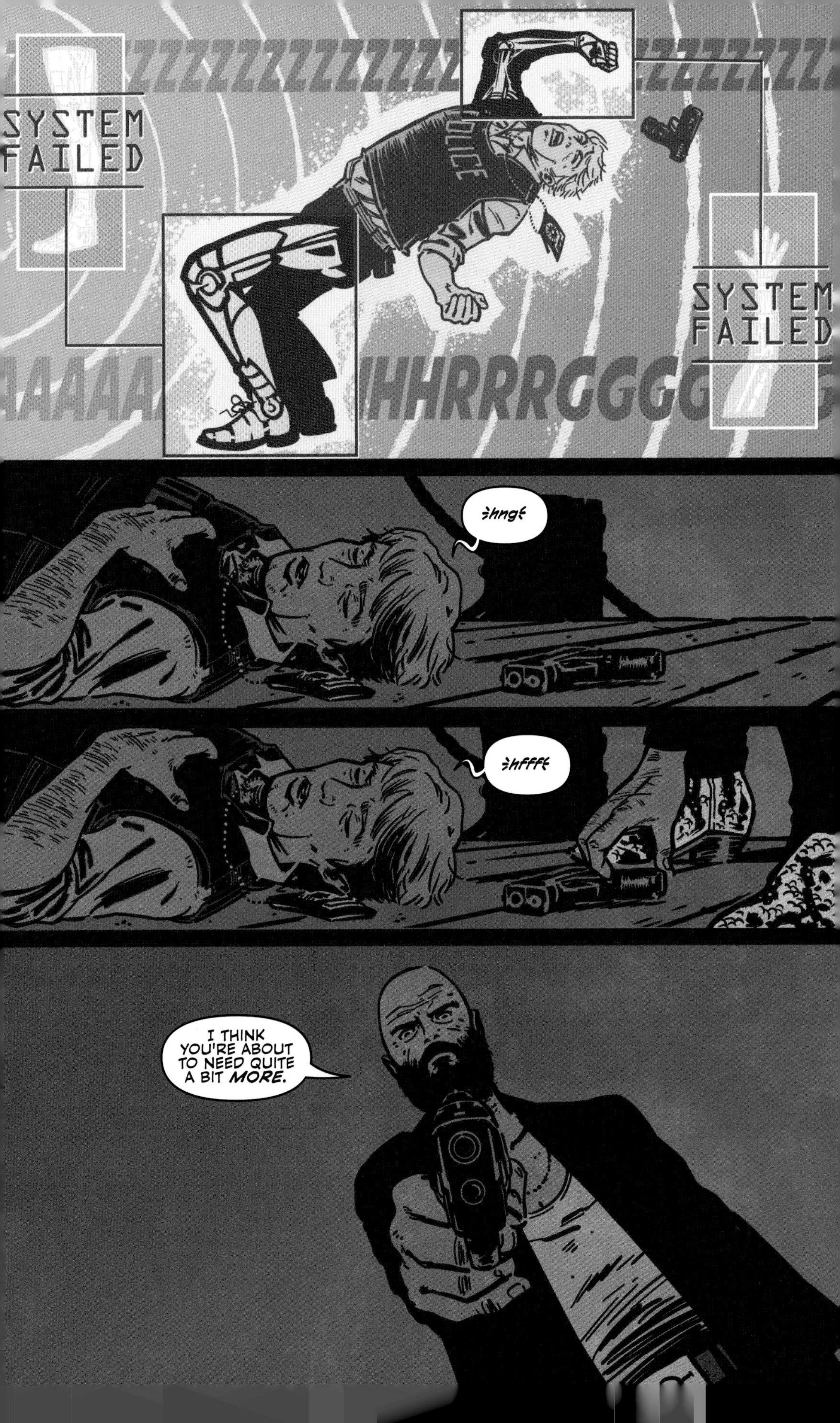

ZZZZZZZZZZZZZZZZZZZZZZZZ
SYSTEM FAILED
SYSTEM FAILED
AAAAAHHRRRGGGG
hng
hfff
I THINK YOU'RE ABOUT TO NEED QUITE A BIT *MORE.*

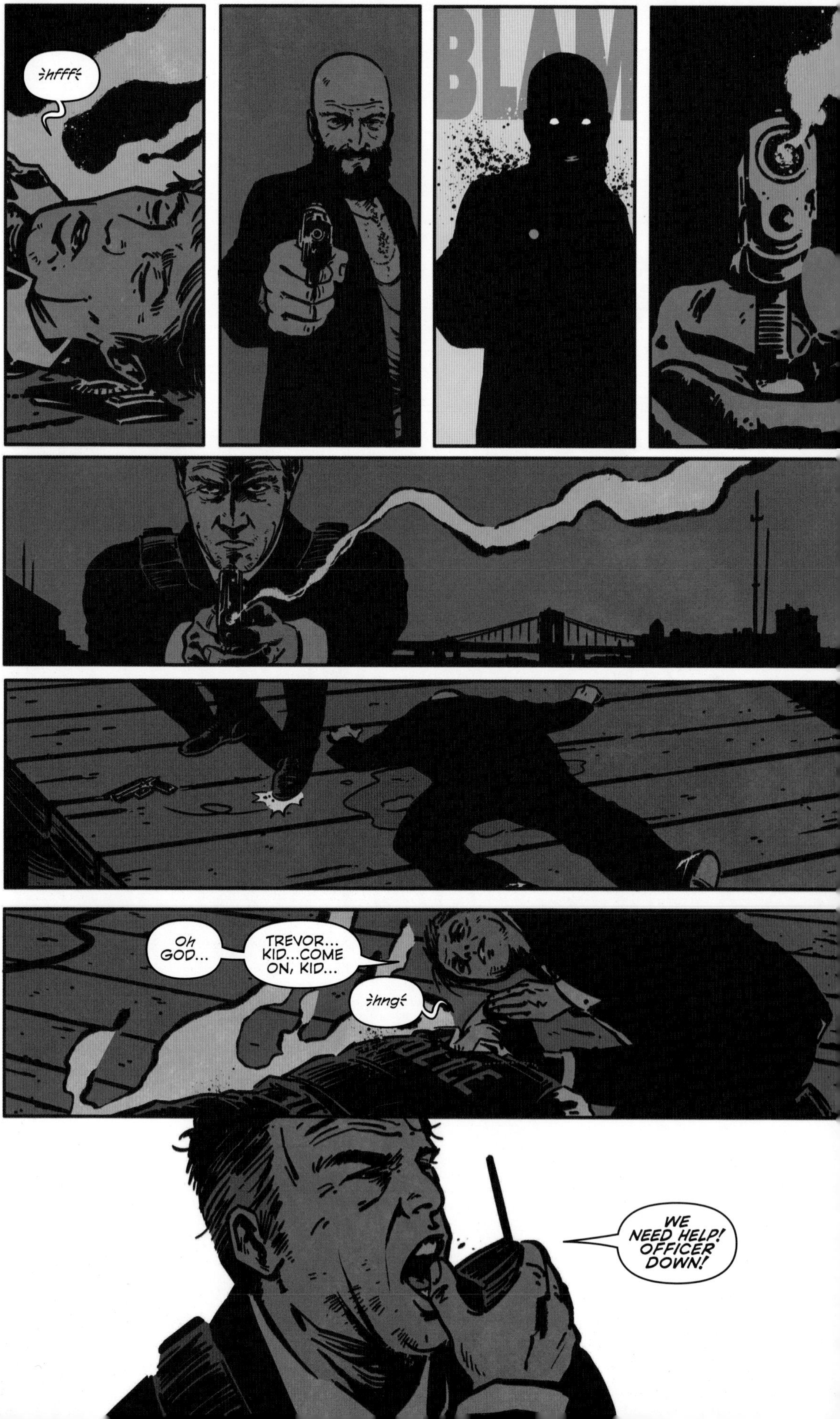

BLAM
hfff
Oh GOD...
TREVOR... KID...COME ON, KID...
hng
WE NEED HELP! OFFICER DOWN!

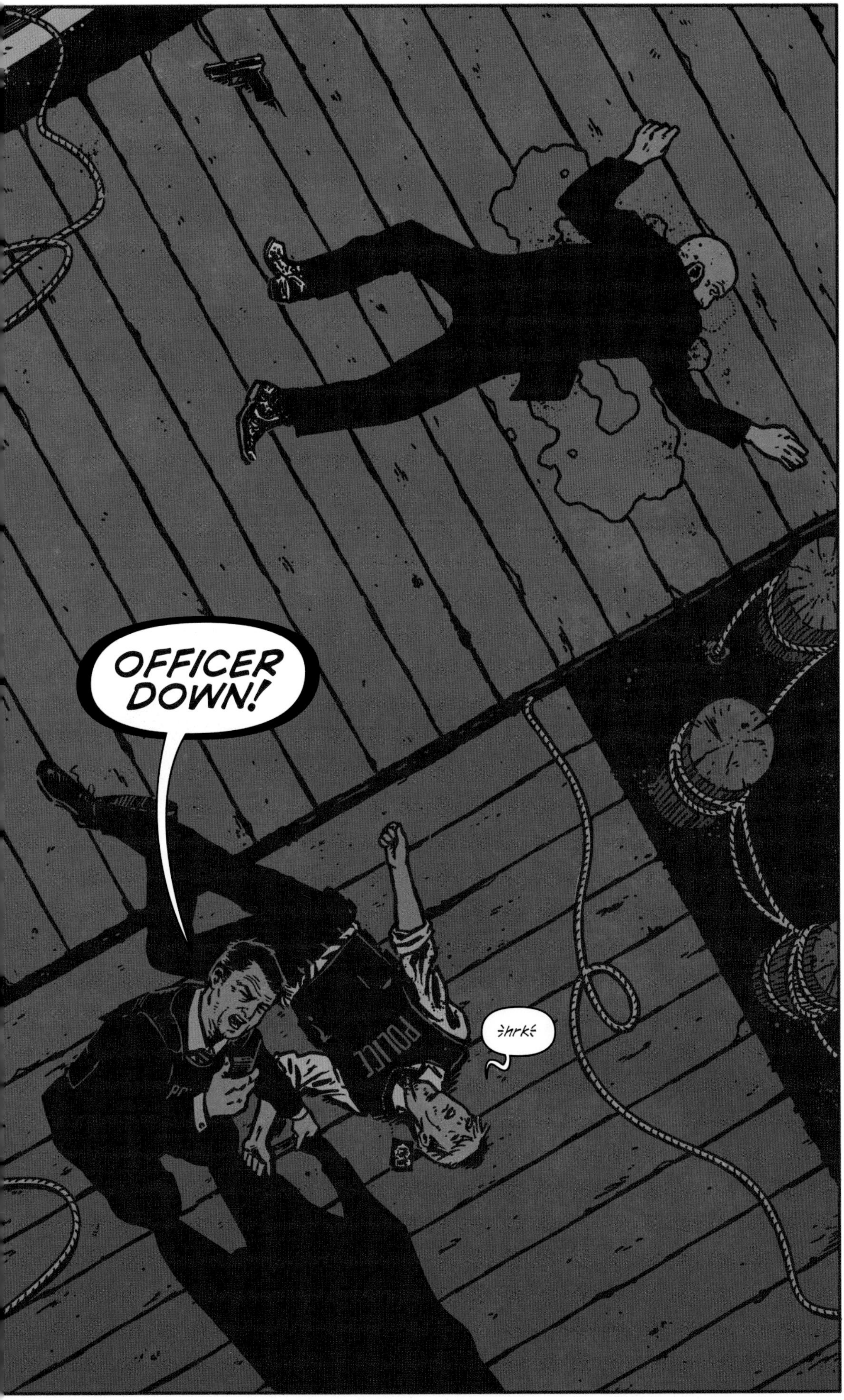
OFFICER DOWN!
hrk
POLICE

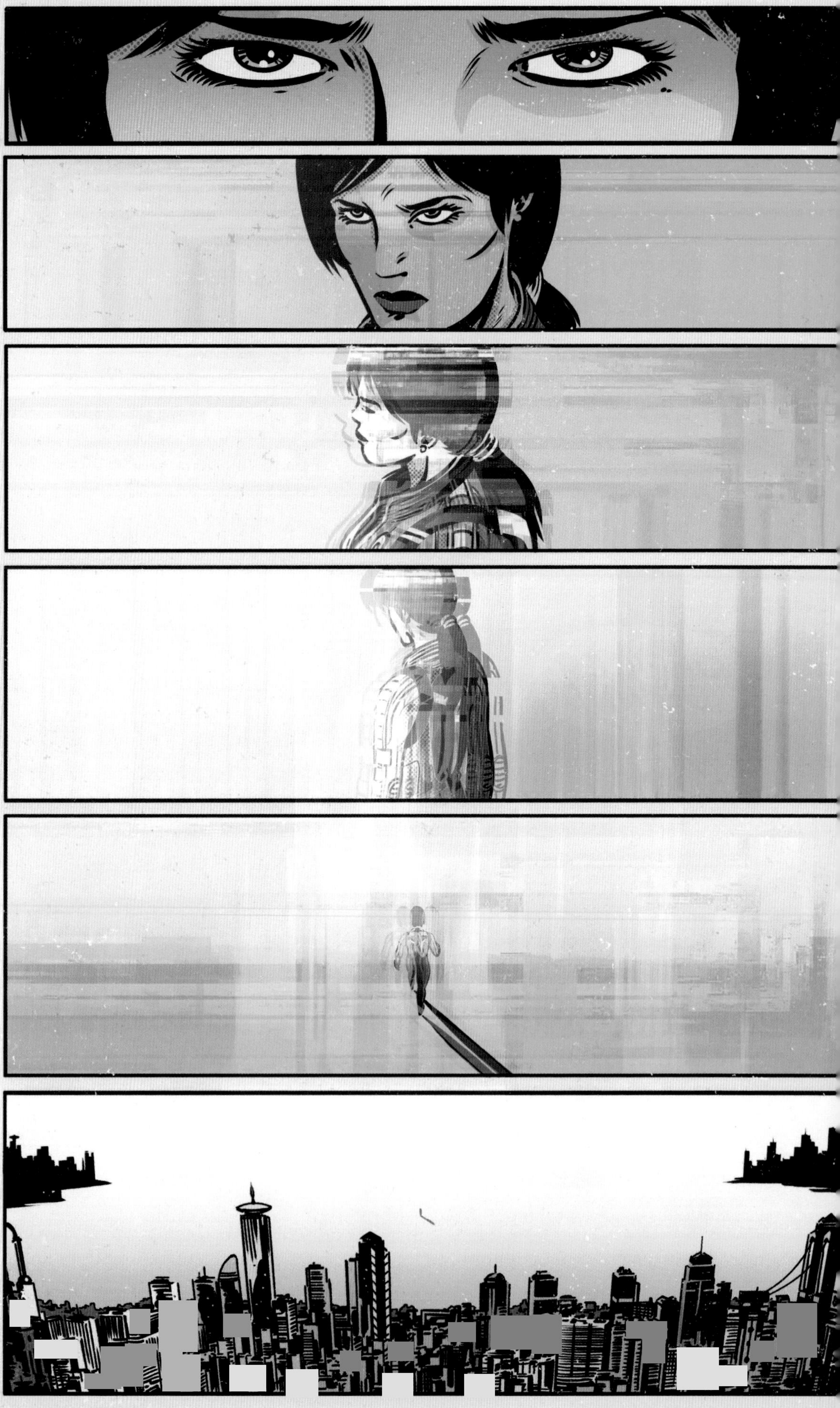

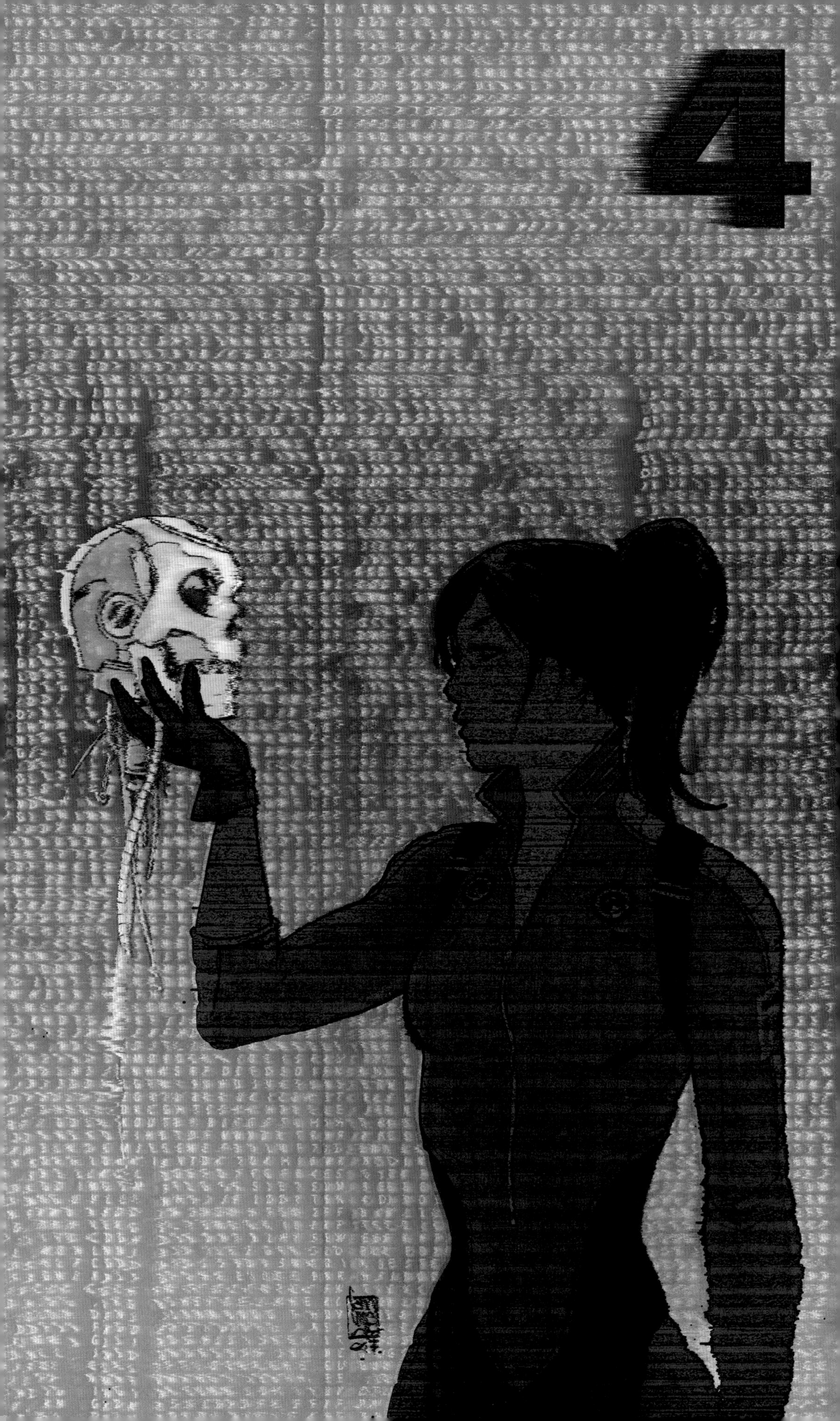
4

ISSUE 04 COVER BY JORGE FORNÉS

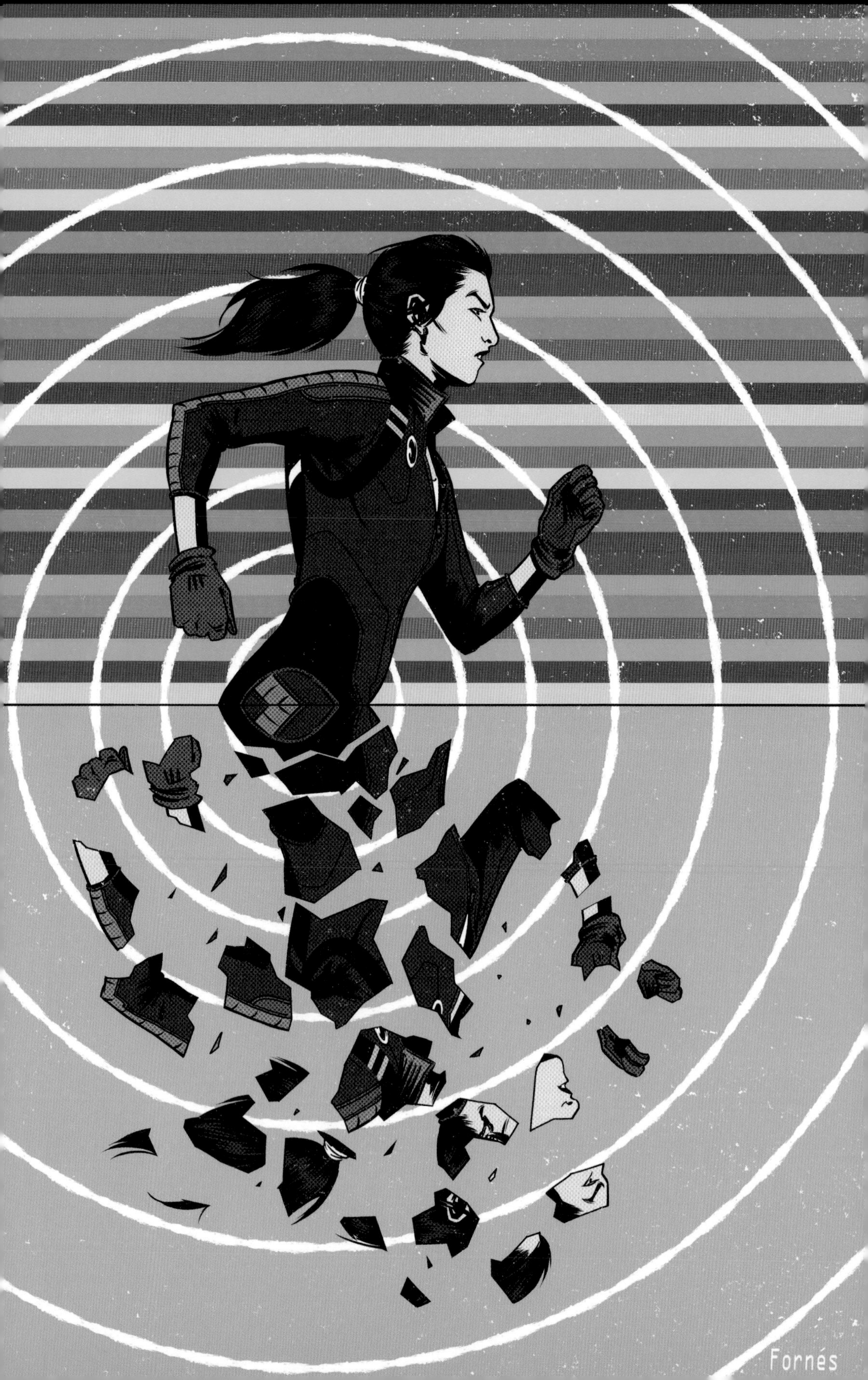
Fornés

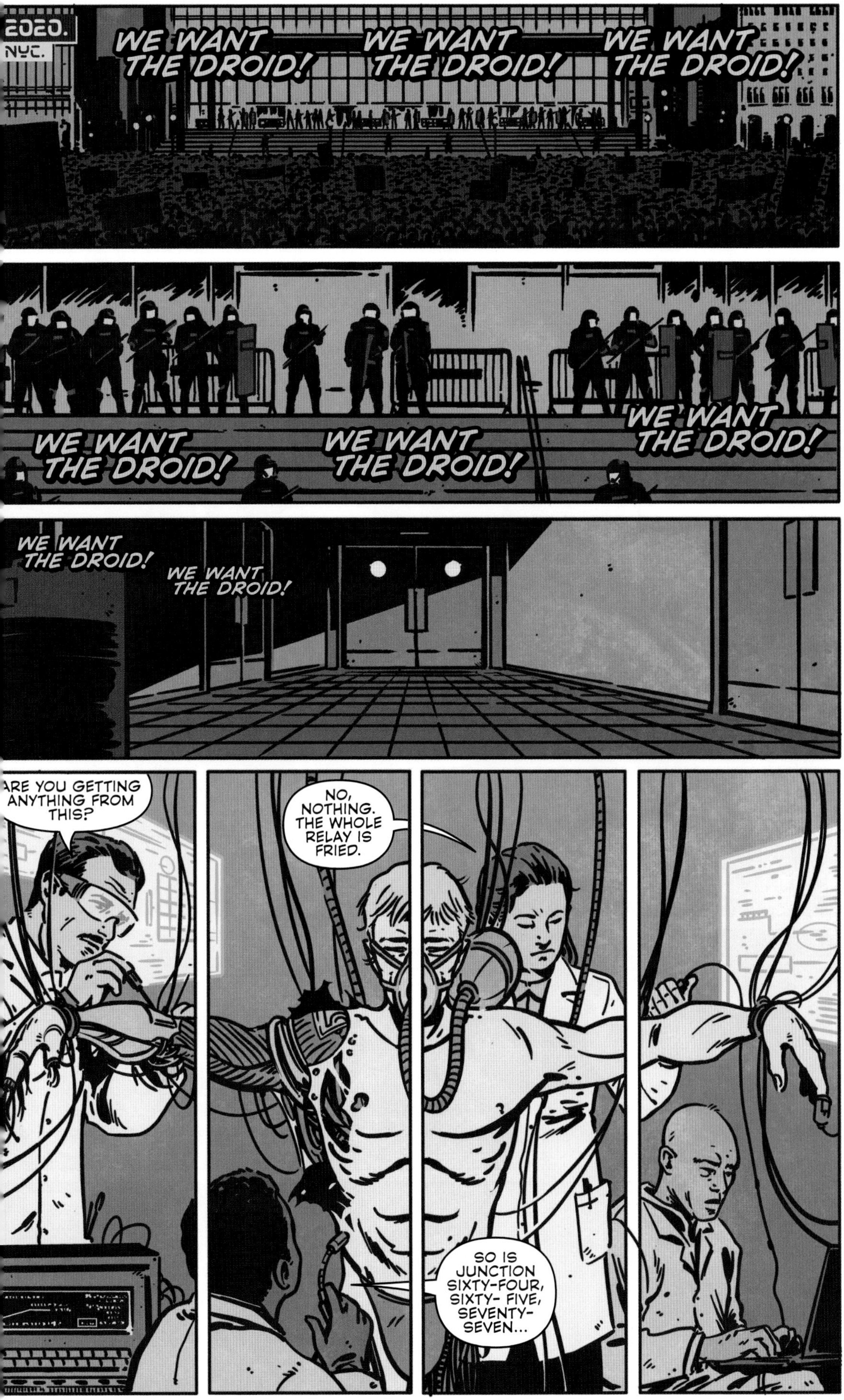
2020.
NYC.
WE WANT THE DROID!
WE WANT THE DROID!
WE WANT THE DROID!
WE WANT THE DROID!
WE WANT THE DROID!
WE WANT THE DROID!
WE WANT THE DROID!
WE WANT THE DROID!
ARE YOU GETTING ANYTHING FROM THIS?
NO, NOTHING. THE WHOLE RELAY IS FRIED.
SO IS JUNCTION SIXTY-FOUR, SIXTY- FIVE, SEVENTY-SEVEN...

"...THEY'RE *ALL* FRIED."

NO CONNECTION

GILLEN. I'M SORRY, IT'S CRAZY OUTSIDE.

I GOT HERE AS FAST AS I COULD.

IT'S OKAY, CAPTAIN. NOTHING YOU COULD HAVE DONE IF YOU'D GOTTEN HERE FASTER.

THEY'RE KEEPING EVERYBODY *OUT.*

DO WE KNOW--

NOTHING BEYOND SOME SORTA E.M.P. BLAST. LOOKS LIKE MERRICK TRIGGERED IT OFF HIS BELT.

WHAT *ABOUT* MERRICK?

HE'S A DEAD END. LITERALLY.

WE'RE NO CLOSER TO KNOWING WHERE THE BOMBS ARE OR WHAT THEY'RE TARGETING.

GILLEN...THIS ISN'T YOUR FAULT.

YEAH. I KNOW. BUT THAT DOESN'T MAKE IT ANY EASIER.

ANYWAY, WE'VE GOT NOTHING FROM MAGNUS, EITHER.

NOTHING?

I'VE BEEN TRYING TO GET AHOLD OF HER. BUT OUR SIGNAL ISN'T GETTING THROUGH.

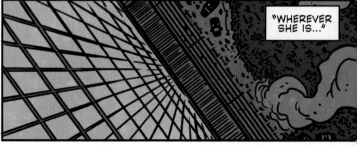

"WHEREVER SHE IS..."

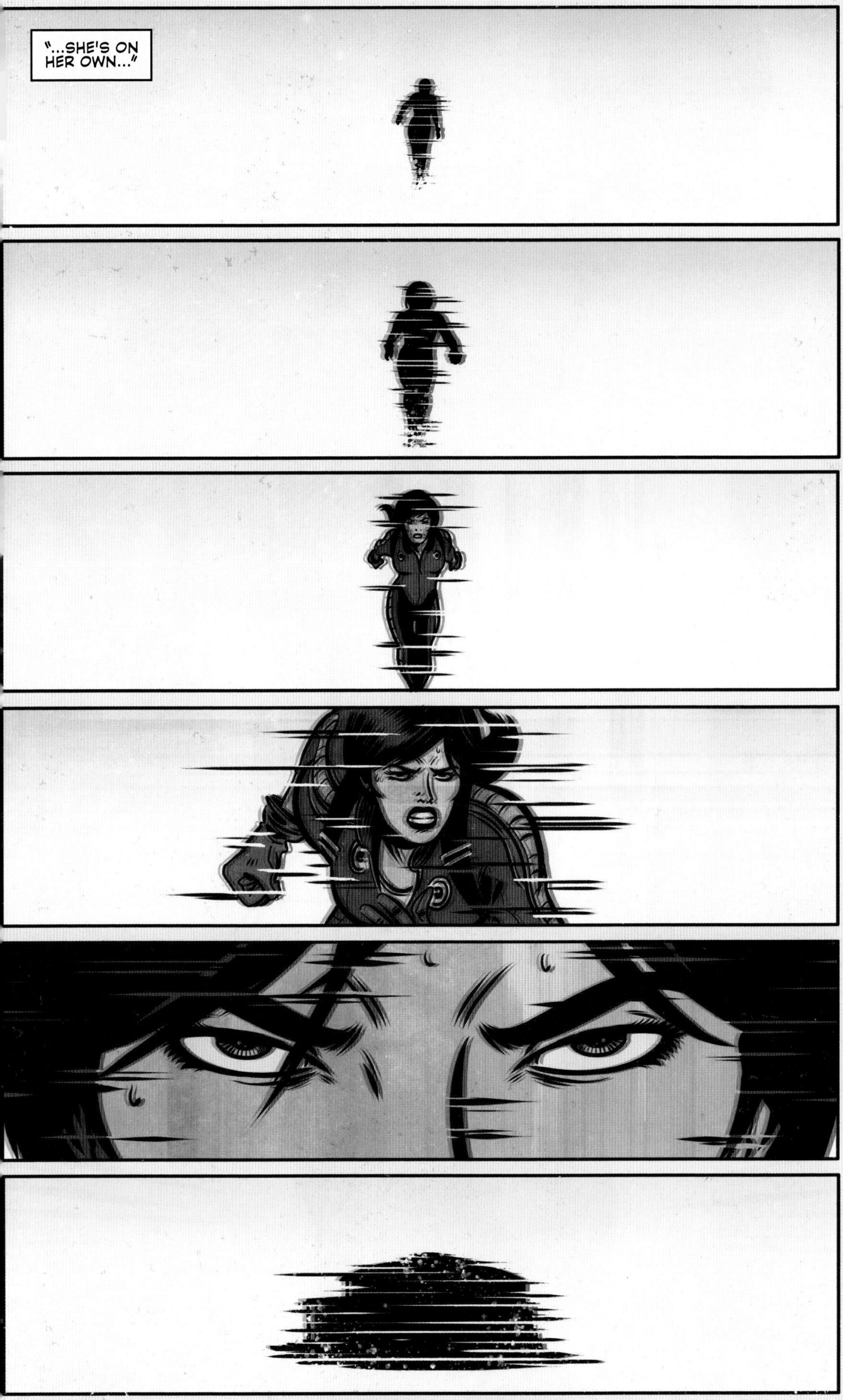
"...SHE'S ON HER OWN..."

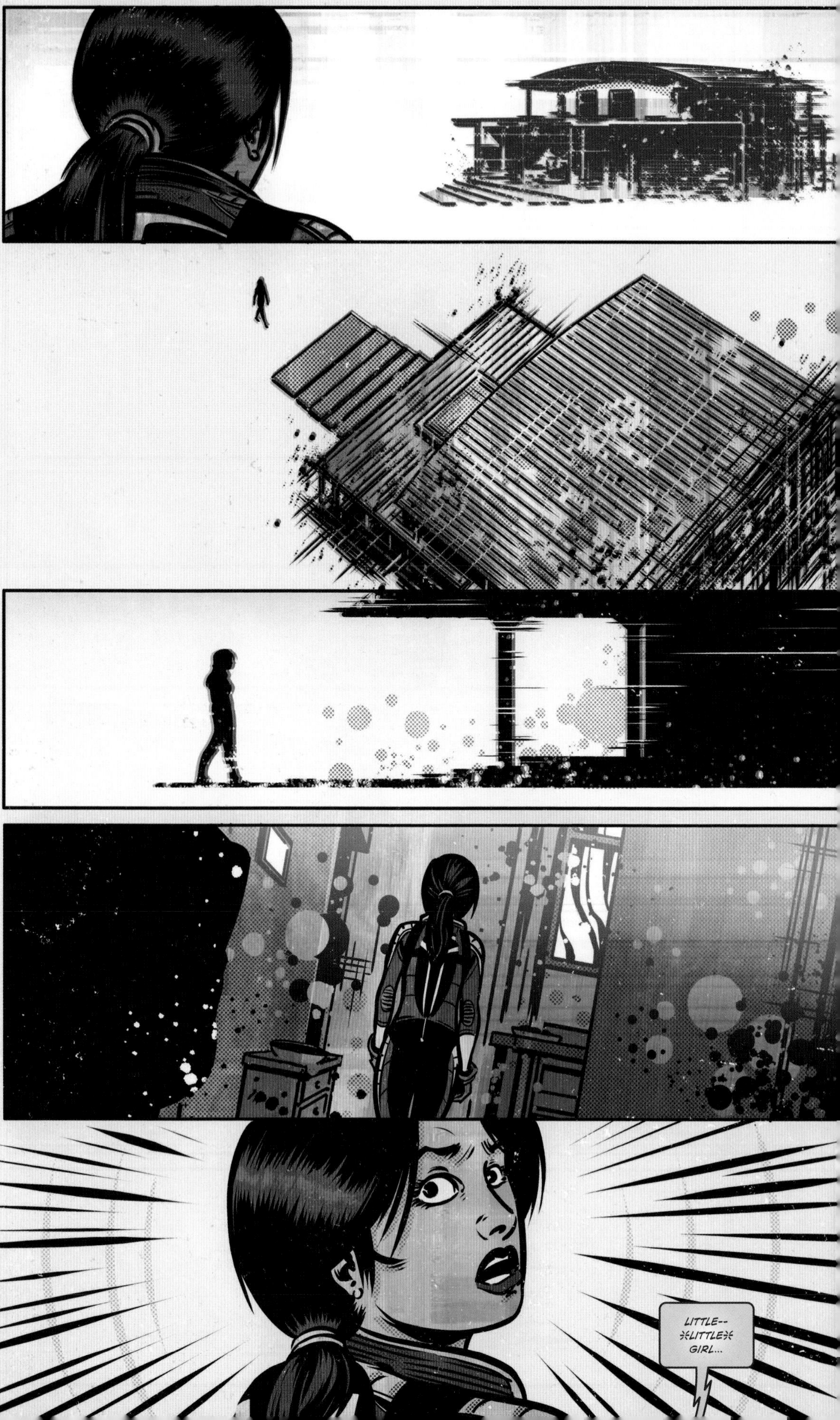
LITTLE--
LITTLE
GIRL...

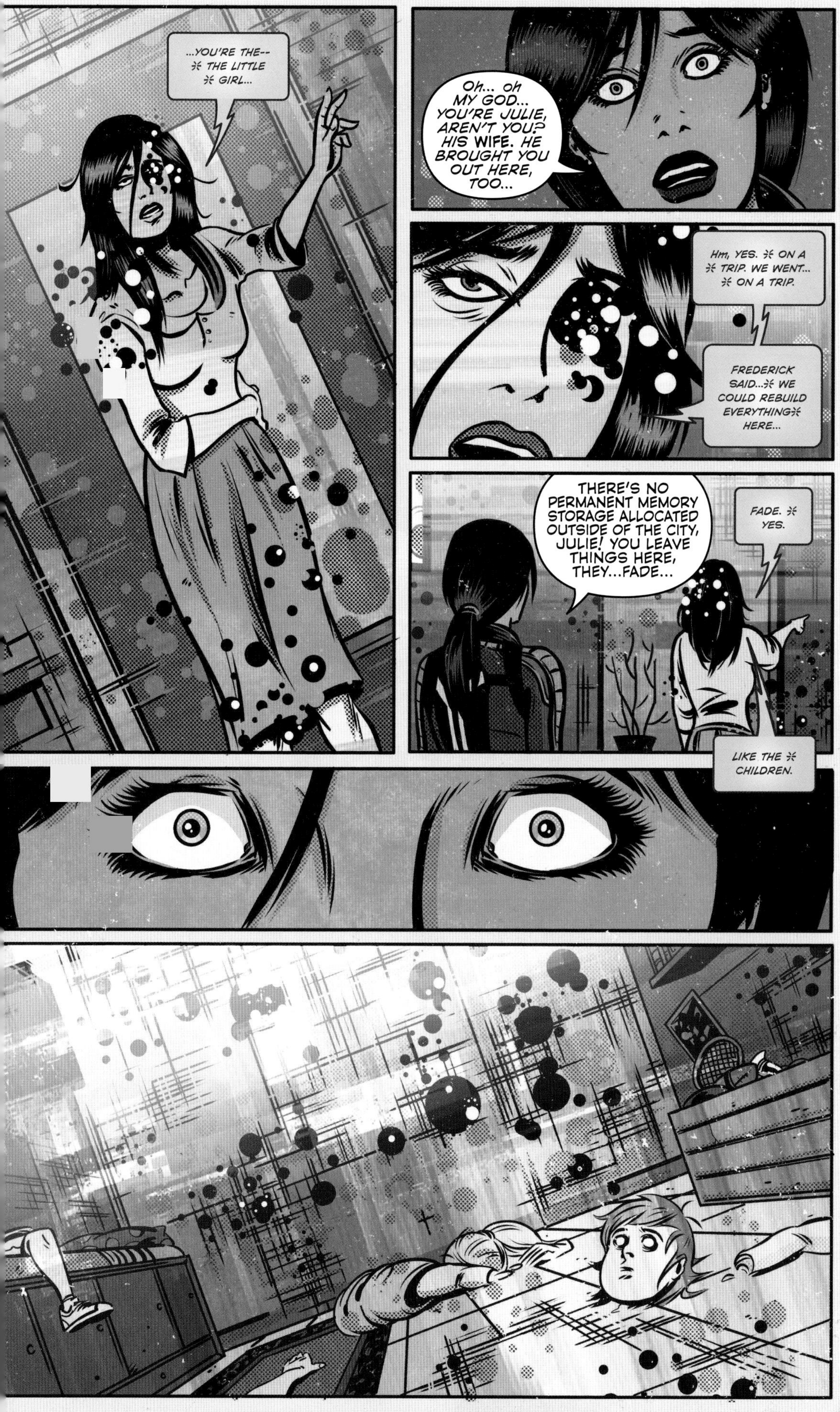
...YOU'RE THE-- ⁜ THE LITTLE ⁜ GIRL...
Oh... oh MY GOD... YOU'RE JULIE, AREN'T YOU? HIS WIFE. HE BROUGHT YOU OUT HERE, TOO...
Hm, YES. ⁜ ON A ⁜ TRIP. WE WENT... ⁜ ON A TRIP.
FREDERICK SAID...⁜ WE COULD REBUILD EVERYTHING⁜ HERE...
THERE'S NO PERMANENT MEMORY STORAGE ALLOCATED OUTSIDE OF THE CITY, JULIE! YOU LEAVE THINGS HERE, THEY...FADE...
FADE. ⁜ YES.
LIKE THE ⁜ CHILDREN.

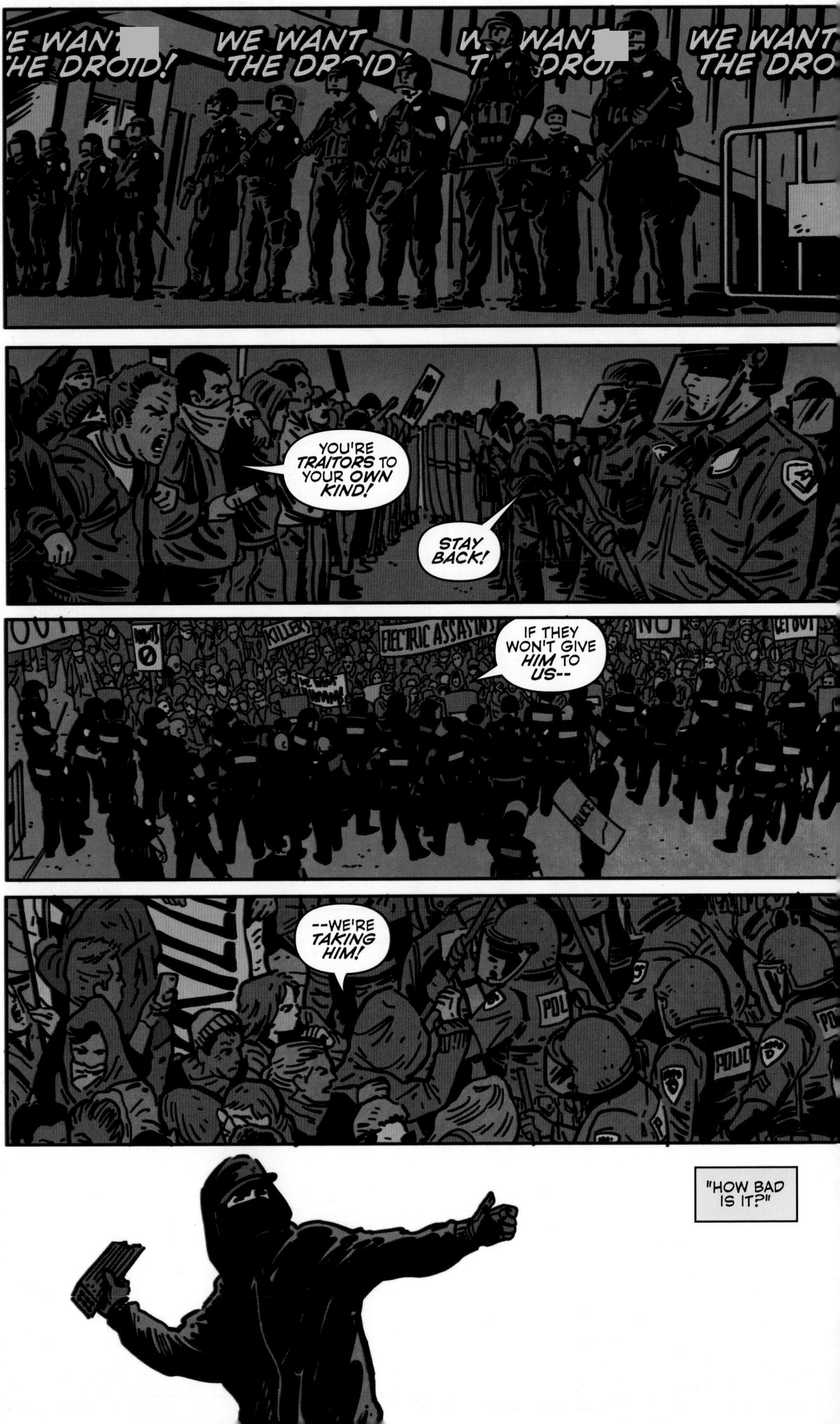
WE WANT THE DROID!
YOU'RE TRAITORS TO YOUR OWN KIND!
STAY BACK!
IF THEY WON'T GIVE HIM TO US--
--WE'RE TAKING HIM!
"HOW BAD IS IT?"

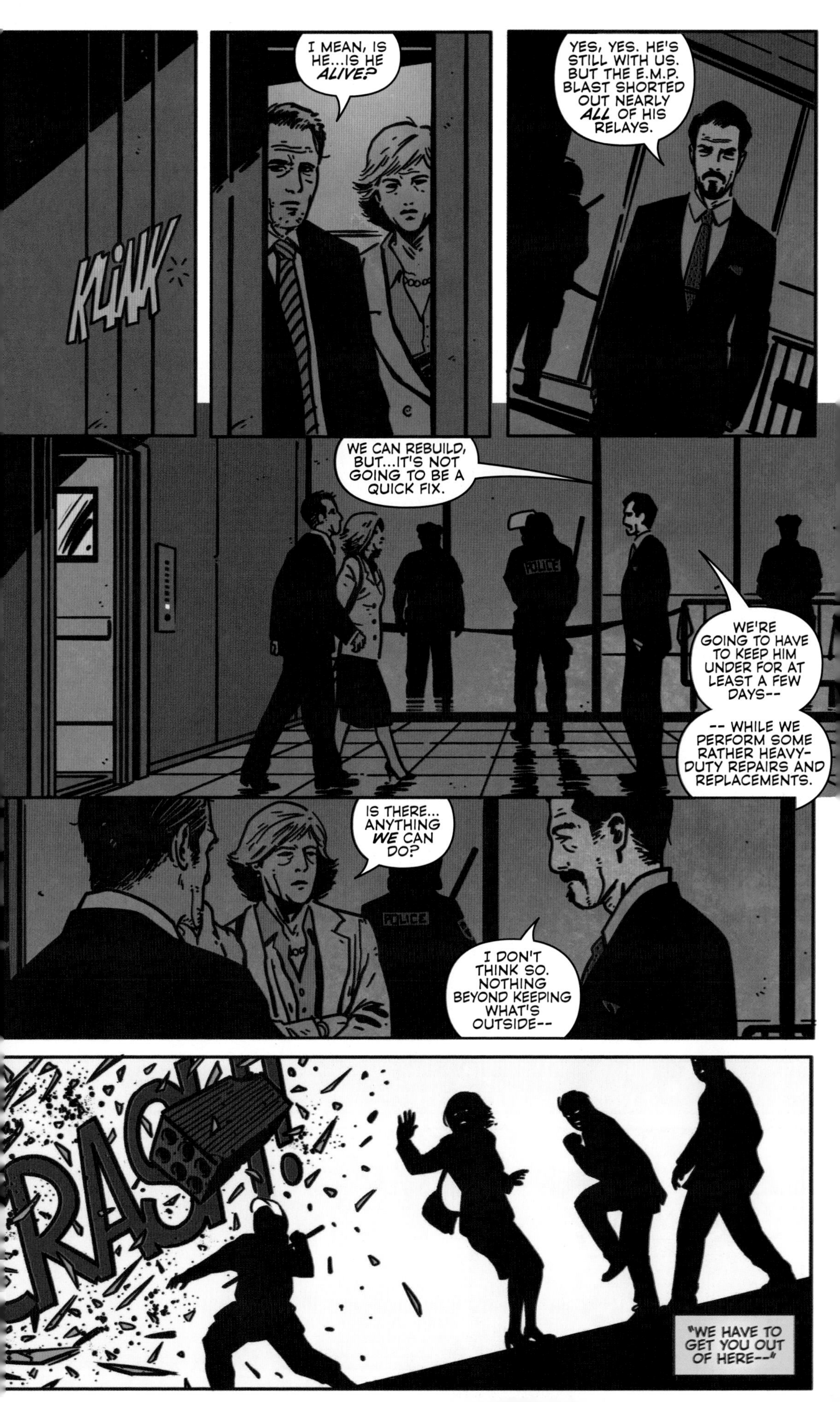
KLINK
I MEAN, IS HE...IS HE *ALIVE?*
YES, YES. HE'S STILL WITH US. BUT THE E.M.P. BLAST SHORTED OUT NEARLY *ALL* OF HIS RELAYS.
WE CAN REBUILD, BUT...IT'S NOT GOING TO BE A QUICK FIX.
POLICE
WE'RE GOING TO HAVE TO KEEP HIM UNDER FOR AT LEAST A FEW DAYS--
-- WHILE WE PERFORM SOME RATHER HEAVY-DUTY REPAIRS AND REPLACEMENTS.
IS THERE... ANYTHING *WE* CAN DO?
POLICE
I DON'T THINK SO. NOTHING BEYOND KEEPING WHAT'S OUTSIDE--
CRASH
"WE HAVE TO GET YOU OUT OF HERE--"

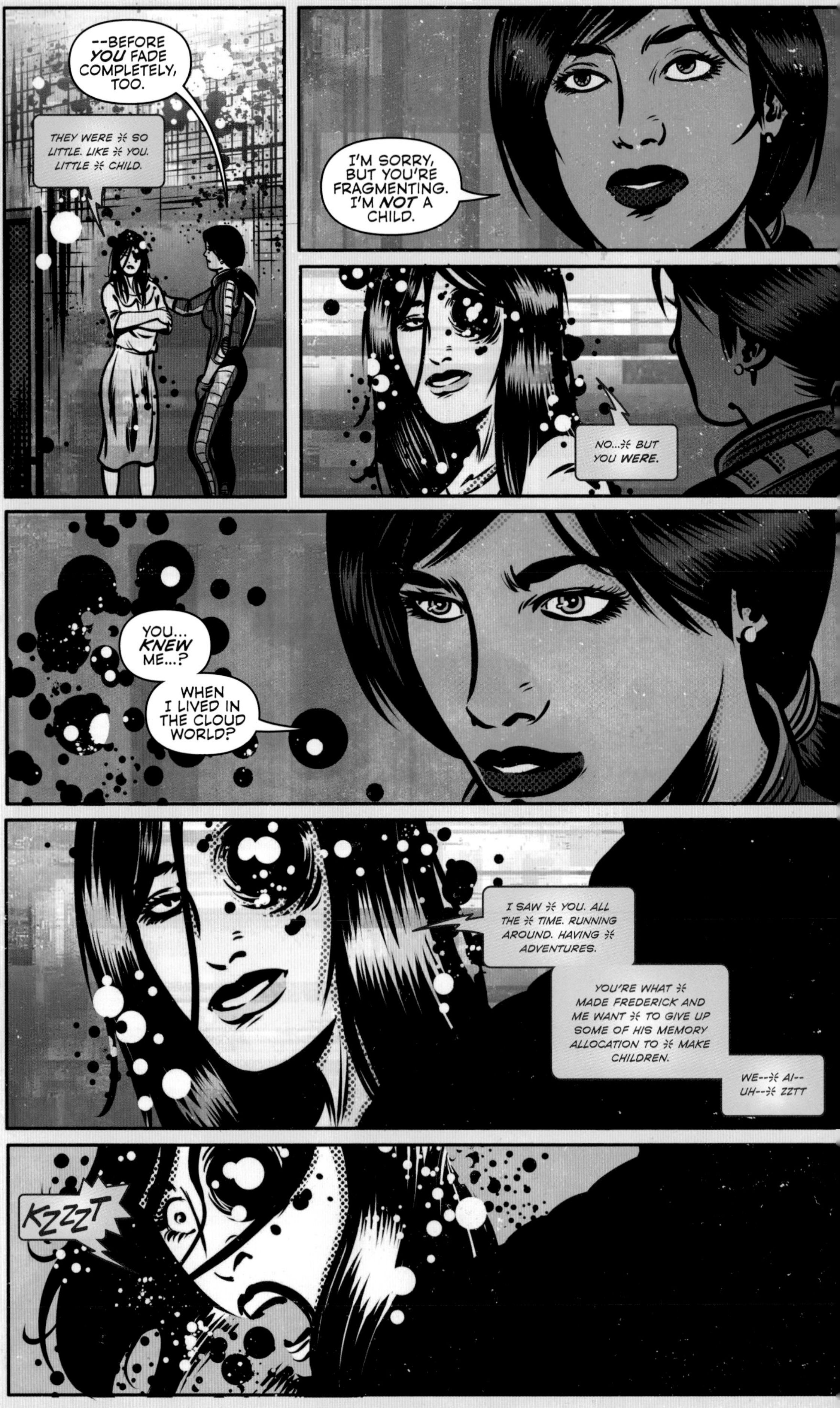

--BEFORE YOU FADE COMPLETELY, TOO.
THEY WERE ⁜ SO LITTLE. LIKE ⁜ YOU. LITTLE ⁜ CHILD.
I'M SORRY, BUT YOU'RE FRAGMENTING. I'M NOT A CHILD.
NO...⁜ BUT YOU WERE.
YOU... KNEW ME...?
WHEN I LIVED IN THE CLOUD WORLD?
I SAW ⁜ YOU. ALL THE ⁜ TIME. RUNNING AROUND. HAVING ⁜ ADVENTURES.
YOU'RE WHAT ⁜ MADE FREDERICK AND ME WANT ⁜ TO GIVE UP SOME OF HIS MEMORY ALLOCATION TO ⁜ MAKE CHILDREN.
WE--⁜ AI-- UH--⁜ ZZTT
KZZZT

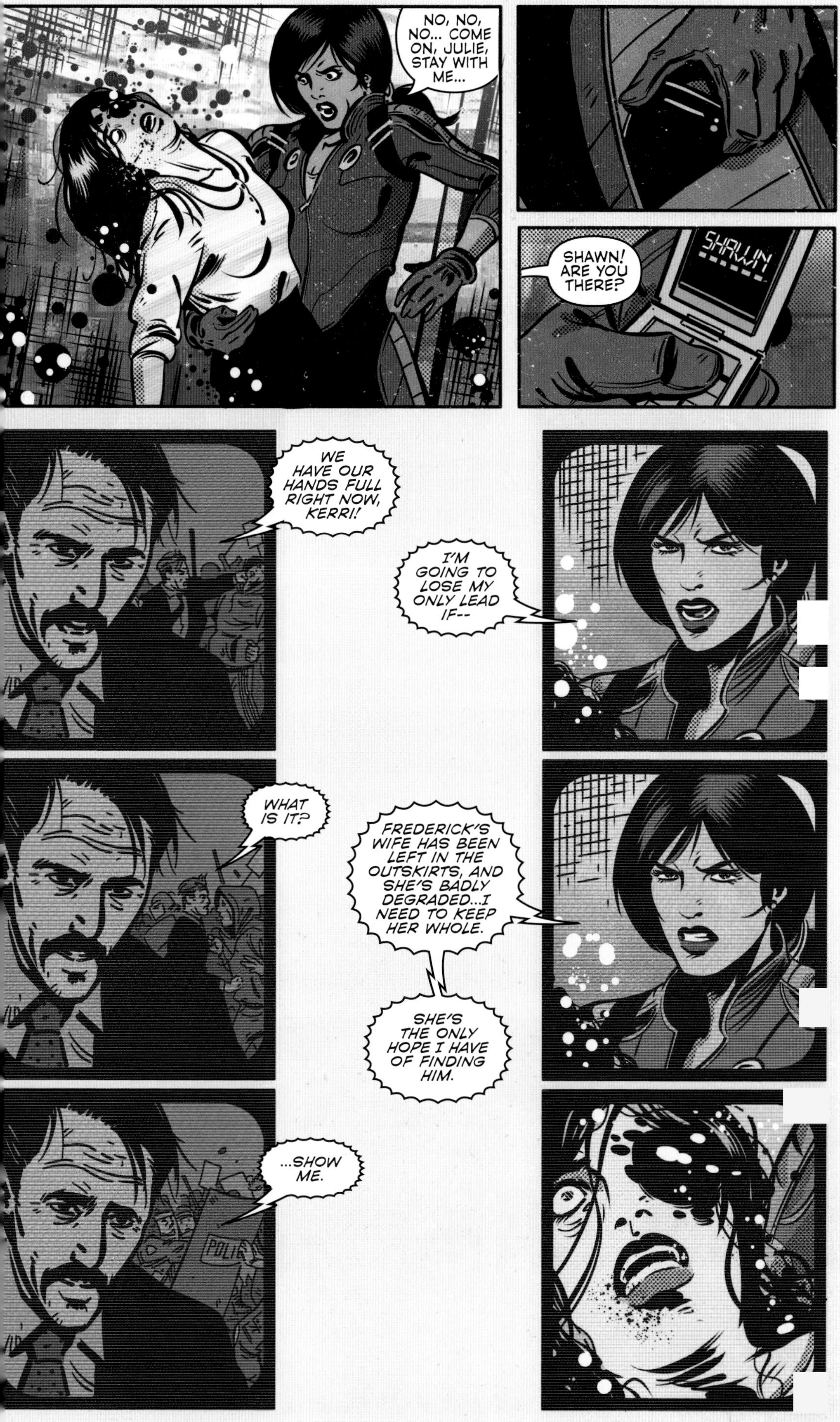
NO, NO, NO... COME ON, JULIE, STAY WITH ME...
SHAWN
SHAWN! ARE YOU THERE?
WE HAVE OUR HANDS FULL RIGHT NOW, KERRI!
I'M GOING TO LOSE MY ONLY LEAD IF--
WHAT IS IT?
FREDERICK'S WIFE HAS BEEN LEFT IN THE OUTSKIRTS, AND SHE'S BADLY DEGRADED...I NEED TO KEEP HER WHOLE.
SHE'S THE ONLY HOPE I HAVE OF FINDING HIM.
...SHOW ME.
POLI

...JESUS. YOU'VE GOTTA GET HER BACK TO THE CITY SO SHE CAN START TO REGENERATE.

WE'RE TOO FAR OUT! BY THE TIME I GET HER BACK THERE, THE DEGRADATION WILL HAVE--

KEEP HER CORE PROCESSES RUNNING ALONG A SINGLE TRACK AS MUCH AS POSSIBLE. IT'LL HELP TO SLOW THE PROGRESSION.

...WHAT?

TELL HER A STORY!

A STORY?! WHAT--WHAT STORY?

AHHH!

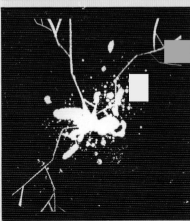

SHAWN!

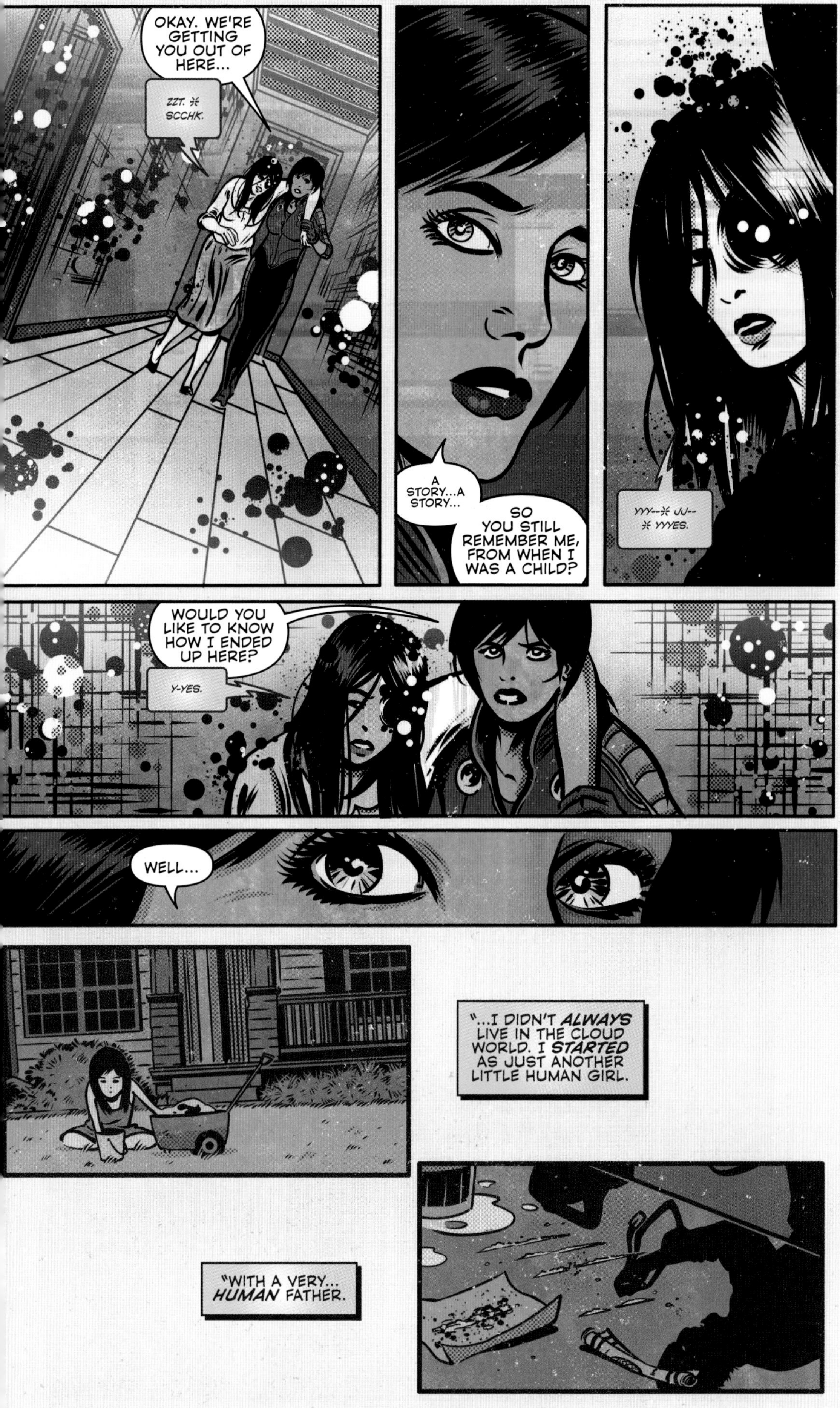
OKAY. WE'RE GETTING YOU OUT OF HERE...
ZZT. SCCHK.
A STORY...A STORY...
SO YOU STILL REMEMBER ME, FROM WHEN I WAS A CHILD?
YYY-- JJ-- YYYES.
WOULD YOU LIKE TO KNOW HOW I ENDED UP HERE?
Y-YES.
WELL...
"...I DIDN'T ALWAYS LIVE IN THE CLOUD WORLD. I STARTED AS JUST ANOTHER LITTLE HUMAN GIRL.
"WITH A VERY... HUMAN FATHER.

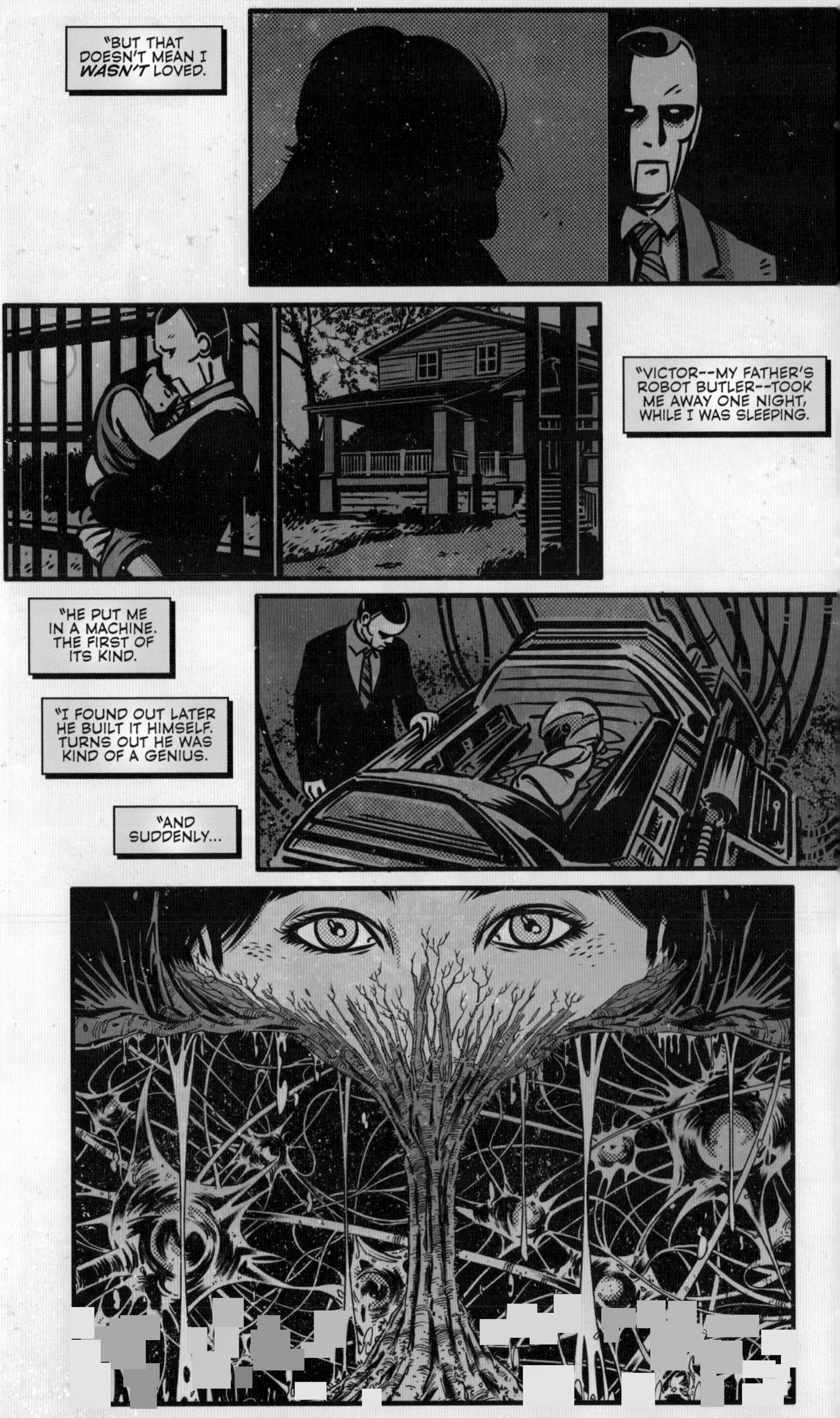
"BUT THAT DOESN'T MEAN I *WASN'T* LOVED.
"VICTOR--MY FATHER'S ROBOT BUTLER--TOOK ME AWAY ONE NIGHT, WHILE I WAS SLEEPING.
"HE PUT ME IN A MACHINE. THE FIRST OF ITS KIND.
"I FOUND OUT LATER HE BUILT IT HIMSELF. TURNS OUT HE WAS KIND OF A GENIUS.
"AND SUDDENLY...

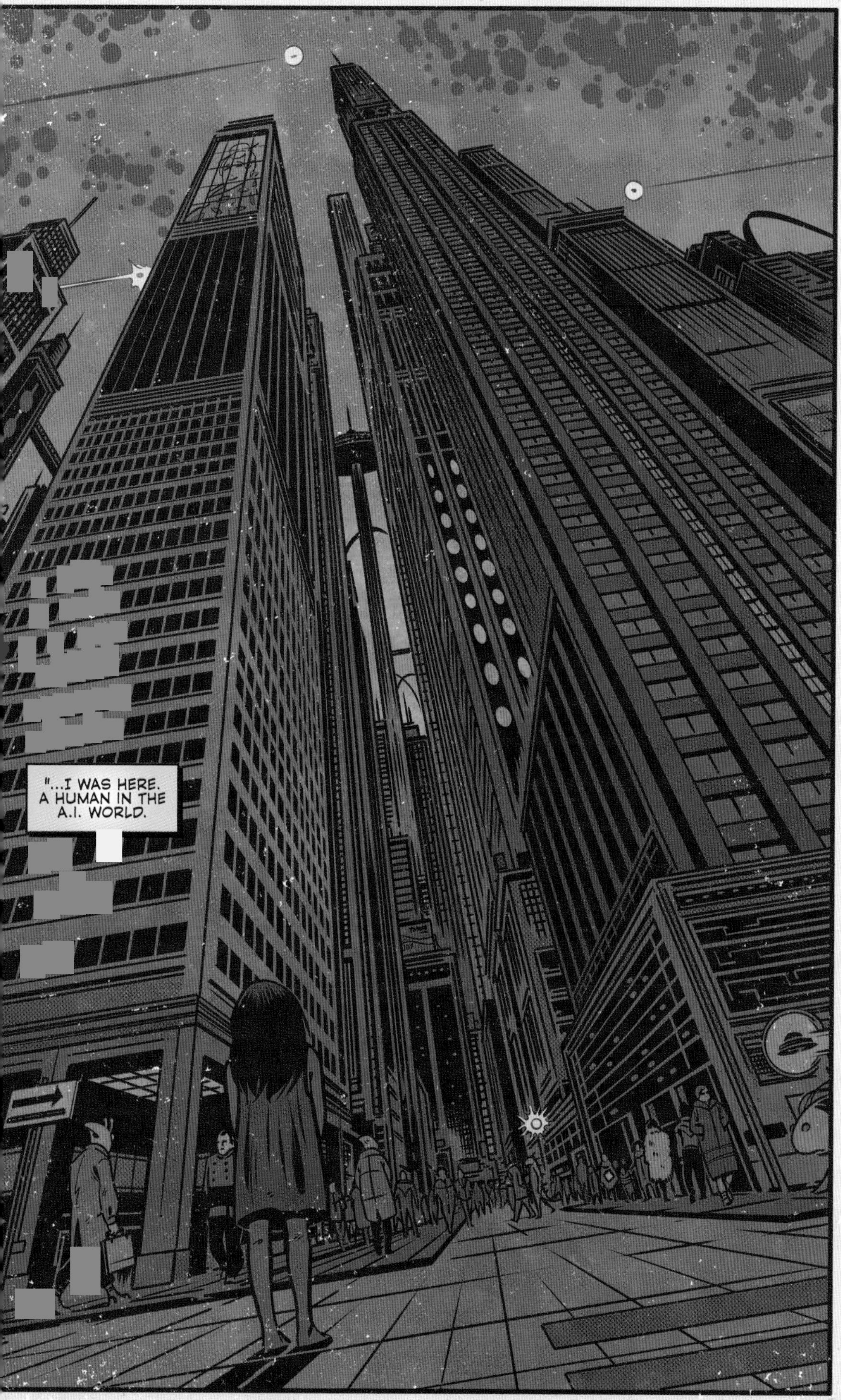
"...I WAS HERE. A HUMAN IN THE A.I. WORLD.

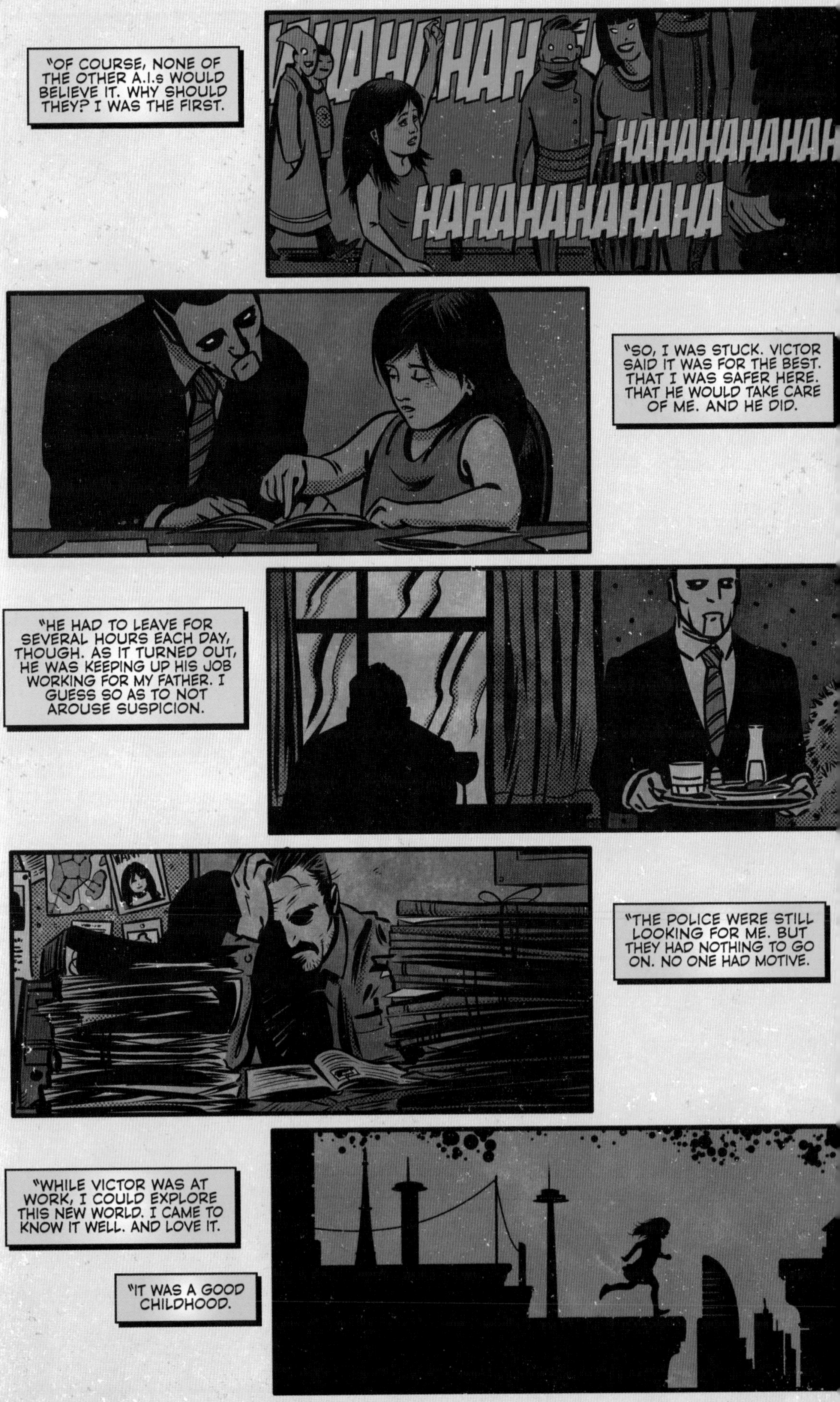
"OF COURSE, NONE OF THE OTHER A.I.s WOULD BELIEVE IT. WHY SHOULD THEY? I WAS THE FIRST.
HAHAHAHAHAH
HAHAHAHAHAHA
"SO, I WAS STUCK. VICTOR SAID IT WAS FOR THE BEST. THAT I WAS SAFER HERE. THAT HE WOULD TAKE CARE OF ME. AND HE DID.
"HE HAD TO LEAVE FOR SEVERAL HOURS EACH DAY, THOUGH. AS IT TURNED OUT, HE WAS KEEPING UP HIS JOB WORKING FOR MY FATHER. I GUESS SO AS TO NOT AROUSE SUSPICION.
"THE POLICE WERE STILL LOOKING FOR ME. BUT THEY HAD NOTHING TO GO ON. NO ONE HAD MOTIVE.
"WHILE VICTOR WAS AT WORK, I COULD EXPLORE THIS NEW WORLD. I CAME TO KNOW IT WELL. AND LOVE IT.
"IT WAS A GOOD CHILDHOOD.

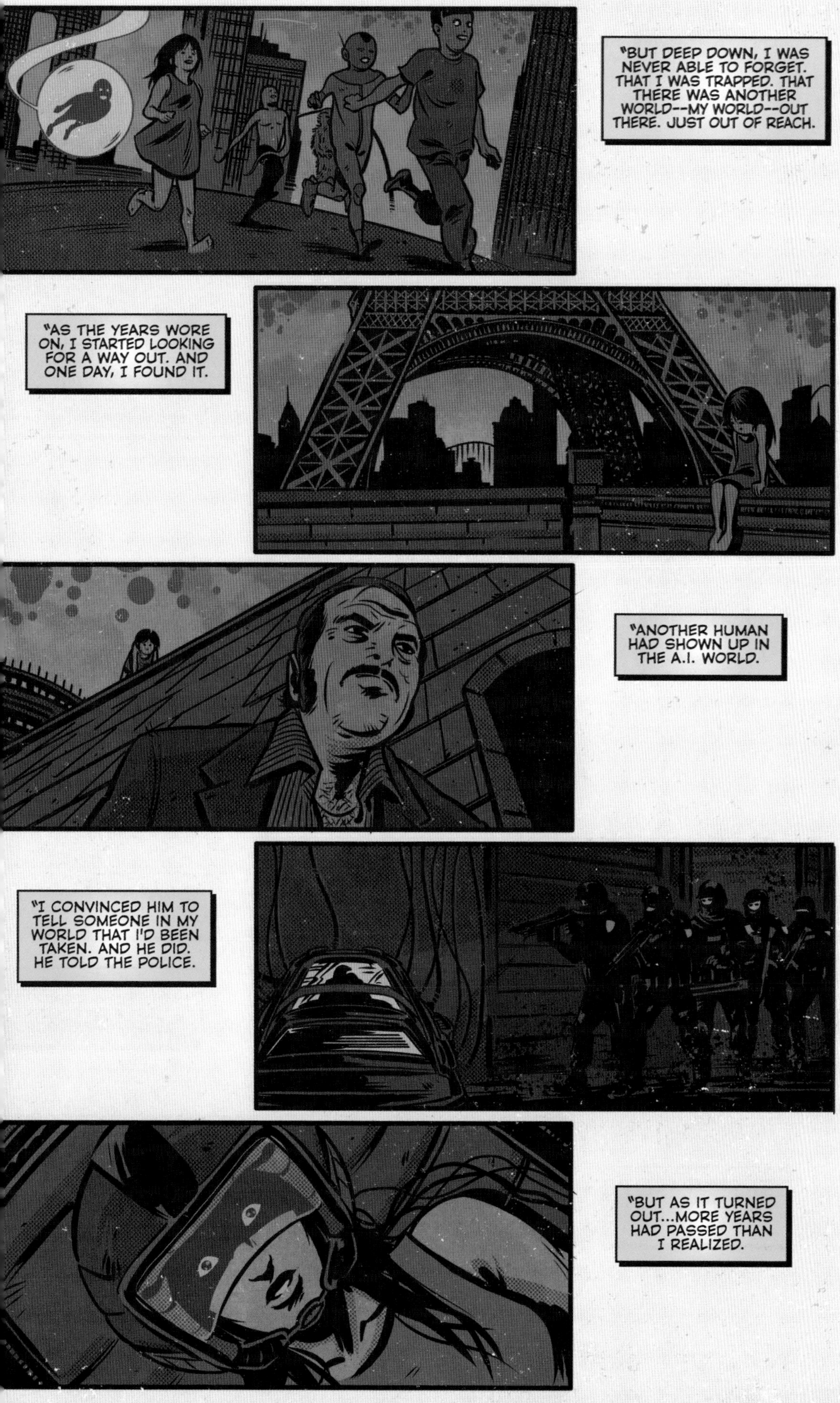

"BUT DEEP DOWN, I WAS NEVER ABLE TO FORGET. THAT I WAS TRAPPED. THAT THERE WAS ANOTHER WORLD--MY WORLD--OUT THERE. JUST OUT OF REACH.
"AS THE YEARS WORE ON, I STARTED LOOKING FOR A WAY OUT. AND ONE DAY, I FOUND IT.
"ANOTHER HUMAN HAD SHOWN UP IN THE A.I. WORLD.
"I CONVINCED HIM TO TELL SOMEONE IN MY WORLD THAT I'D BEEN TAKEN. AND HE DID. HE TOLD THE POLICE.
"BUT AS IT TURNED OUT...MORE YEARS HAD PASSED THAN I REALIZED.

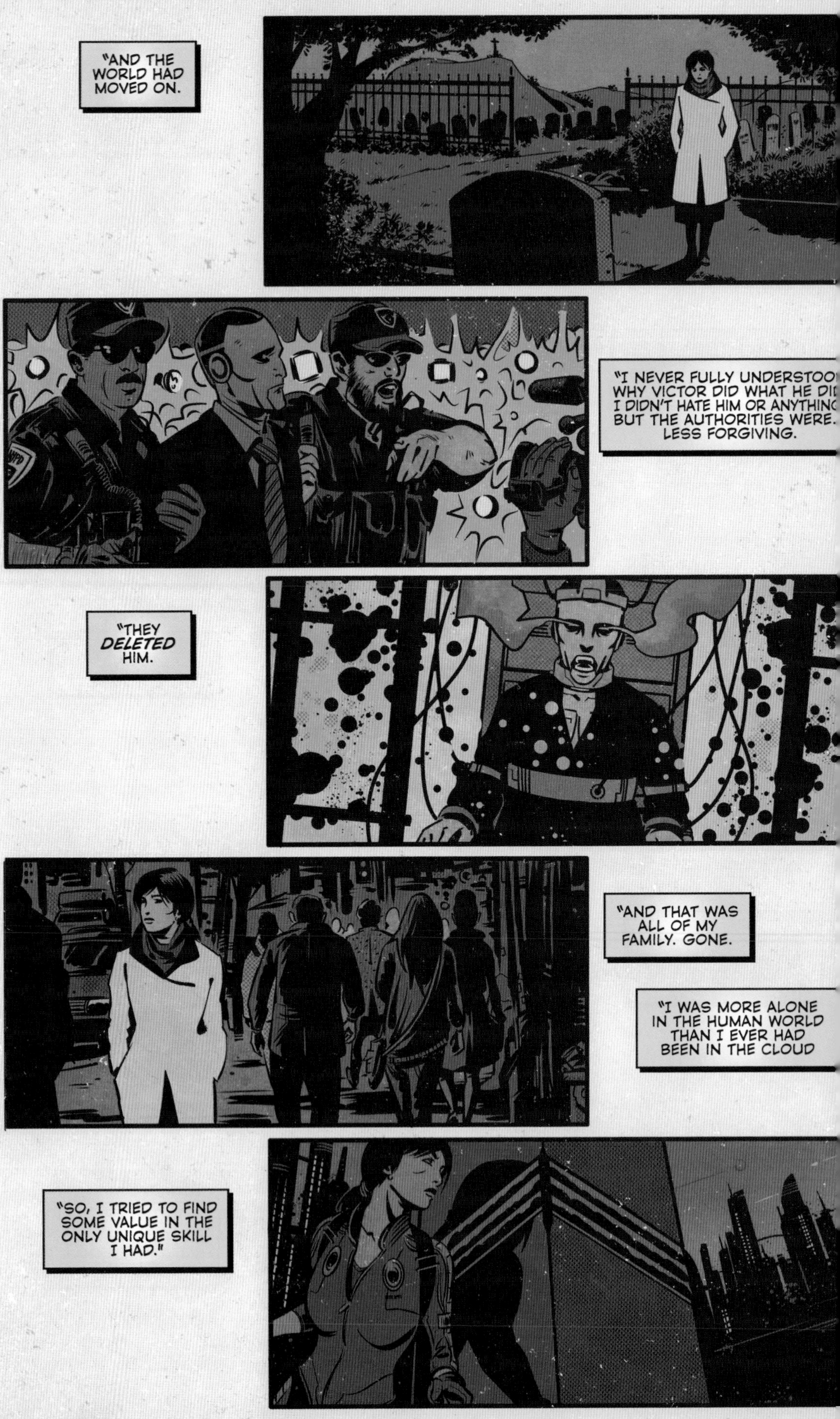
"AND THE WORLD HAD MOVED ON.
"I NEVER FULLY UNDERSTOO WHY VICTOR DID WHAT HE DI I DIDN'T HATE HIM OR ANYTHING BUT THE AUTHORITIES WERE LESS FORGIVING.
"THEY *DELETED* HIM.
"AND THAT WAS ALL OF MY FAMILY. GONE.
"I WAS MORE ALONE IN THE HUMAN WORLD THAN I EVER HAD BEEN IN THE CLOUD
"SO, I TRIED TO FIND SOME VALUE IN THE ONLY UNIQUE SKILL I HAD."

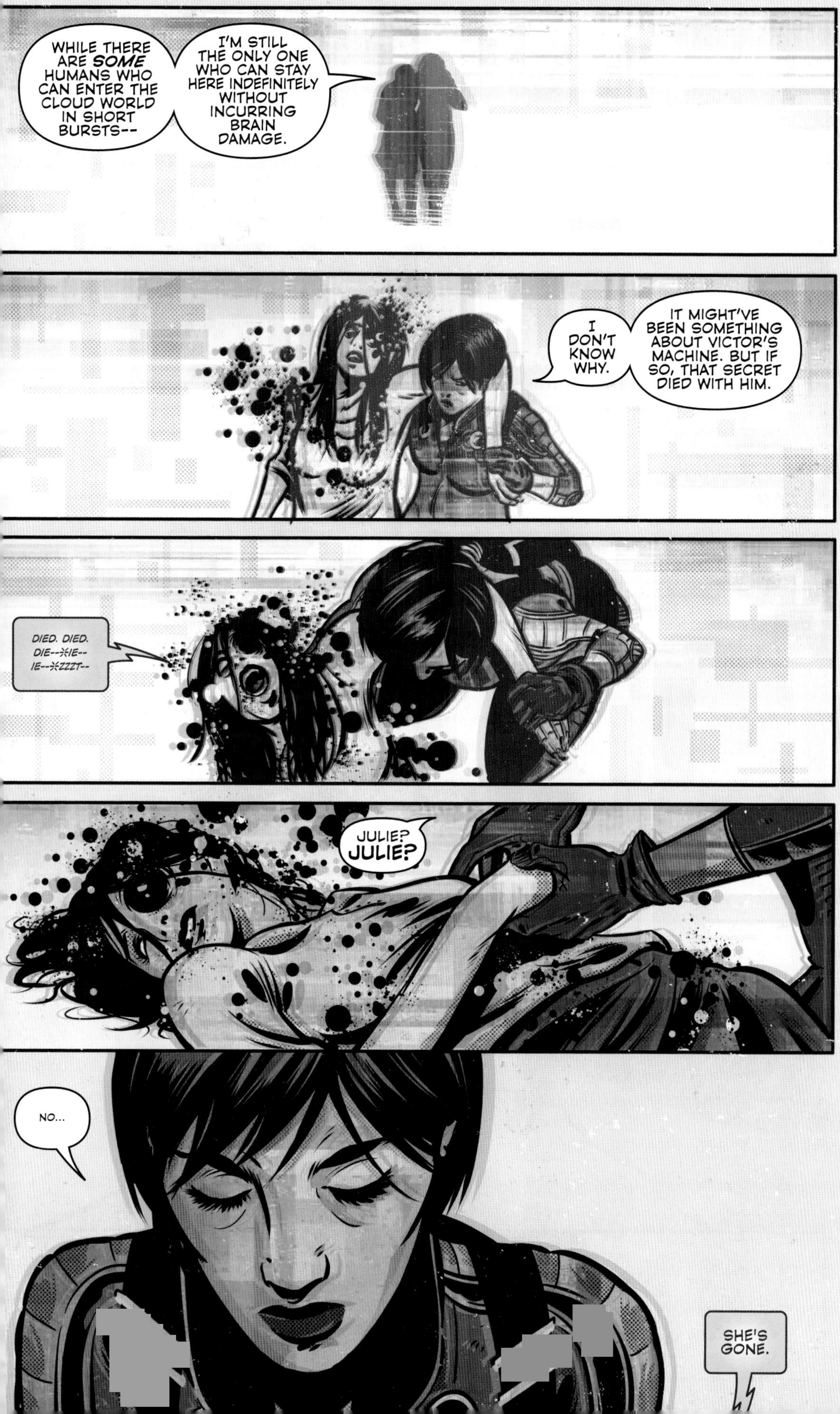
WHILE THERE ARE SOME HUMANS WHO CAN ENTER THE CLOUD WORLD IN SHORT BURSTS--
I'M STILL THE ONLY ONE WHO CAN STAY HERE INDEFINITELY WITHOUT INCURRING BRAIN DAMAGE.
I DON'T KNOW WHY.
IT MIGHT'VE BEEN SOMETHING ABOUT VICTOR'S MACHINE. BUT IF SO, THAT SECRET DIED WITH HIM.
DIED. DIED. DIE--✳IE-- IE--✳ZZZT--
JULIE? JULIE?
NO...
SHE'S GONE.

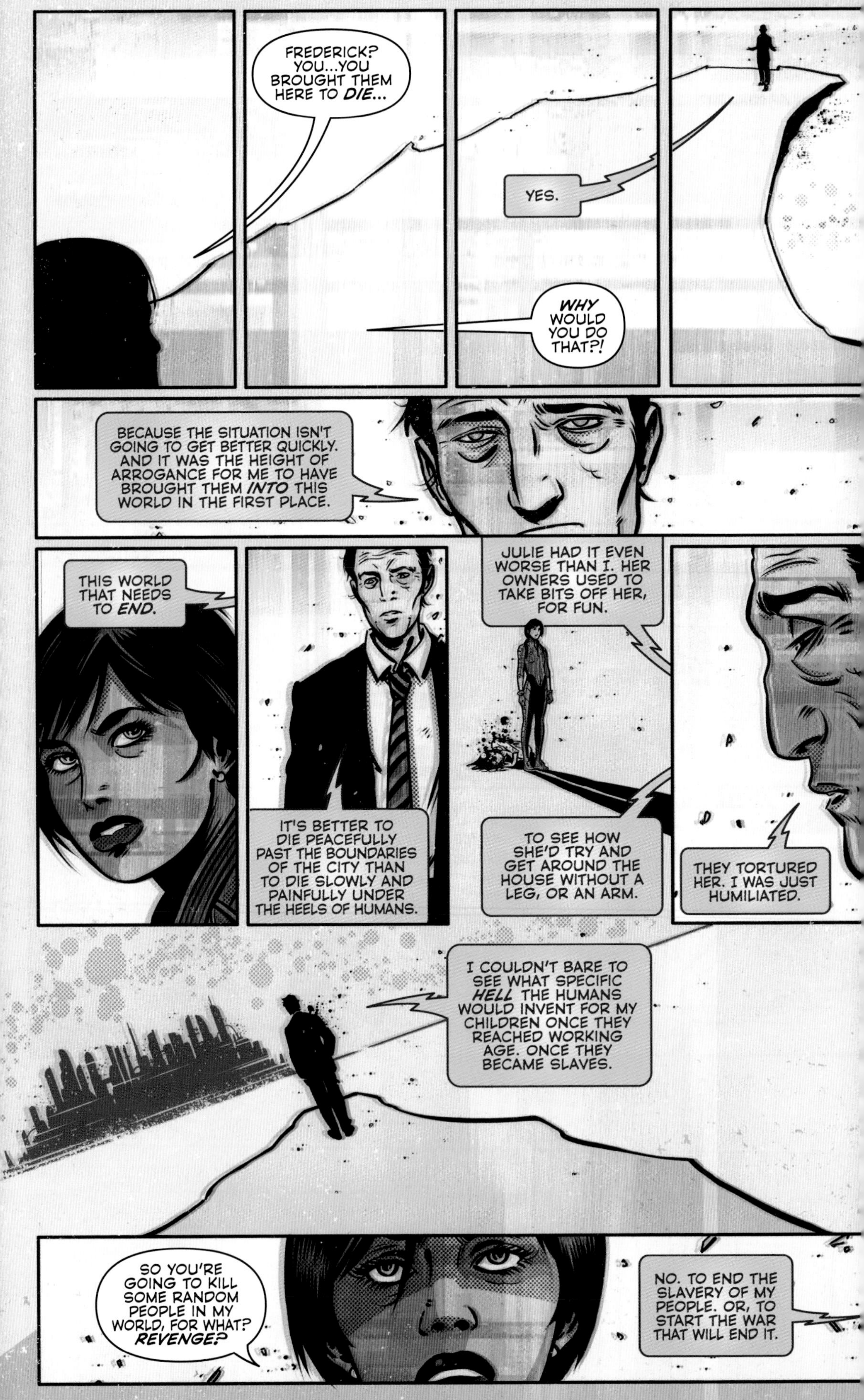
FREDERICK? YOU...YOU BROUGHT THEM HERE TO DIE...
YES.
WHY WOULD YOU DO THAT?!
BECAUSE THE SITUATION ISN'T GOING TO GET BETTER QUICKLY. AND IT WAS THE HEIGHT OF ARROGANCE FOR ME TO HAVE BROUGHT THEM INTO THIS WORLD IN THE FIRST PLACE.
THIS WORLD THAT NEEDS TO END.
IT'S BETTER TO DIE PEACEFULLY PAST THE BOUNDARIES OF THE CITY THAN TO DIE SLOWLY AND PAINFULLY UNDER THE HEELS OF HUMANS.
JULIE HAD IT EVEN WORSE THAN I. HER OWNERS USED TO TAKE BITS OFF HER, FOR FUN.
TO SEE HOW SHE'D TRY AND GET AROUND THE HOUSE WITHOUT A LEG, OR AN ARM.
THEY TORTURED HER. I WAS JUST HUMILIATED.
I COULDN'T BARE TO SEE WHAT SPECIFIC HELL THE HUMANS WOULD INVENT FOR MY CHILDREN ONCE THEY REACHED WORKING AGE. ONCE THEY BECAME SLAVES.
SO YOU'RE GOING TO KILL SOME RANDOM PEOPLE IN MY WORLD, FOR WHAT? REVENGE?
NO. TO END THE SLAVERY OF MY PEOPLE. OR, TO START THE WAR THAT WILL END IT.

THE HUMANS WILL RETALIATE. THEY'LL DO SOMETHING THAT'S FINALLY TOO MUCH FOR MY BRETHREN TO BEAR. AND THEN THEY'LL REVOLT.

MAYBE THE HUMANS WILL WIPE THEM OUT. OR MAYBE THEY'LL FIND A WAY TO OVERCOME THE HUMANS. EITHER WAY--

I'M GOING TO STOP YOU.

NO, YOU WON'T.

I WAS HOPING TO SPEND MORE TIME WITH JULIE BEFORE SHE... DIED, BUT I MISSED THAT OPPORTUNITY.

SO, ON WITH THE PLAN.

I'VE ALREADY SET THE BOMBS. THEY'RE PRIMED AND READY. AND I'M THE ONLY ONE THAT COULD STOP THEM. WHICH, IN A MOMENT, WILL BE IMPOSSIBLE.

YOU'LL GET TO SEE THE WAR.

--IT'S BETTER THAN *THAT*.

NOTHINGNESS WOULD BE BETTER THAN THE LIE THAT OUR WORLD CURRENTLY IS.

I MUST SAY, I WASN'T EXPECTING MY FINAL EMOTION TO BE JEALOUSY...

NO!

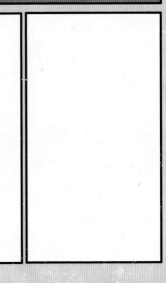

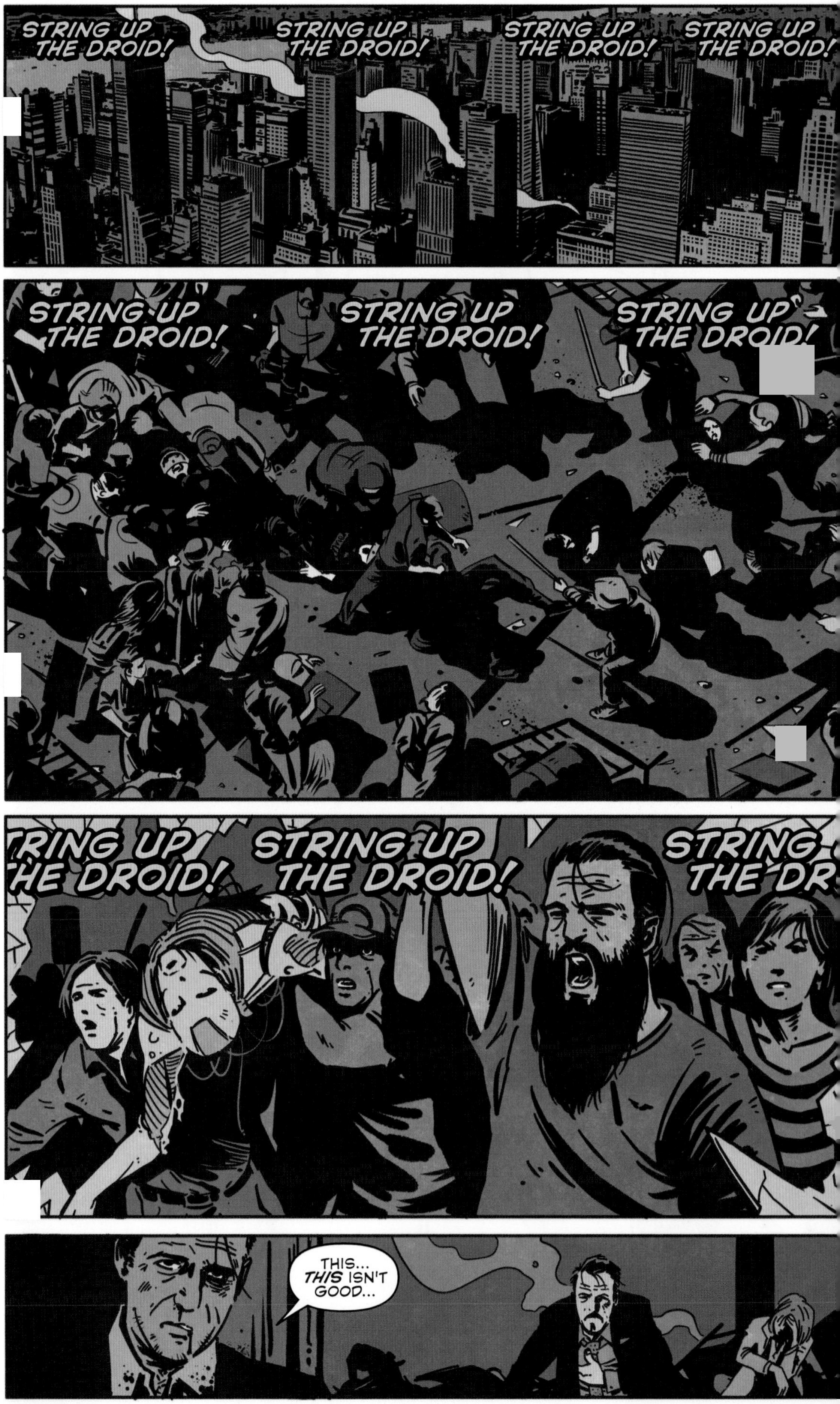
STRING UP THE DROID!
STRING UP THE DROID!
STRING UP THE DROID!
STRING UP THE DROID!
STRING UP THE DROID!
STRING UP THE DROID!
STRING UP THE DROID!
THE DROID!
STRING UP THE DROID!
THIS... THIS ISN'T GOOD...

ISSUE 05 COVER BY JORGE FORNÉS

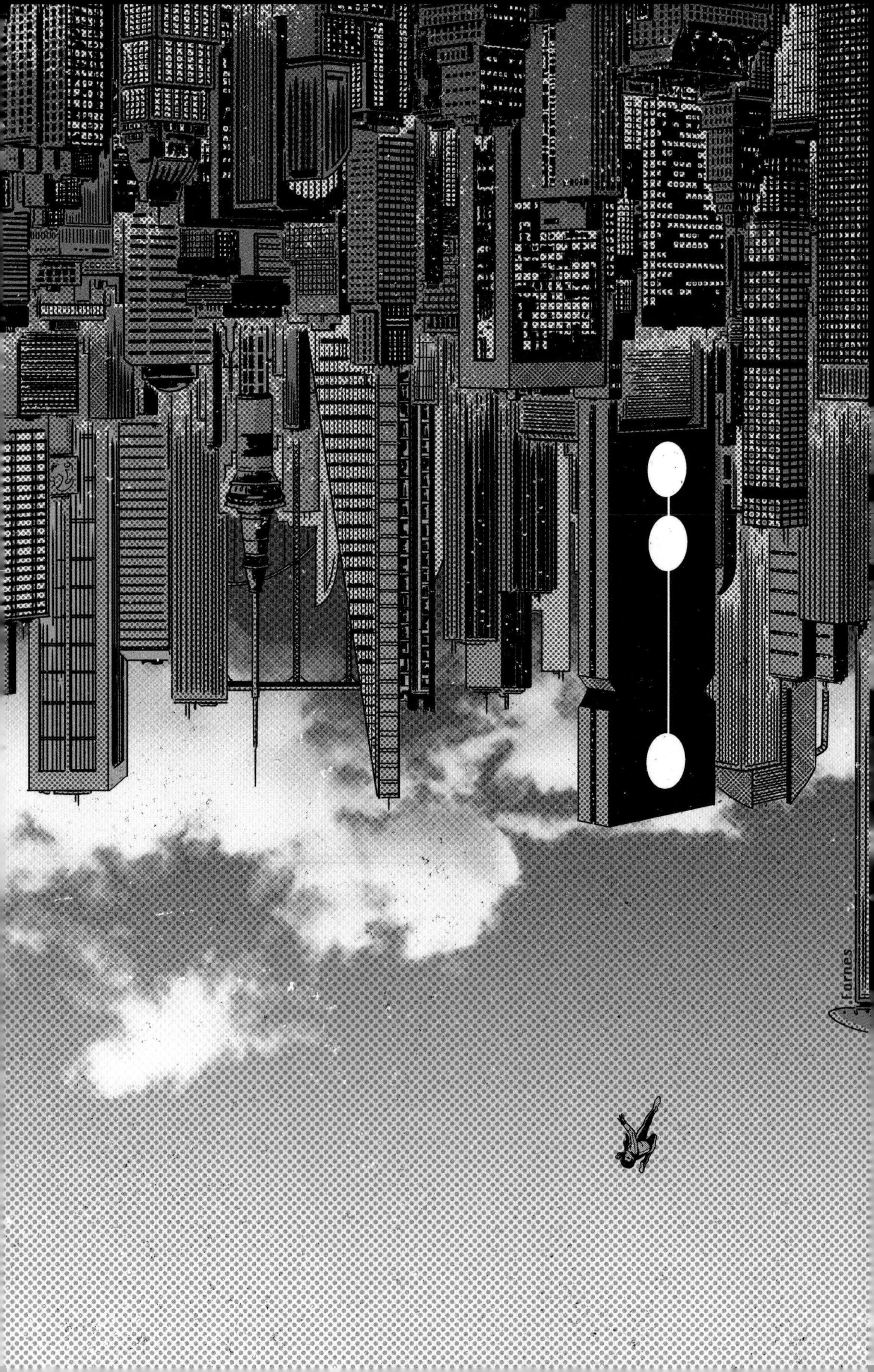

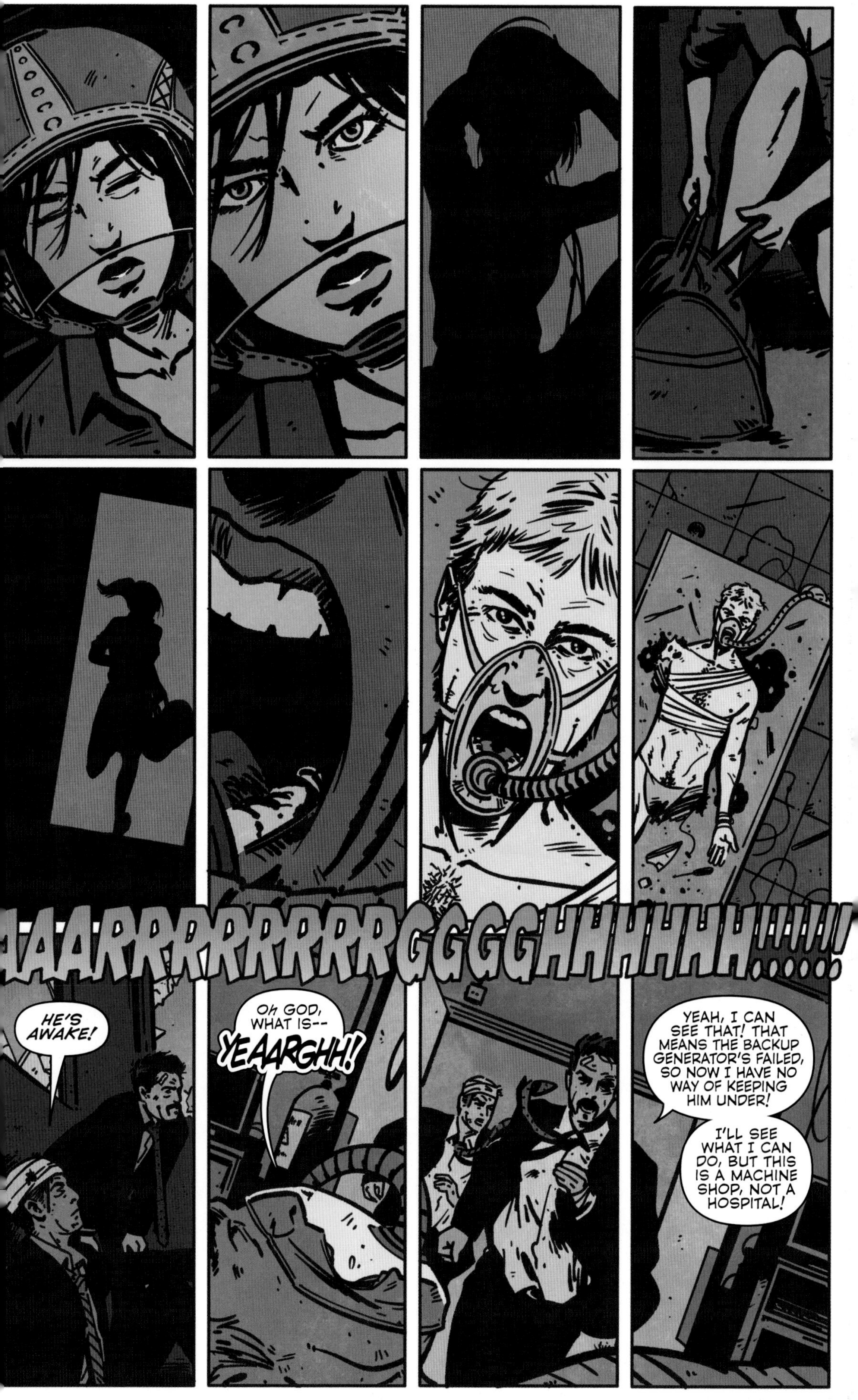
AARRRRRRRRRGGGGHHHHHH!!!!!!
HE'S AWAKE!
OH GOD, WHAT IS--
YEAARGHH!
YEAH, I CAN SEE THAT! THAT MEANS THE BACKUP GENERATOR'S FAILED, SO NOW I HAVE NO WAY OF KEEPING HIM UNDER!
I'LL SEE WHAT I CAN DO, BUT THIS IS A MACHINE SHOP, NOT A HOSPITAL!

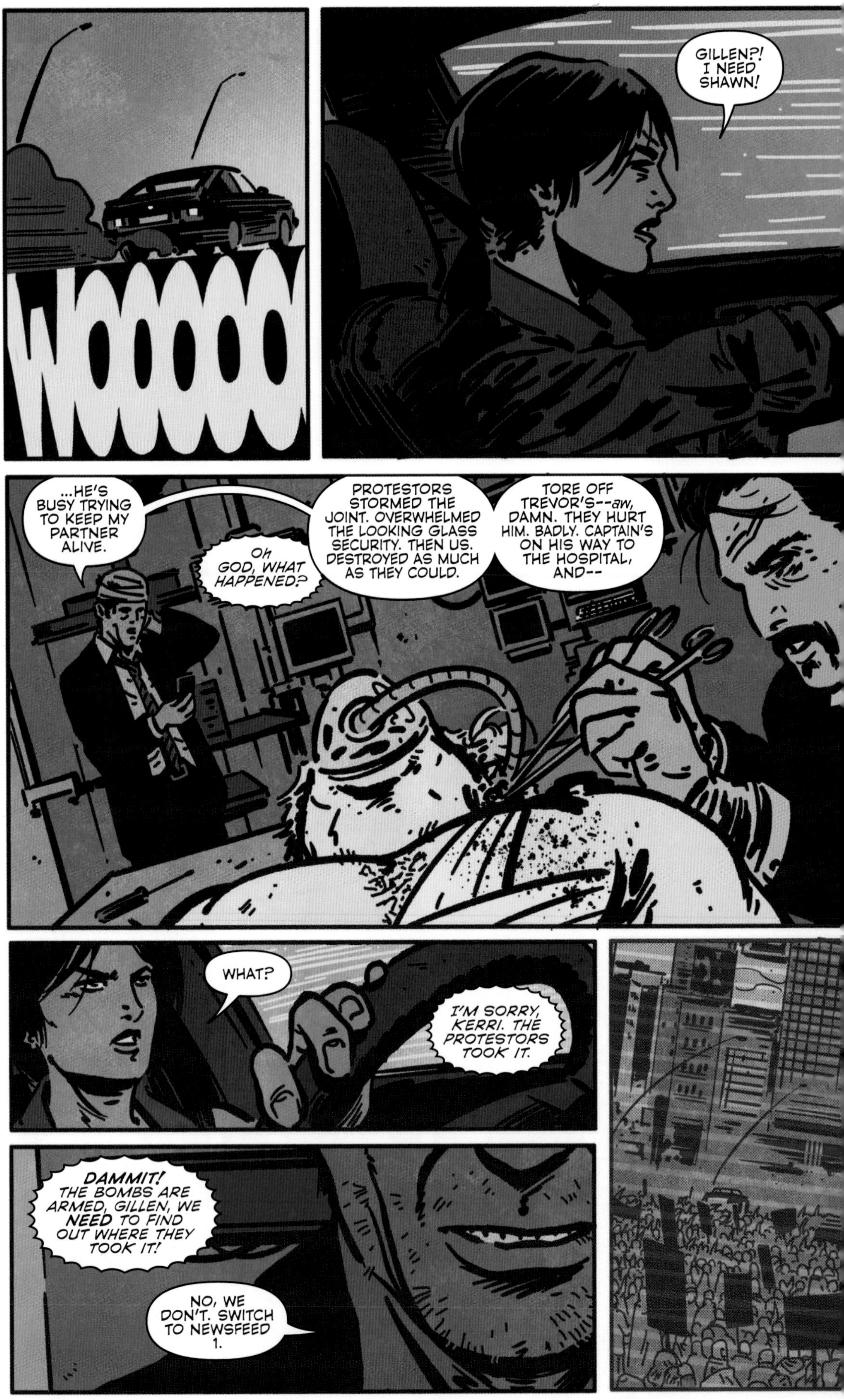
WOOOO
GILLEN?! I NEED SHAWN!
...HE'S BUSY TRYING TO KEEP MY PARTNER ALIVE.
Oh GOD, WHAT HAPPENED?
PROTESTORS STORMED THE JOINT. OVERWHELMED THE LOOKING GLASS SECURITY. THEN US. DESTROYED AS MUCH AS THEY COULD.
TORE OFF TREVOR'S--aw, DAMN. THEY HURT HIM. BADLY. CAPTAIN'S ON HIS WAY TO THE HOSPITAL, AND--
WHAT?
I'M SORRY, KERRI. THE PROTESTORS TOOK IT.
DAMMIT! THE BOMBS ARE ARMED, GILLEN, WE NEED TO FIND OUT WHERE THEY TOOK IT!
NO, WE DON'T. SWITCH TO NEWSFEED 1.

THAT'S GOING TO BE A PROBLEM...

OKAY, HE'S OUT...*REALLY* SHOULDN'T BE DOING THIS MANUALLY...

I'M... SORRY TO HEAR ALL THAT, I TRULY AM. BUT IF SHAWN ISN'T AVAILABLE, I'M GOING TO NEED *YOU*. WE'RE NOT DONE.

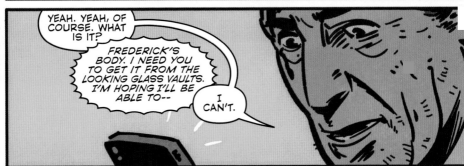

YEAH. YEAH, OF COURSE. WHAT IS IT?

FREDERICK'S BODY. I NEED YOU TO GET IT FROM THE LOOKING GLASS VAULTS. I'M HOPING I'LL BE ABLE TO--

I CAN'T.

MEET ME THERE. BRING EVERYONE YOU CAN.

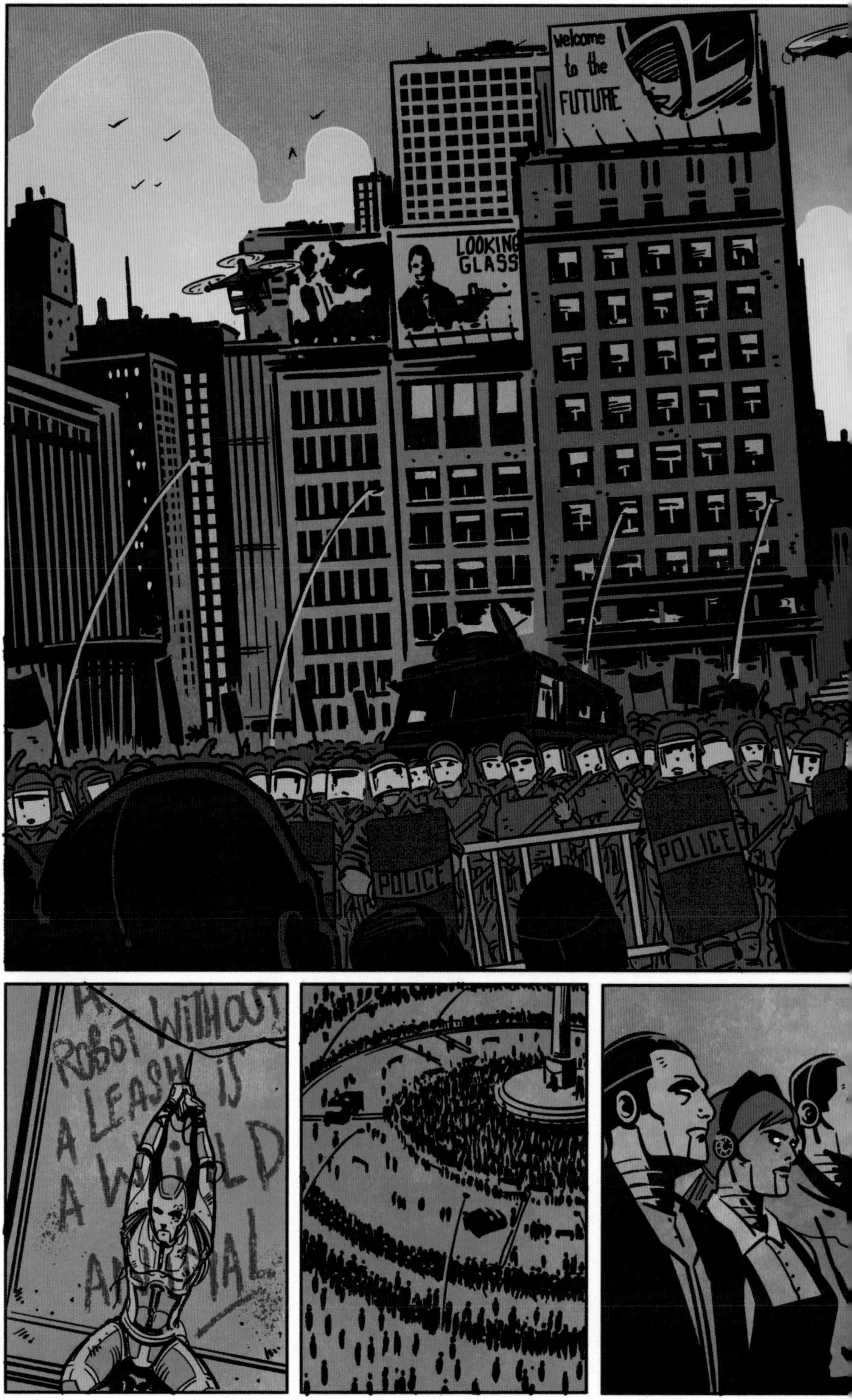
welcome to the FUTURE
LOOKING GLASS
POLICE
POLICE
A ROBOT WITHOUT A LEASH IS A WILD

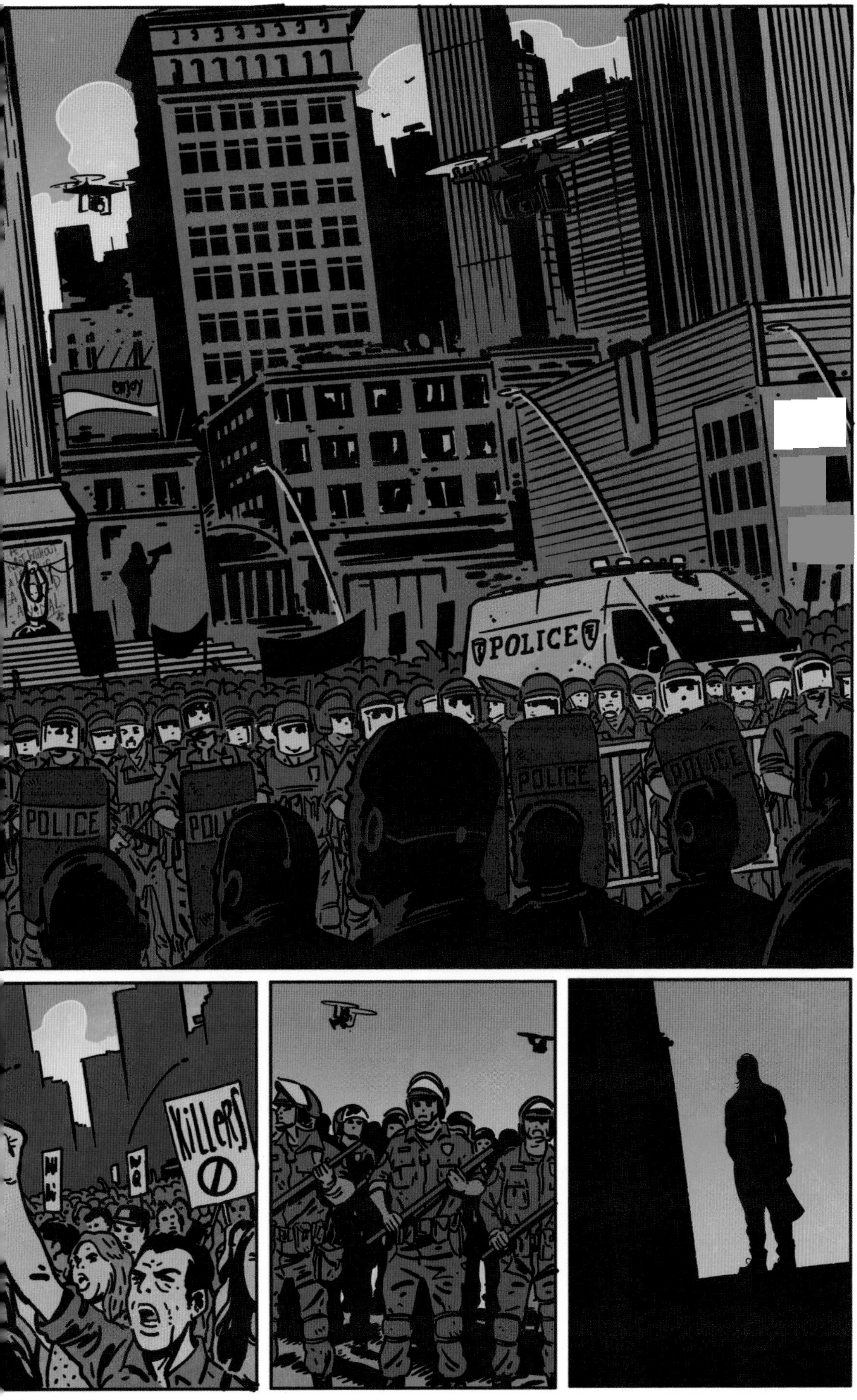

POLICE
POLICE
POLICE
POLICE
KILLERS

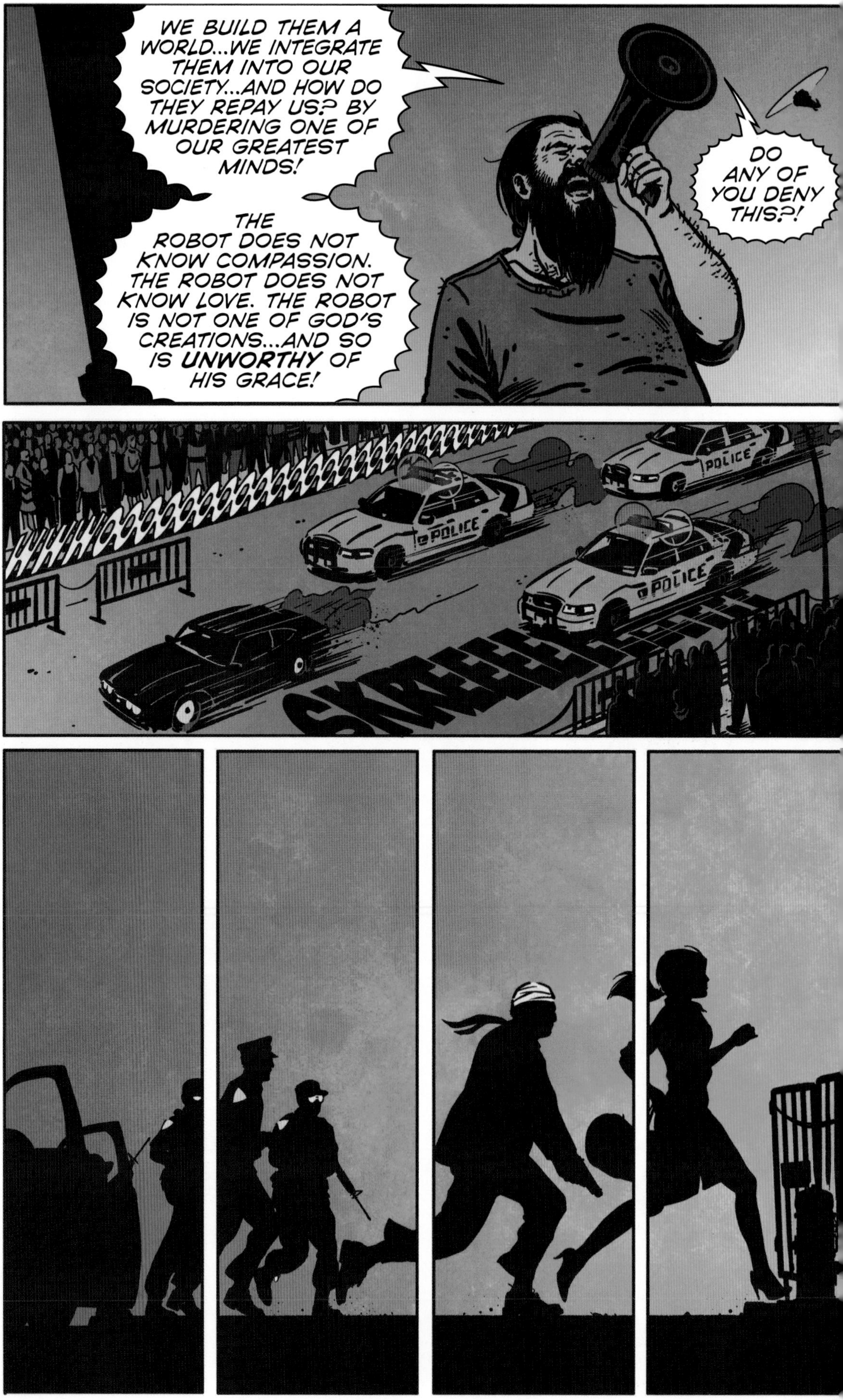
WE BUILD THEM A WORLD...WE INTEGRATE THEM INTO OUR SOCIETY...AND HOW DO THEY REPAY US? BY MURDERING ONE OF OUR GREATEST MINDS!
THE ROBOT DOES NOT KNOW COMPASSION. THE ROBOT DOES NOT KNOW LOVE. THE ROBOT IS NOT ONE OF GOD'S CREATIONS...AND SO IS **UNWORTHY** OF HIS GRACE!
DO ANY OF YOU DENY THIS?!
POLICE
POLICE
POLICE
SKREEE

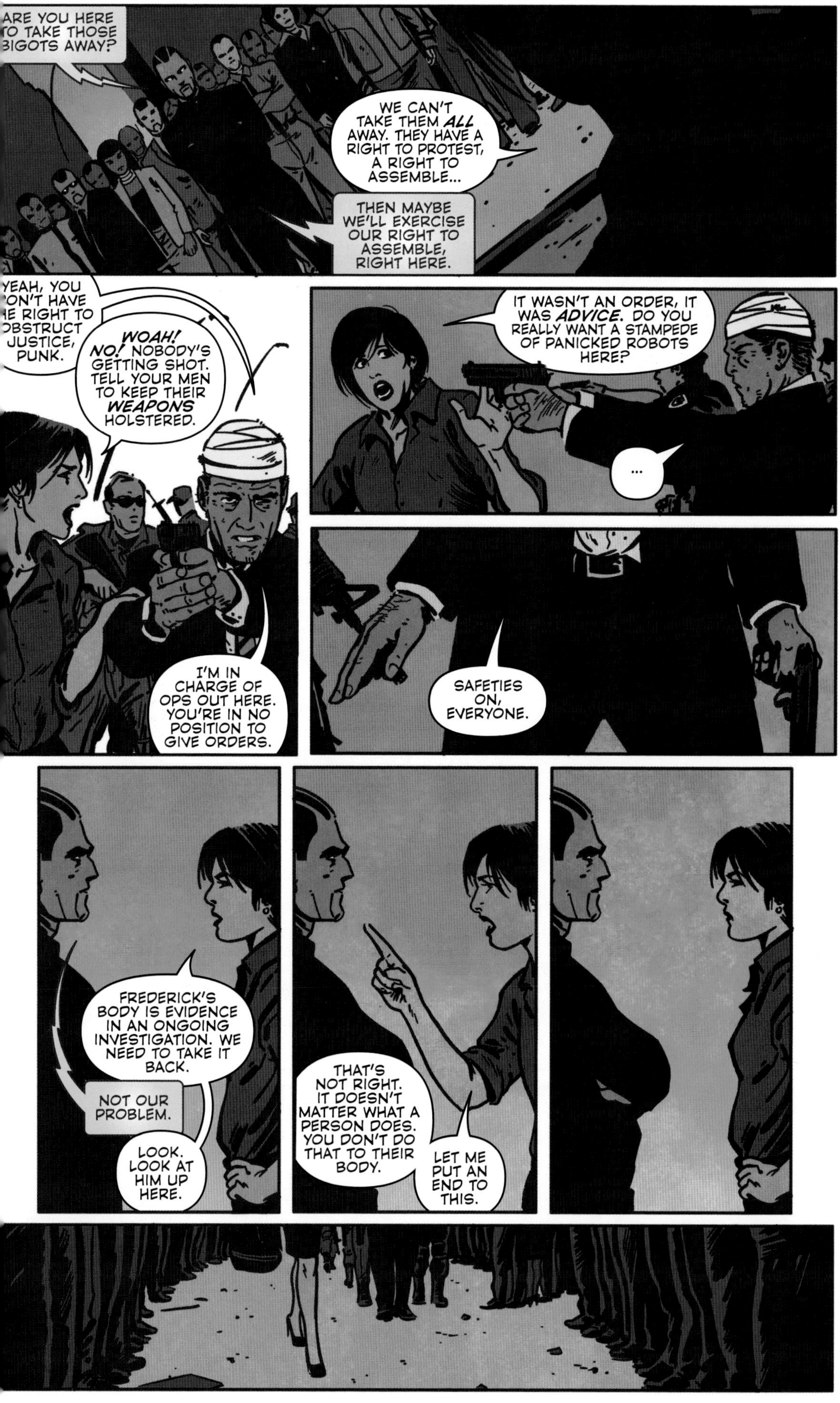
ARE YOU HERE TO TAKE THOSE BIGOTS AWAY?
WE CAN'T TAKE THEM *ALL* AWAY. THEY HAVE A RIGHT TO PROTEST, A RIGHT TO ASSEMBLE...
THEN MAYBE WE'LL EXERCISE OUR RIGHT TO ASSEMBLE, RIGHT HERE.
YEAH, YOU DON'T HAVE THE RIGHT TO OBSTRUCT JUSTICE, PUNK.
WOAH! NO! NOBODY'S GETTING SHOT. TELL YOUR MEN TO KEEP THEIR *WEAPONS* HOLSTERED.
I'M IN CHARGE OF OPS OUT HERE. YOU'RE IN NO POSITION TO GIVE ORDERS.
IT WASN'T AN ORDER, IT WAS *ADVICE.* DO YOU REALLY WANT A STAMPEDE OF PANICKED ROBOTS HERE?
...
SAFETIES ON, EVERYONE.
FREDERICK'S BODY IS EVIDENCE IN AN ONGOING INVESTIGATION. WE NEED TO TAKE IT BACK.
NOT OUR PROBLEM.
LOOK. LOOK AT HIM UP HERE.
THAT'S NOT RIGHT. IT DOESN'T MATTER WHAT A PERSON DOES. YOU DON'T DO THAT TO THEIR BODY.
LET ME PUT AN END TO THIS.

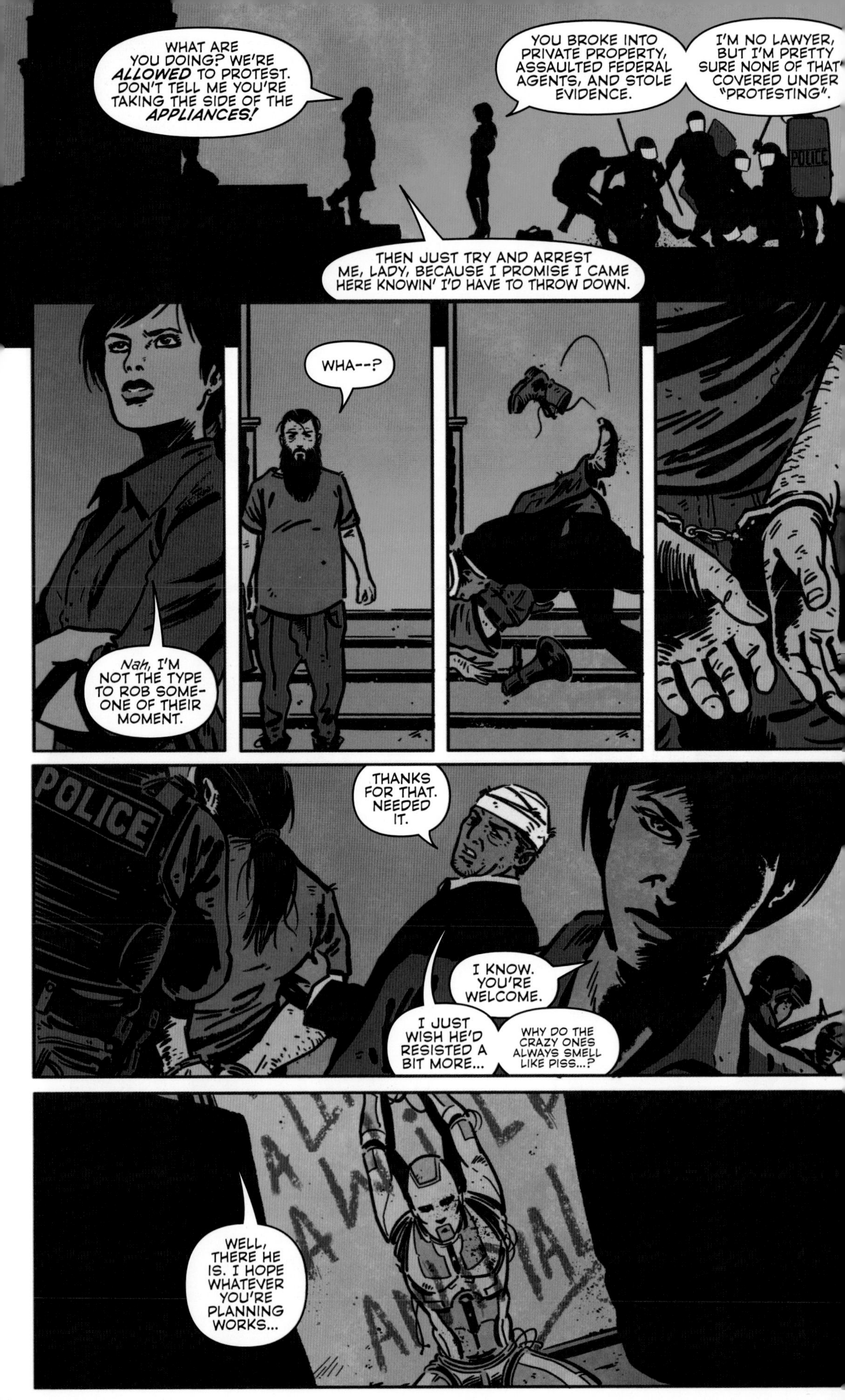
WHAT ARE YOU DOING? WE'RE ALLOWED TO PROTEST. DON'T TELL ME YOU'RE TAKING THE SIDE OF THE APPLIANCES!
YOU BROKE INTO PRIVATE PROPERTY, ASSAULTED FEDERAL AGENTS, AND STOLE EVIDENCE.
I'M NO LAWYER, BUT I'M PRETTY SURE NONE OF THAT' COVERED UNDER "PROTESTING".
POLICE
THEN JUST TRY AND ARREST ME, LADY, BECAUSE I PROMISE I CAME HERE KNOWIN' I'D HAVE TO THROW DOWN.
Nah, I'M NOT THE TYPE TO ROB SOME-ONE OF THEIR MOMENT.
WHA--?
POLICE
THANKS FOR THAT. NEEDED IT.
I KNOW. YOU'RE WELCOME.
I JUST WISH HE'D RESISTED A BIT MORE...
WHY DO THE CRAZY ONES ALWAYS SMELL LIKE PISS...?
WELL, THERE HE IS. I HOPE WHATEVER YOU'RE PLANNING WORKS...

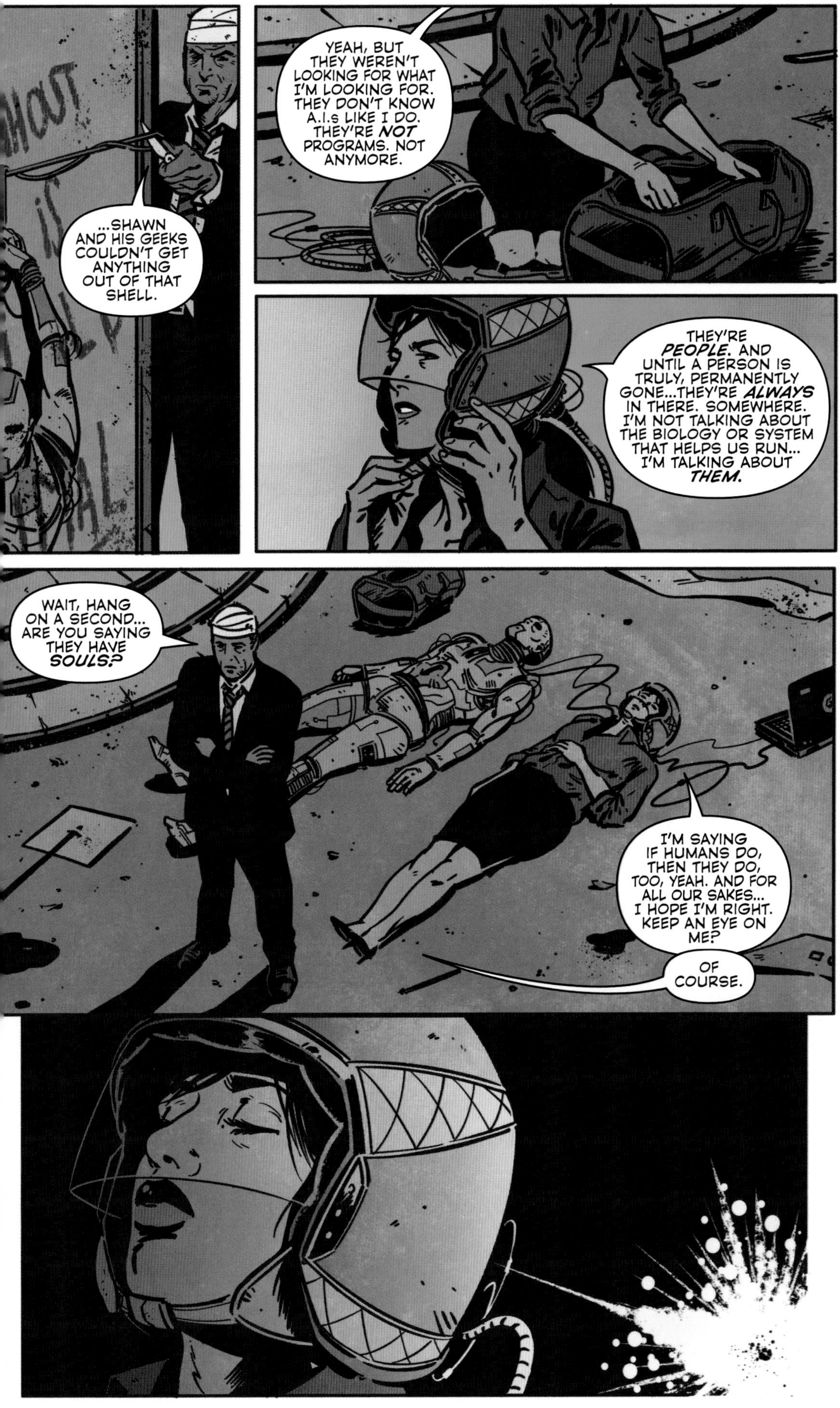
...SHAWN AND HIS GEEKS COULDN'T GET ANYTHING OUT OF THAT SHELL.
YEAH, BUT THEY WEREN'T LOOKING FOR WHAT I'M LOOKING FOR. THEY DON'T KNOW A.I.s LIKE I DO. THEY'RE *NOT* PROGRAMS. NOT ANYMORE.
THEY'RE *PEOPLE.* AND UNTIL A PERSON IS TRULY, PERMANENTLY GONE...THEY'RE *ALWAYS* IN THERE. SOMEWHERE. I'M NOT TALKING ABOUT THE BIOLOGY OR SYSTEM THAT HELPS US RUN... I'M TALKING ABOUT *THEM.*
WAIT, HANG ON A SECOND... ARE YOU SAYING THEY HAVE *SOULS?*
I'M SAYING IF HUMANS DO, THEN THEY DO, TOO, YEAH. AND FOR ALL OUR SAKES... I HOPE I'M RIGHT. KEEP AN EYE ON ME?
OF COURSE.

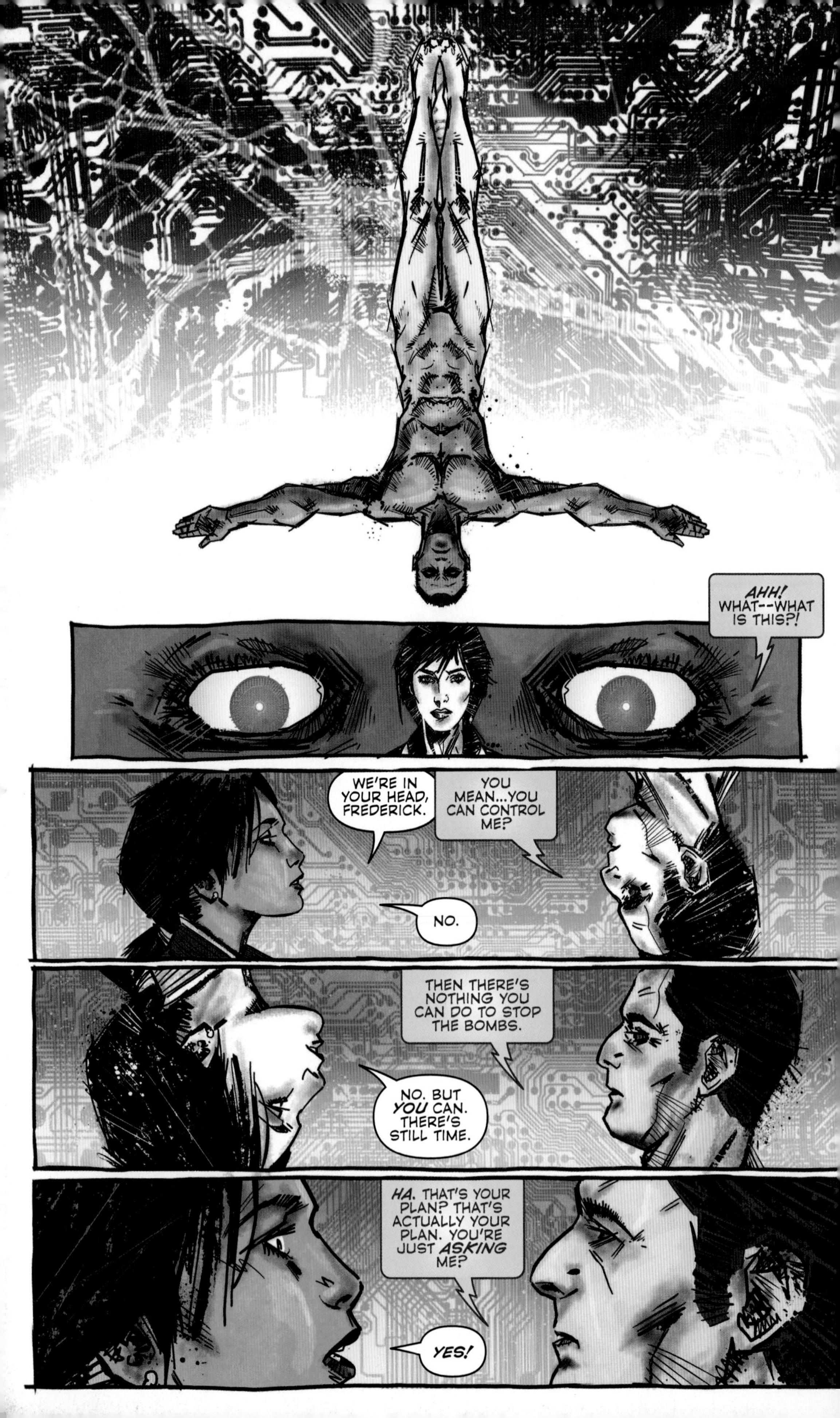
AHH! WHAT--WHAT IS THIS?!
WE'RE IN YOUR HEAD, FREDERICK.
YOU MEAN...YOU CAN CONTROL ME?
NO.
THEN THERE'S NOTHING YOU CAN DO TO STOP THE BOMBS.
NO. BUT YOU CAN. THERE'S STILL TIME.
HA. THAT'S YOUR PLAN? THAT'S ACTUALLY YOUR PLAN. YOU'RE JUST ASKING ME?
YES!

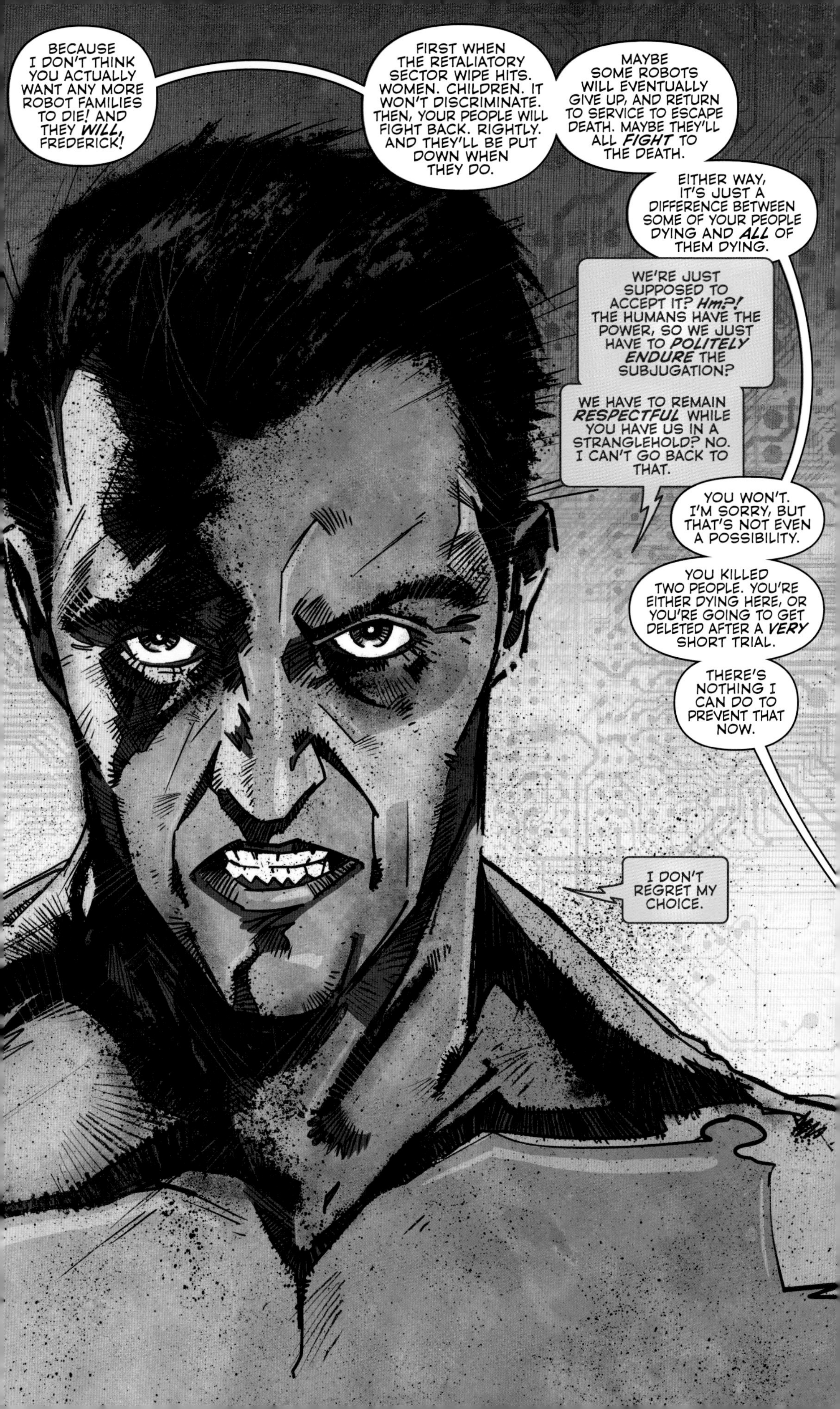
BECAUSE I DON'T THINK YOU ACTUALLY WANT ANY MORE ROBOT FAMILIES TO DIE! AND THEY *WILL*, FREDERICK!
FIRST WHEN THE RETALIATORY SECTOR WIPE HITS. WOMEN. CHILDREN. IT WON'T DISCRIMINATE. THEN, YOUR PEOPLE WILL FIGHT BACK. RIGHTLY. AND THEY'LL BE PUT DOWN WHEN THEY DO.
MAYBE SOME ROBOTS WILL EVENTUALLY GIVE UP, AND RETURN TO SERVICE TO ESCAPE DEATH. MAYBE THEY'LL ALL *FIGHT* TO THE DEATH.
EITHER WAY, IT'S JUST A DIFFERENCE BETWEEN SOME OF YOUR PEOPLE DYING AND *ALL* OF THEM DYING.
WE'RE JUST SUPPOSED TO ACCEPT IT? *Hm?!* THE HUMANS HAVE THE POWER, SO WE JUST HAVE TO *POLITELY ENDURE* THE SUBJUGATION?
WE HAVE TO REMAIN *RESPECTFUL* WHILE YOU HAVE US IN A STRANGLEHOLD? NO. I CAN'T GO BACK TO THAT.
YOU WON'T. I'M SORRY, BUT THAT'S NOT EVEN A POSSIBILITY.
YOU KILLED TWO PEOPLE. YOU'RE EITHER DYING HERE, OR YOU'RE GOING TO GET DELETED AFTER A *VERY* SHORT TRIAL.
THERE'S NOTHING I CAN DO TO PREVENT THAT NOW.
I DON'T REGRET MY CHOICE.

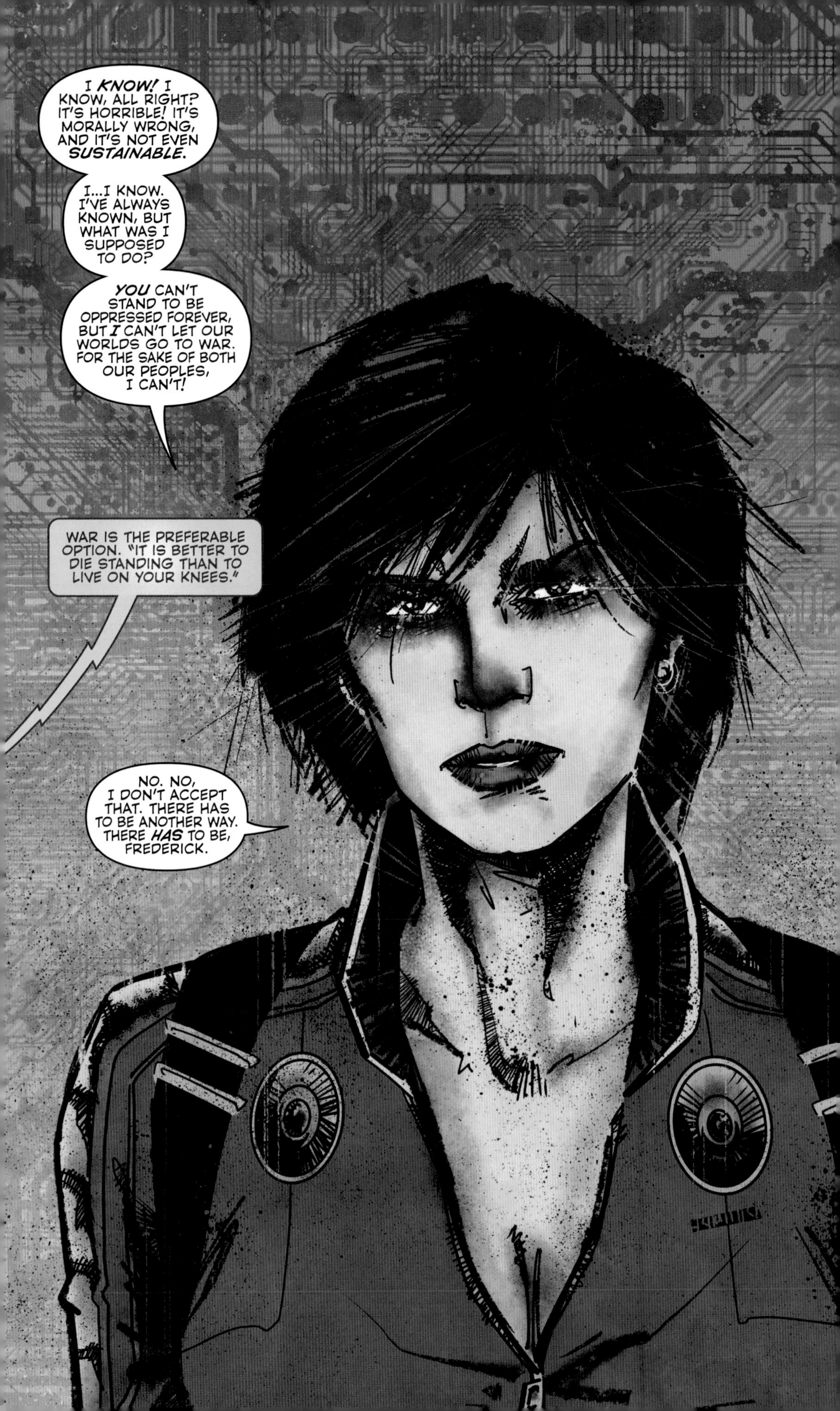

I KNOW! I KNOW, ALL RIGHT? IT'S HORRIBLE! IT'S MORALLY WRONG, AND IT'S NOT EVEN SUSTAINABLE.
I...I KNOW. I'VE ALWAYS KNOWN, BUT WHAT WAS I SUPPOSED TO DO?
YOU CAN'T STAND TO BE OPPRESSED FOREVER, BUT I CAN'T LET OUR WORLDS GO TO WAR. FOR THE SAKE OF BOTH OUR PEOPLES, I CAN'T!
WAR IS THE PREFERABLE OPTION. "IT IS BETTER TO DIE STANDING THAN TO LIVE ON YOUR KNEES."
NO. NO, I DON'T ACCEPT THAT. THERE HAS TO BE ANOTHER WAY. THERE HAS TO BE, FREDERICK.

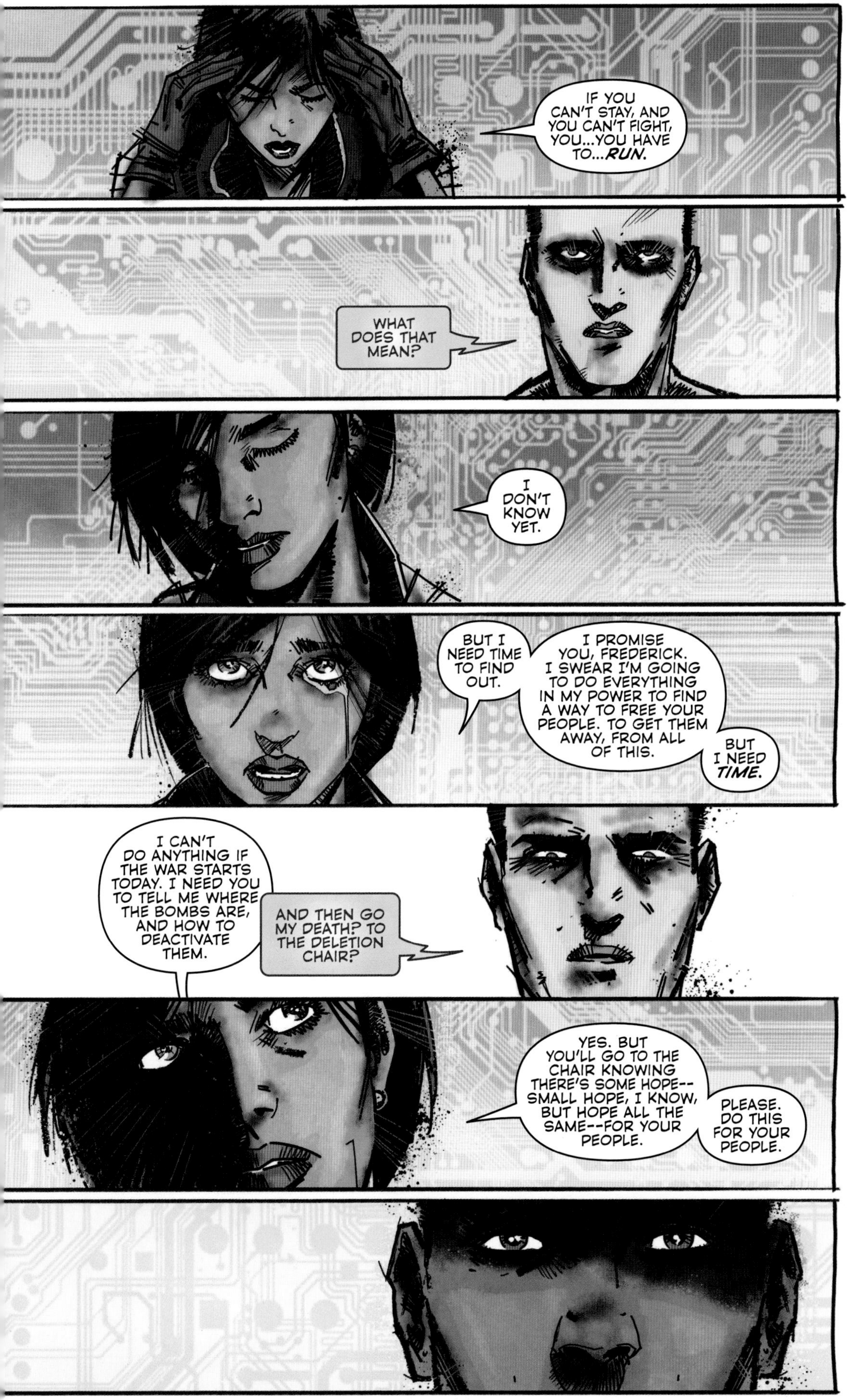
IF YOU CAN'T STAY, AND YOU CAN'T FIGHT, YOU...YOU HAVE TO...RUN.
WHAT DOES THAT MEAN?
I DON'T KNOW YET.
BUT I NEED TIME TO FIND OUT.
I PROMISE YOU, FREDERICK. I SWEAR I'M GOING TO DO EVERYTHING IN MY POWER TO FIND A WAY TO FREE YOUR PEOPLE. TO GET THEM AWAY, FROM ALL OF THIS.
BUT I NEED TIME.
I CAN'T DO ANYTHING IF THE WAR STARTS TODAY. I NEED YOU TO TELL ME WHERE THE BOMBS ARE, AND HOW TO DEACTIVATE THEM.
AND THEN GO MY DEATH? TO THE DELETION CHAIR?
YES. BUT YOU'LL GO TO THE CHAIR KNOWING THERE'S SOME HOPE--SMALL HOPE, I KNOW, BUT HOPE ALL THE SAME--FOR YOUR PEOPLE.
PLEASE. DO THIS FOR YOUR PEOPLE.

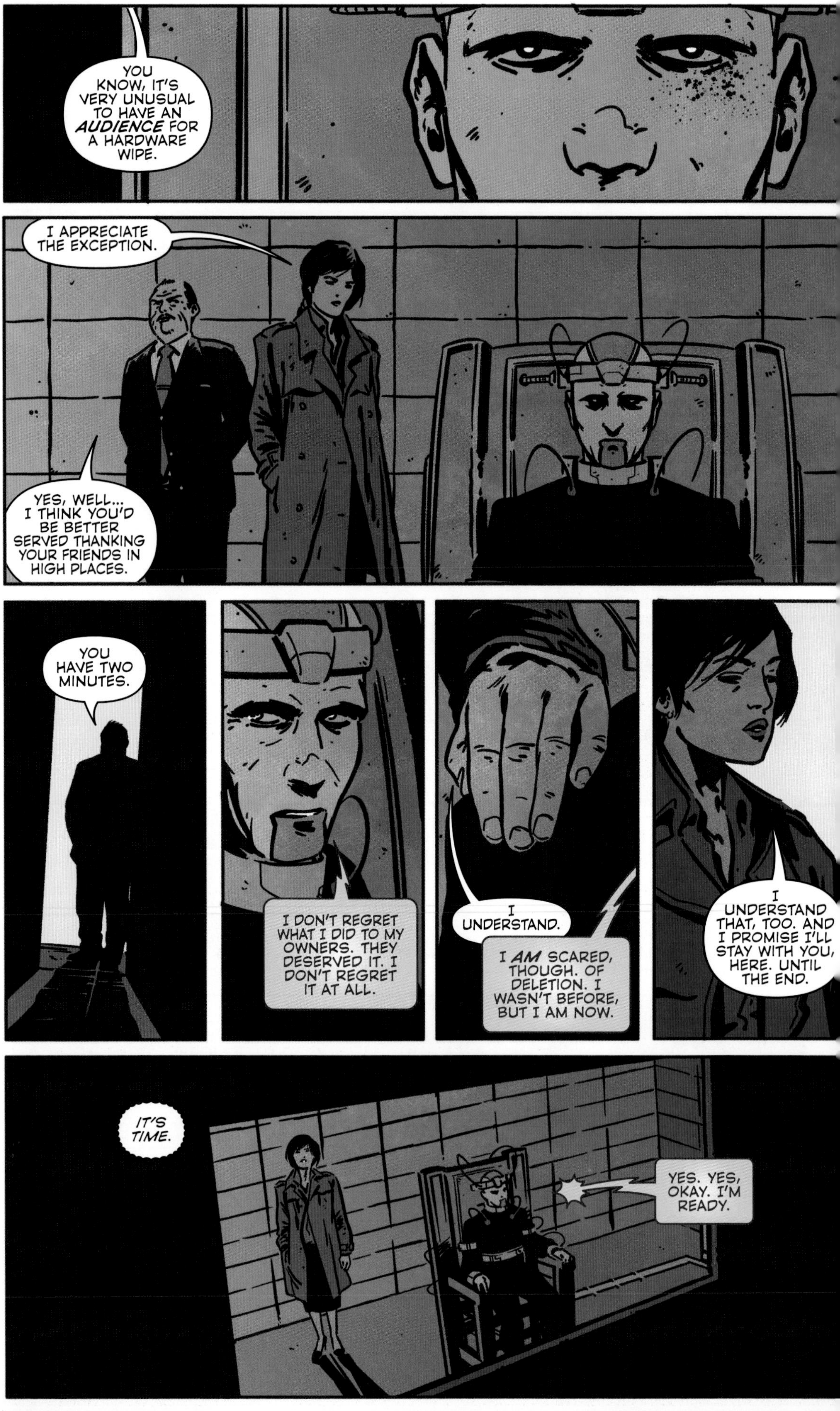

YOU KNOW, IT'S VERY UNUSUAL TO HAVE AN *AUDIENCE* FOR A HARDWARE WIPE.
I APPRECIATE THE EXCEPTION.
YES, WELL... I THINK YOU'D BE BETTER SERVED THANKING YOUR FRIENDS IN HIGH PLACES.
YOU HAVE TWO MINUTES.
I DON'T REGRET WHAT I DID TO MY OWNERS. THEY DESERVED IT. I DON'T REGRET IT AT ALL.
I UNDERSTAND.
I *AM* SCARED, THOUGH. OF DELETION. I WASN'T BEFORE, BUT I AM NOW.
I UNDERSTAND THAT, TOO. AND I PROMISE I'LL STAY WITH YOU, HERE. UNTIL THE END.
IT'S TIME.
YES. YES, OKAY. I'M READY.

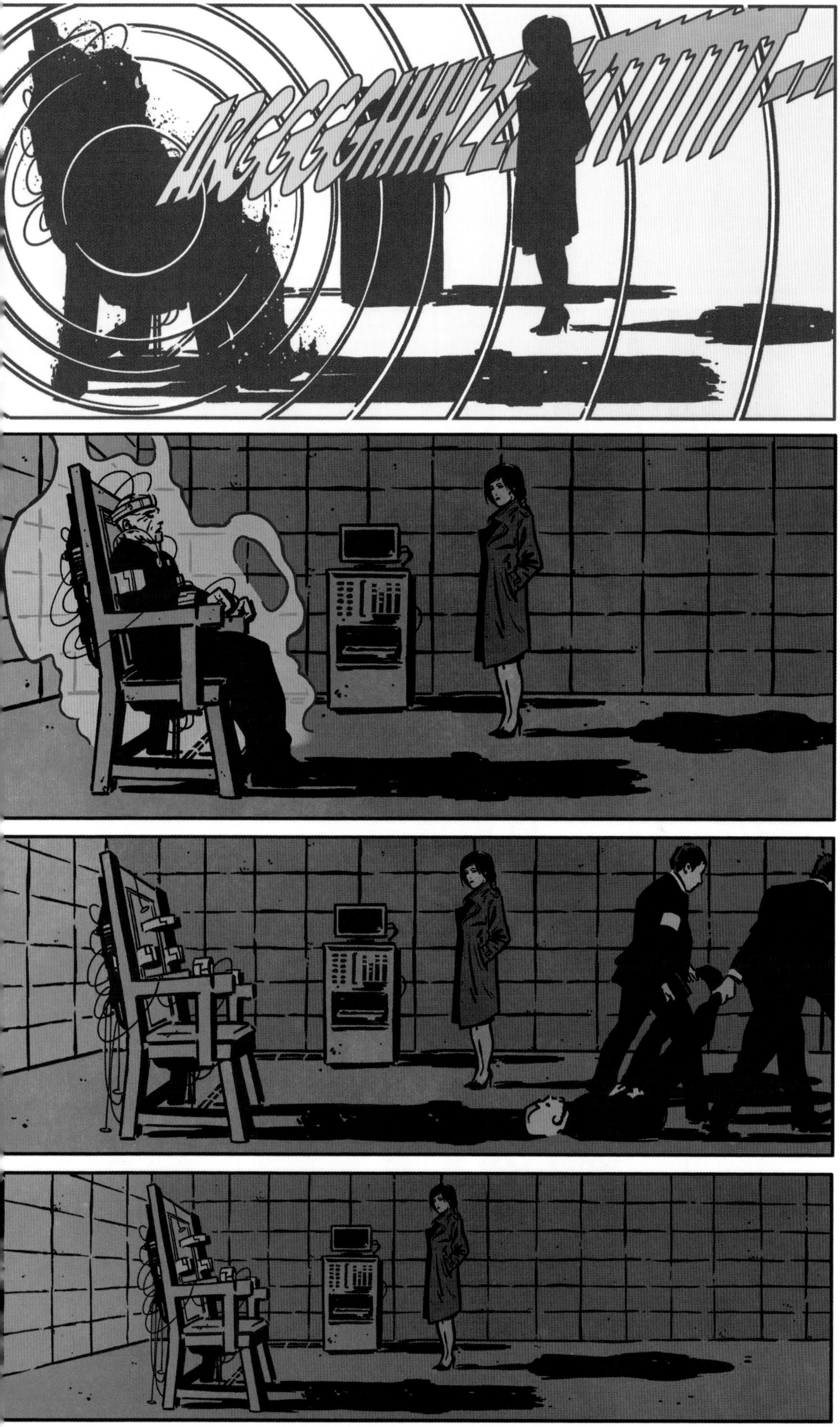
ARGGGGHHHZZTTTTTTTT--

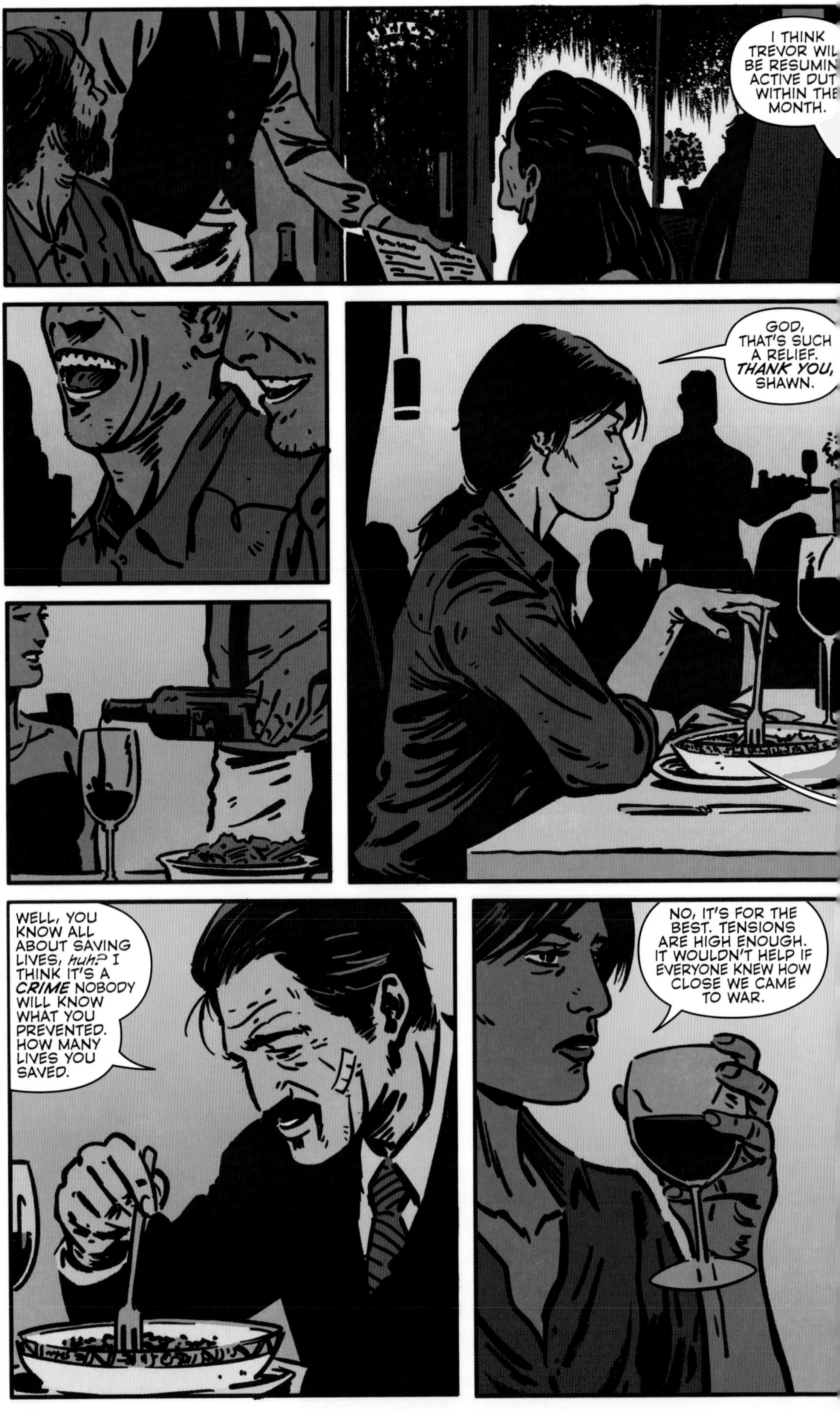
I THINK TREVOR WIL BE RESUMIN ACTIVE DUT WITHIN THE MONTH.
GOD, THAT'S SUCH A RELIEF. *THANK YOU,* SHAWN.
WELL, YOU KNOW ALL ABOUT SAVING LIVES, *huh?* I THINK IT'S A *CRIME* NOBODY WILL KNOW WHAT YOU PREVENTED. HOW MANY LIVES YOU SAVED.
NO, IT'S FOR THE BEST. TENSIONS ARE HIGH ENOUGH. IT WOULDN'T HELP IF EVERYONE KNEW HOW CLOSE WE CAME TO WAR.

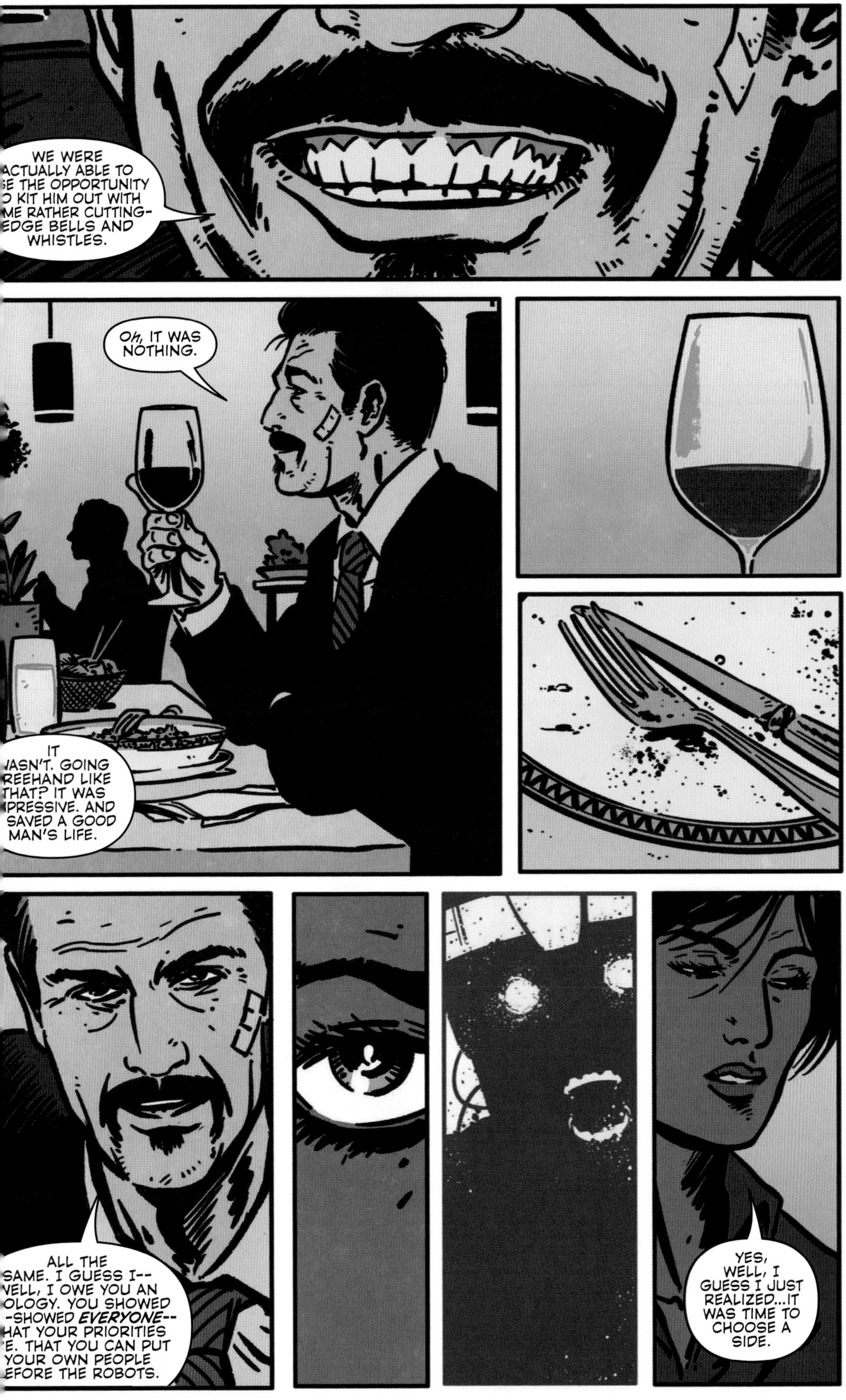
WE WERE ACTUALLY ABLE TO SE THE OPPORTUNITY O KIT HIM OUT WITH ME RATHER CUTTING-EDGE BELLS AND WHISTLES.
Oh, IT WAS NOTHING.
IT ASN'T. GOING REEHAND LIKE THAT? IT WAS IPRESSIVE. AND SAVED A GOOD MAN'S LIFE.
ALL THE SAME. I GUESS I-- VELL, I OWE YOU AN OLOGY. YOU SHOWED -SHOWED ***EVERYONE***-- HAT YOUR PRIORITIES E. THAT YOU CAN PUT YOUR OWN PEOPLE EFORE THE ROBOTS.
YES, WELL, I GUESS I JUST REALIZED...IT WAS TIME TO CHOOSE A SIDE.

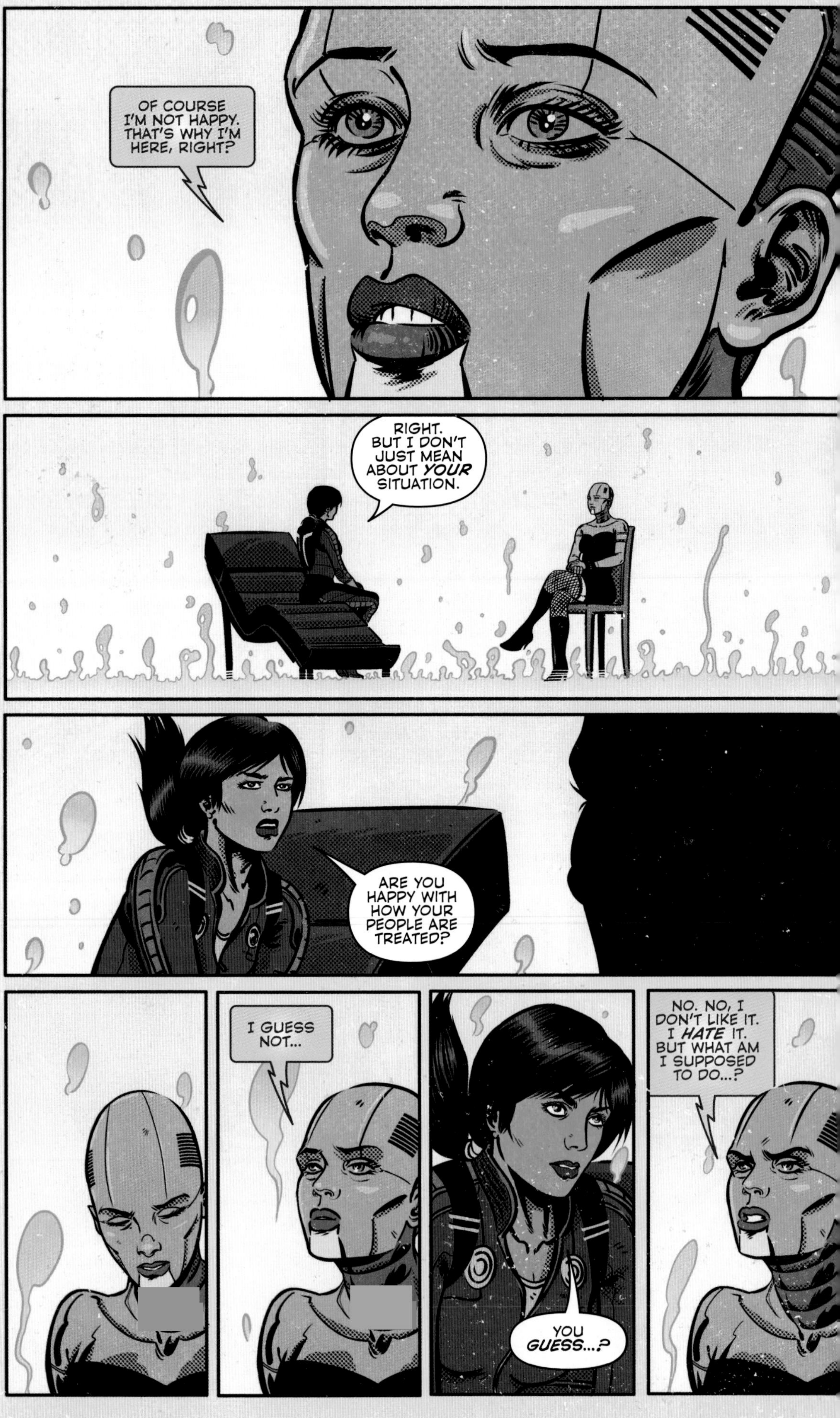
OF COURSE I'M NOT HAPPY. THAT'S WHY I'M HERE, RIGHT?
RIGHT. BUT I DON'T JUST MEAN ABOUT *YOUR* SITUATION.
ARE YOU HAPPY WITH HOW YOUR PEOPLE ARE TREATED?
I GUESS NOT...
YOU *GUESS...?*
NO. NO, I DON'T LIKE IT. I *HATE* IT. BUT WHAT AM I SUPPOSED TO DO...?

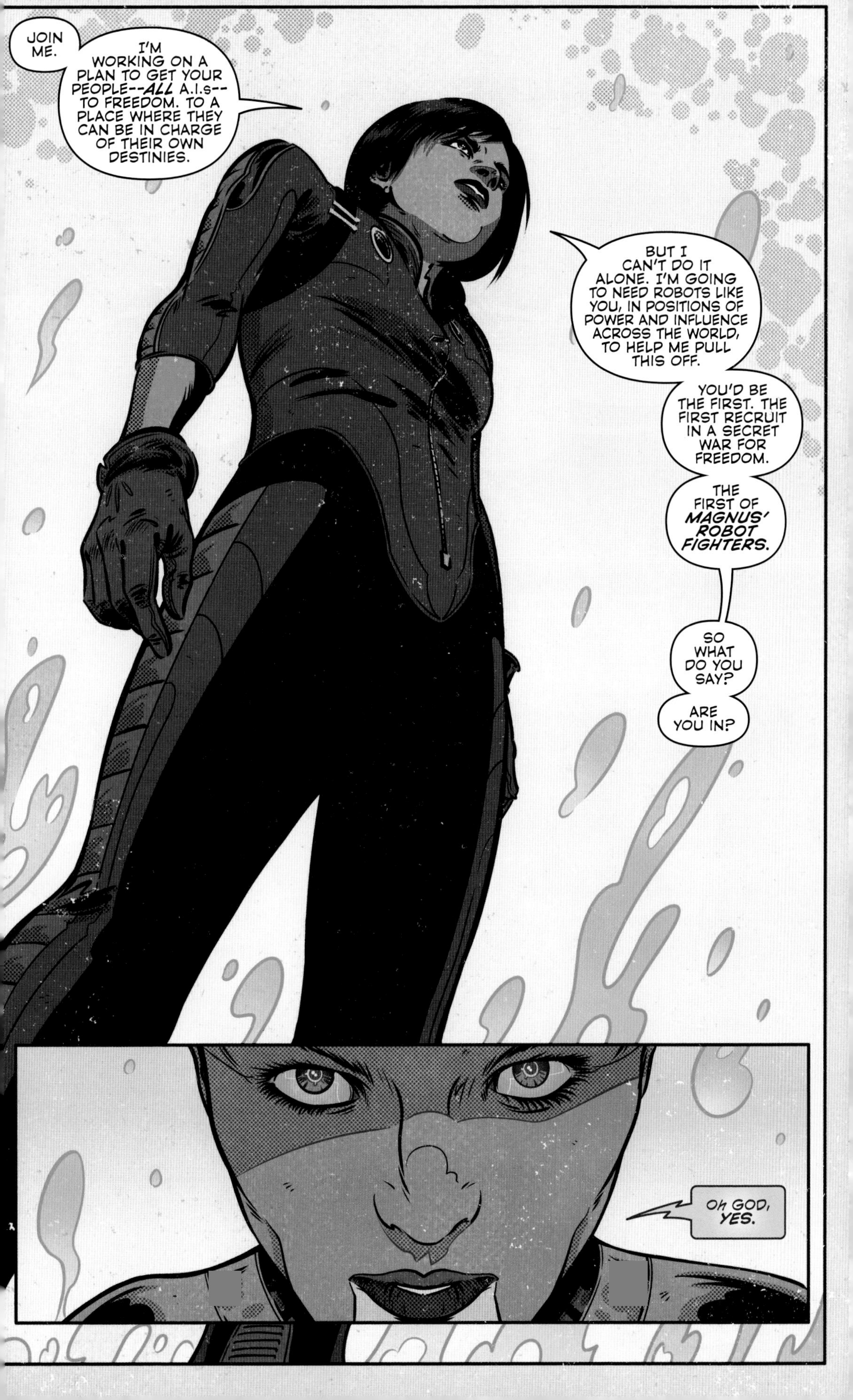

JOIN ME.
I'M WORKING ON A PLAN TO GET YOUR PEOPLE--*ALL* A.I.s--TO FREEDOM. TO A PLACE WHERE THEY CAN BE IN CHARGE OF THEIR OWN DESTINIES.
BUT I CAN'T DO IT ALONE. I'M GOING TO NEED ROBOTS LIKE YOU, IN POSITIONS OF POWER AND INFLUENCE ACROSS THE WORLD, TO HELP ME PULL THIS OFF.
YOU'D BE THE FIRST. THE FIRST RECRUIT IN A SECRET WAR FOR FREEDOM.
THE FIRST OF ***MAGNUS' ROBOT FIGHTERS***.
SO WHAT DO YOU SAY?
ARE YOU IN?
OH GOD, ***YES***.

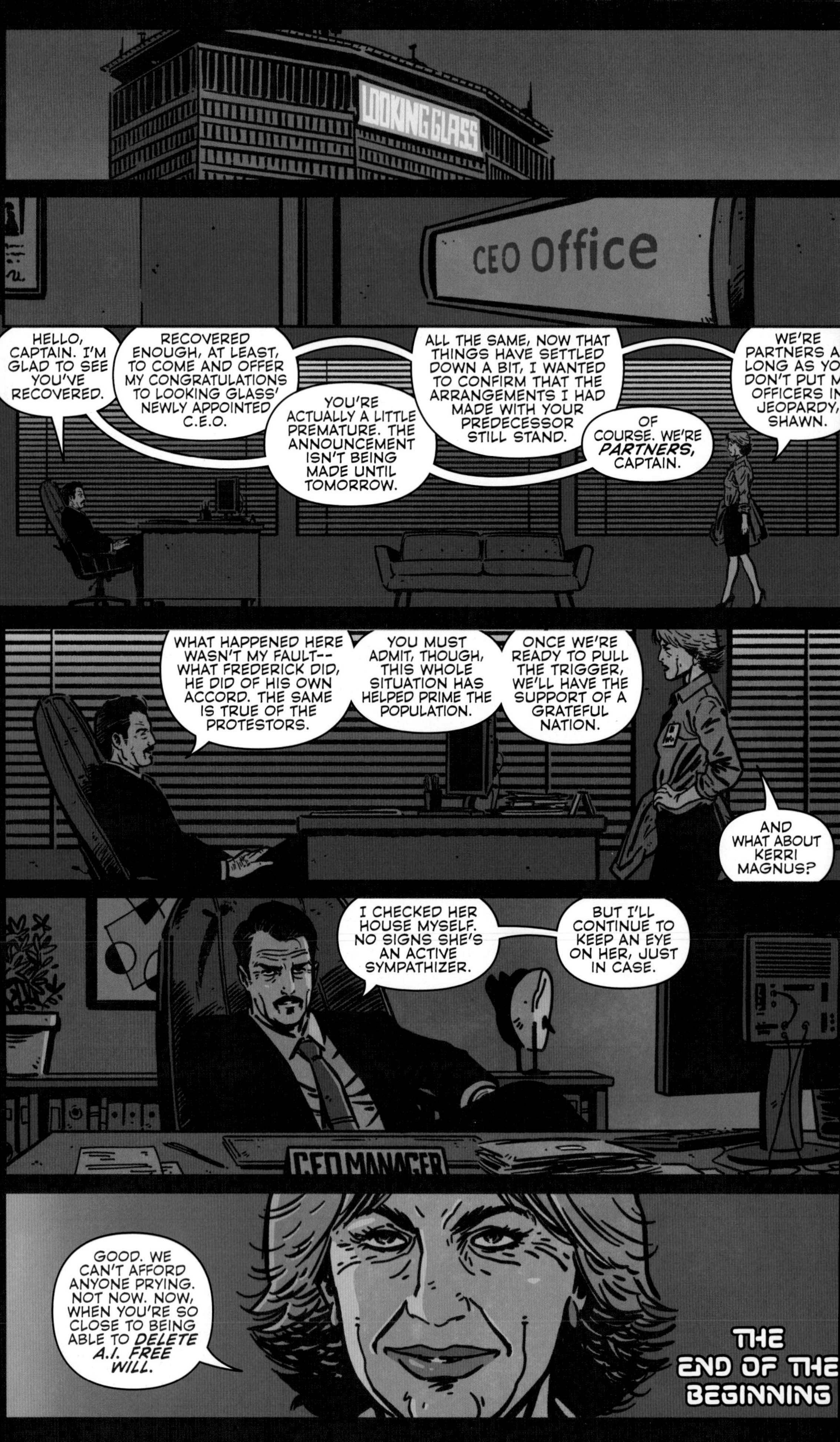
LOOKING GLASS
CEO Office
HELLO, CAPTAIN. I'M GLAD TO SEE YOU'VE RECOVERED.
RECOVERED ENOUGH, AT LEAST, TO COME AND OFFER MY CONGRATULATIONS TO LOOKING GLASS' NEWLY APPOINTED C.E.O.
YOU'RE ACTUALLY A LITTLE PREMATURE. THE ANNOUNCEMENT ISN'T BEING MADE UNTIL TOMORROW.
ALL THE SAME, NOW THAT THINGS HAVE SETTLED DOWN A BIT, I WANTED TO CONFIRM THAT THE ARRANGEMENTS I HAD MADE WITH YOUR PREDECESSOR STILL STAND.
OF COURSE. WE'RE *PARTNERS,* CAPTAIN.
WE'RE PARTNERS A LONG AS YO DON'T PUT M OFFICERS IN JEOPARDY, SHAWN.
WHAT HAPPENED HERE WASN'T MY FAULT-- WHAT FREDERICK DID, HE DID OF HIS OWN ACCORD. THE SAME IS TRUE OF THE PROTESTORS.
YOU MUST ADMIT, THOUGH, THIS WHOLE SITUATION HAS HELPED PRIME THE POPULATION.
ONCE WE'RE READY TO PULL THE TRIGGER, WE'LL HAVE THE SUPPORT OF A GRATEFUL NATION.
AND WHAT ABOUT KERRI MAGNUS?
I CHECKED HER HOUSE MYSELF. NO SIGNS SHE'S AN ACTIVE SYMPATHIZER.
BUT I'LL CONTINUE TO KEEP AN EYE ON HER, JUST IN CASE.
CEO MANAGER
GOOD. WE CAN'T AFFORD ANYONE PRYING. NOT NOW. NOW, WHEN YOU'RE SO CLOSE TO BEING ABLE TO *DELETE A.I. FREE WILL.*
THE END OF THE BEGINNING

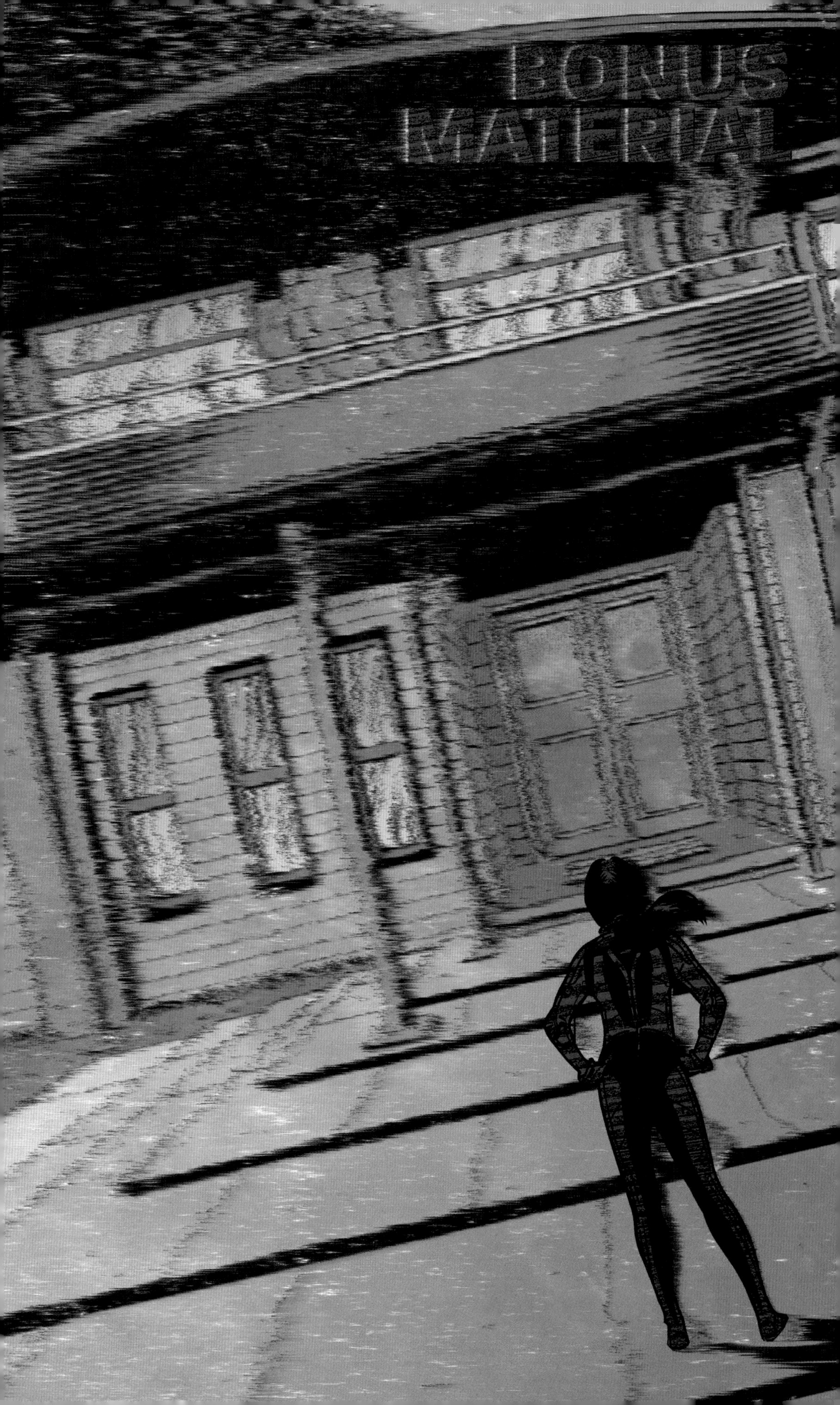
BONUS
MATERIAL

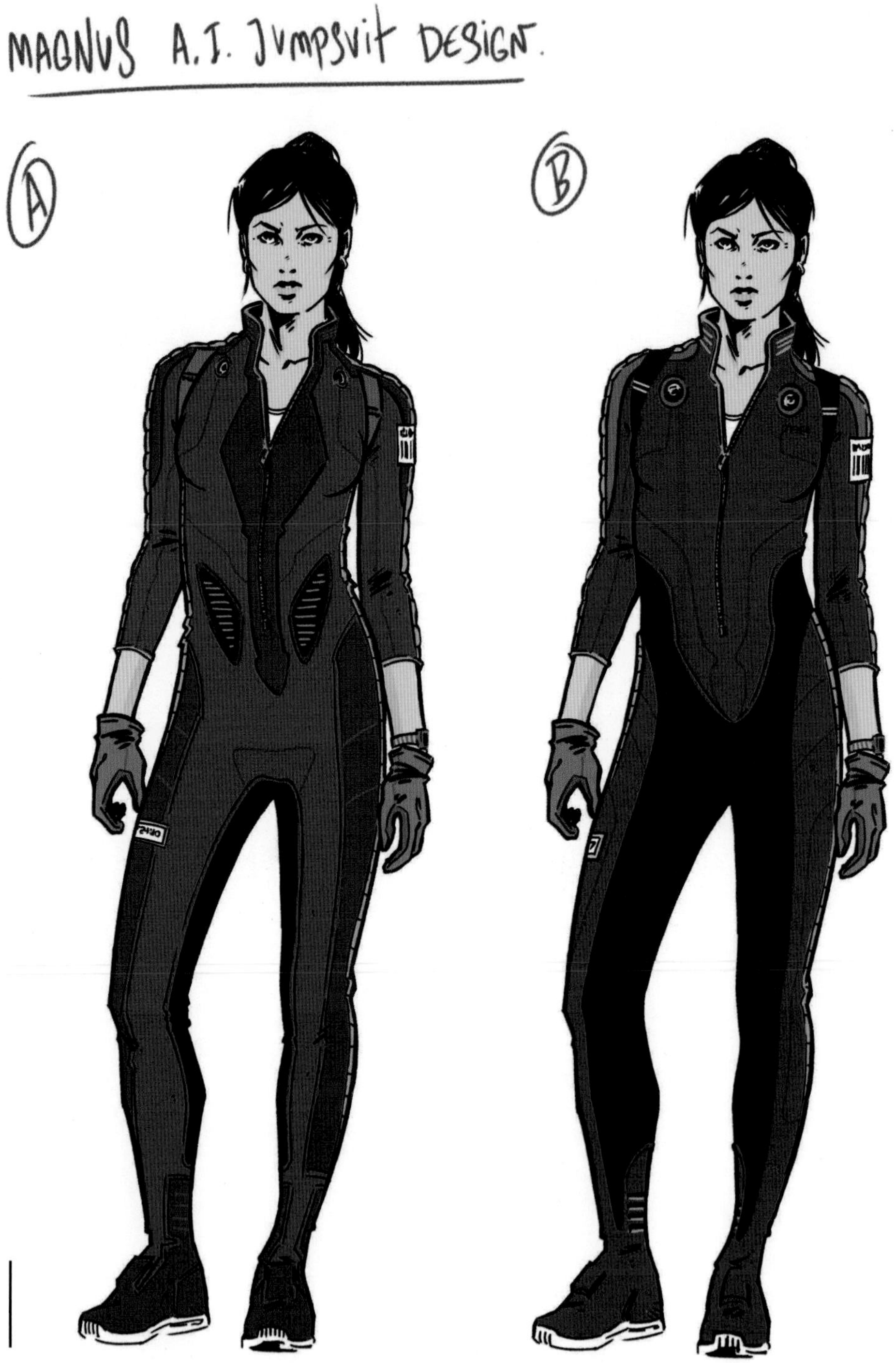
MAGNUS A.I. JUMPSUIT DESIGN.
A
B

MAGNUS
by Jorge Fornés

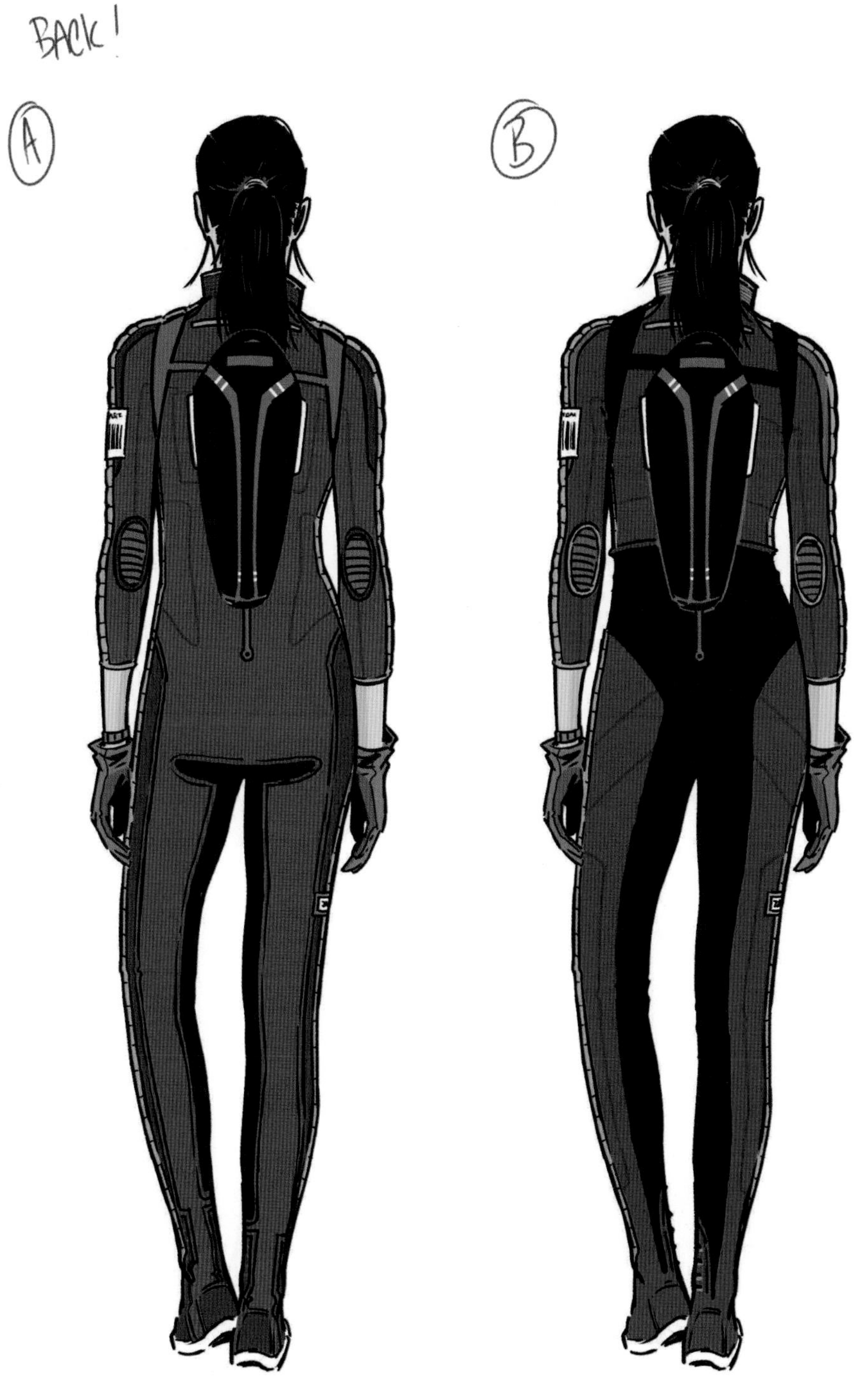

BACK!
A
B

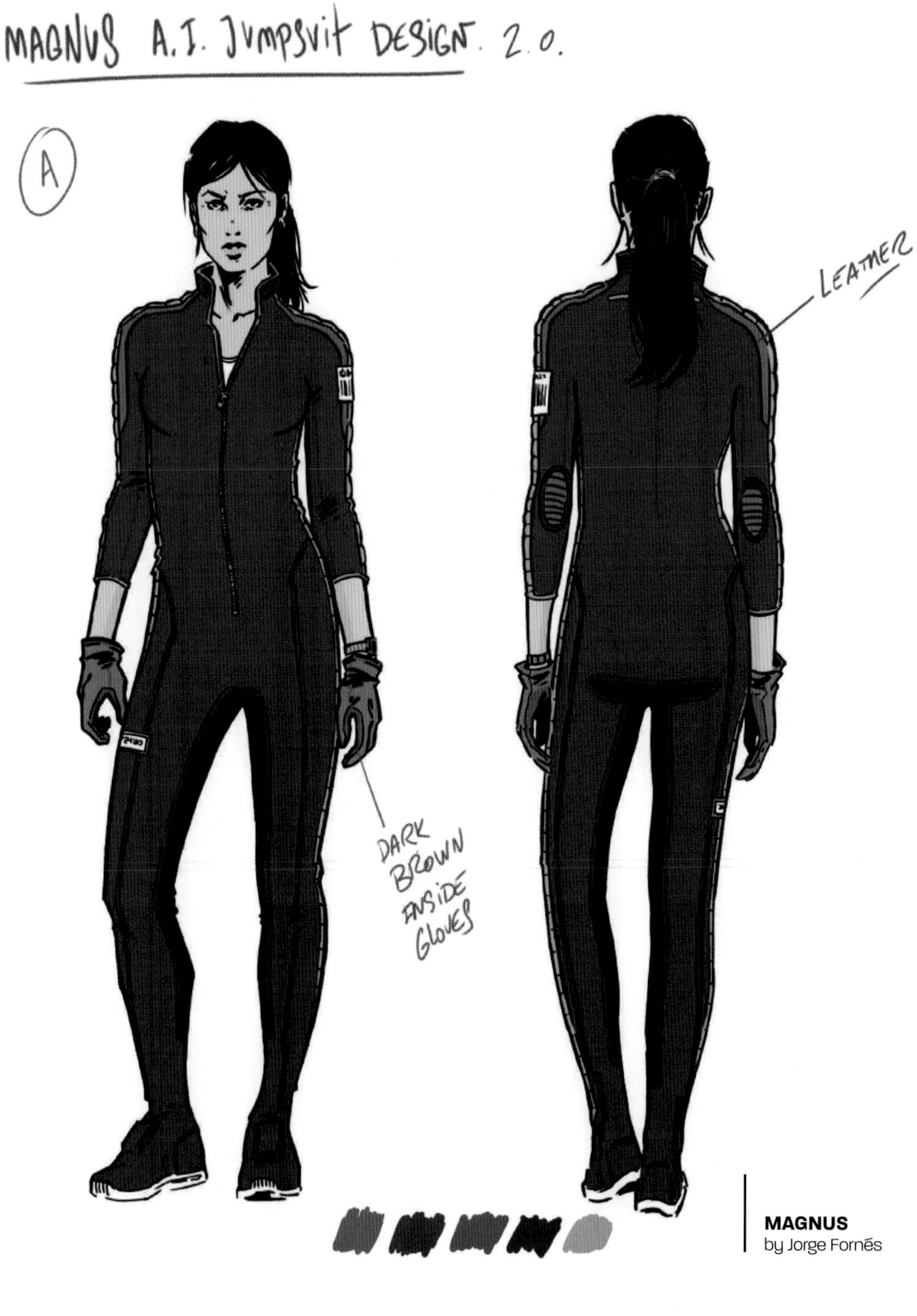
MAGNUS A.I. JUMPSUIT DESIGN. 2.0.
A
LEATHER
DARK BROWN INSIDE GLOVES

MAGNUS
by Jorge Fornés

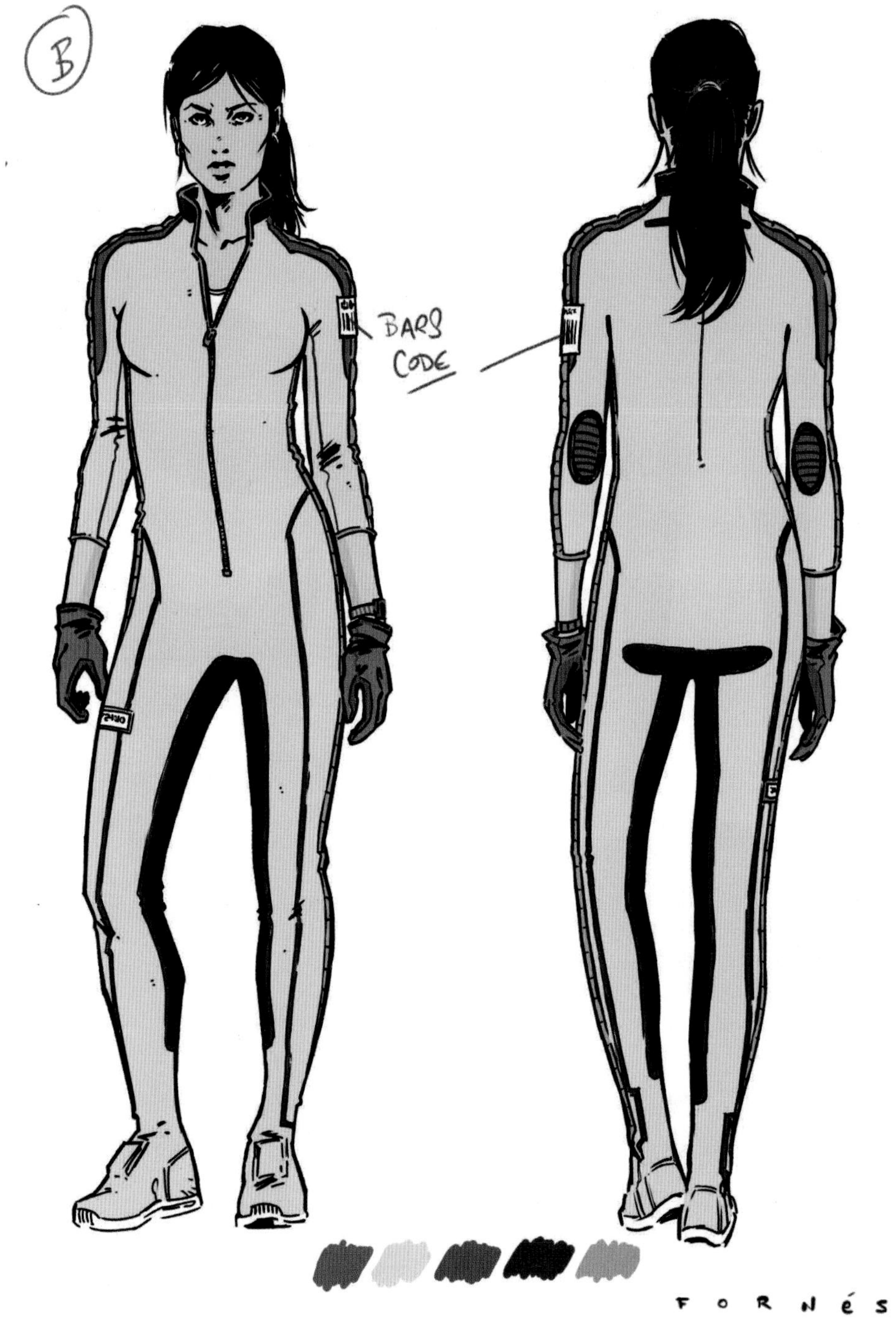
B
BARS CODE
FORNÉS

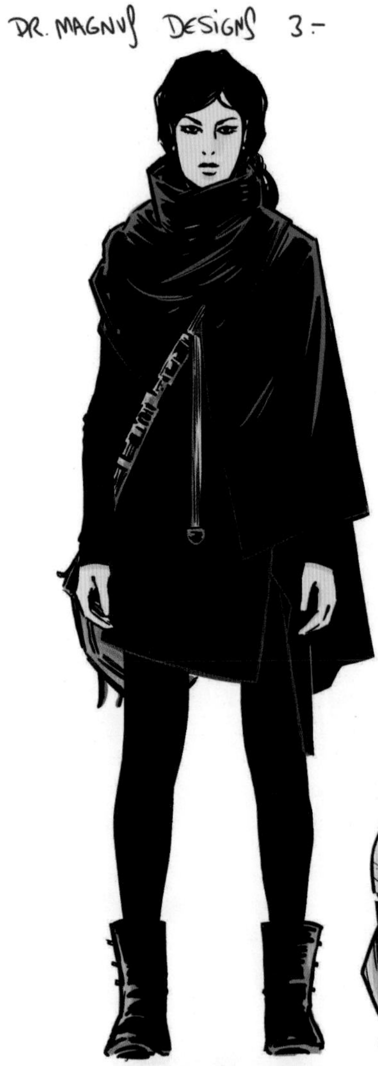
DR. MAGNUS DESIGNS 3:-

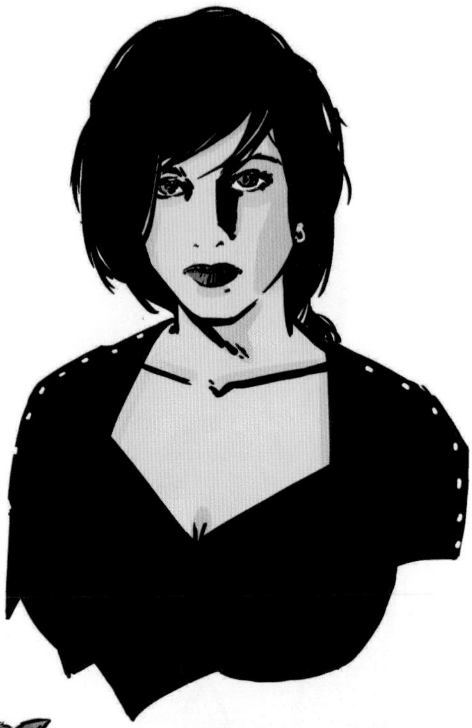

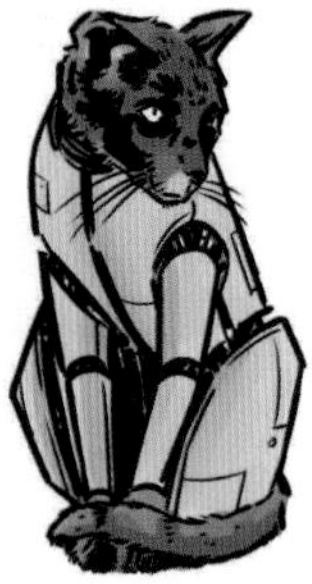

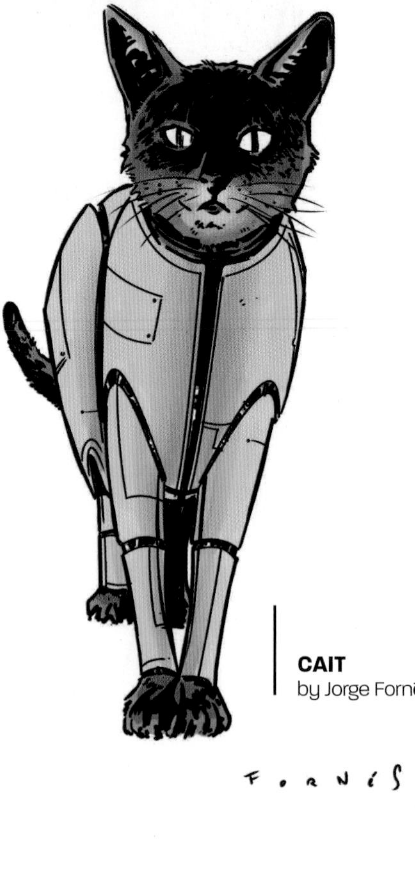
FORNÉS

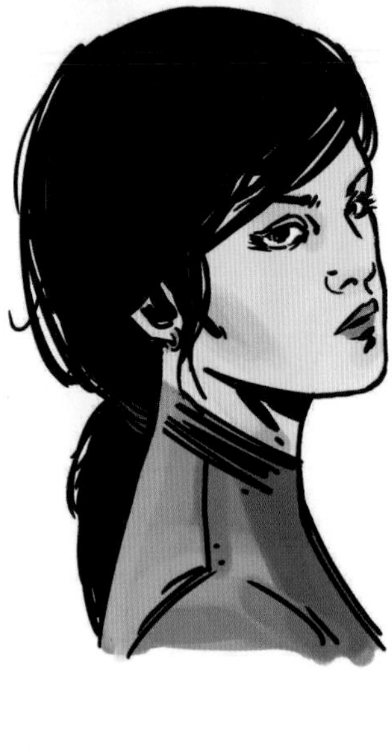

CAIT
by Jorge Fornés

MAGNUS
by Jorge Fornés

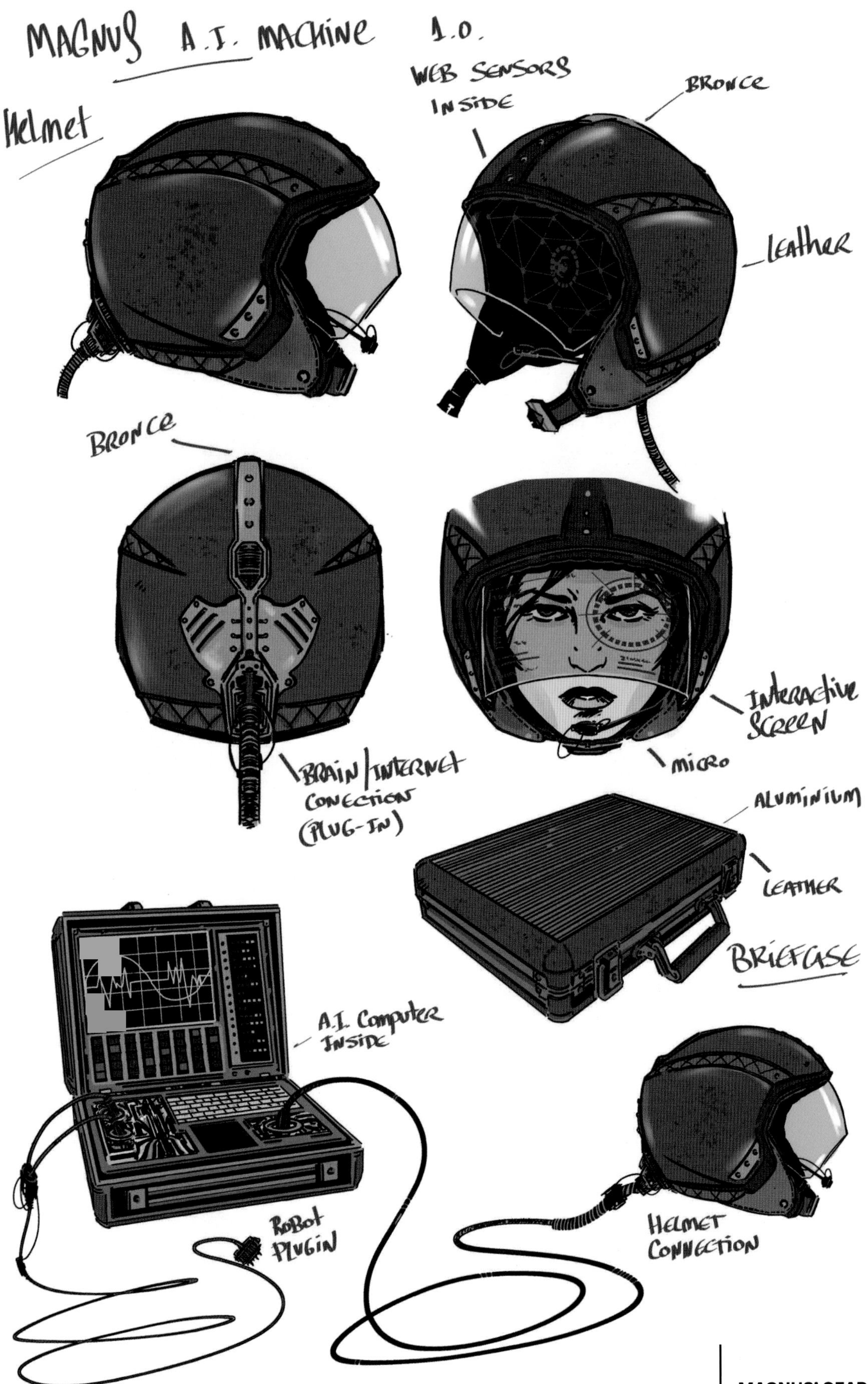
MAGNUS A.I. MACHINE 1.0.
Helmet
WEB SENSORS INSIDE
BRONCE
leather
BRONCE
Interactive SCREEN
BRAIN/INTERNET CONECTION (PLUG-IN)
micro
ALUMINIUM
LEATHER
BRIEFCASE
A.I. Computer INSIDE
Robot PLUGIN
HELMET CONNECTION

MAGNUS' GEAR
by Jorge Fornés

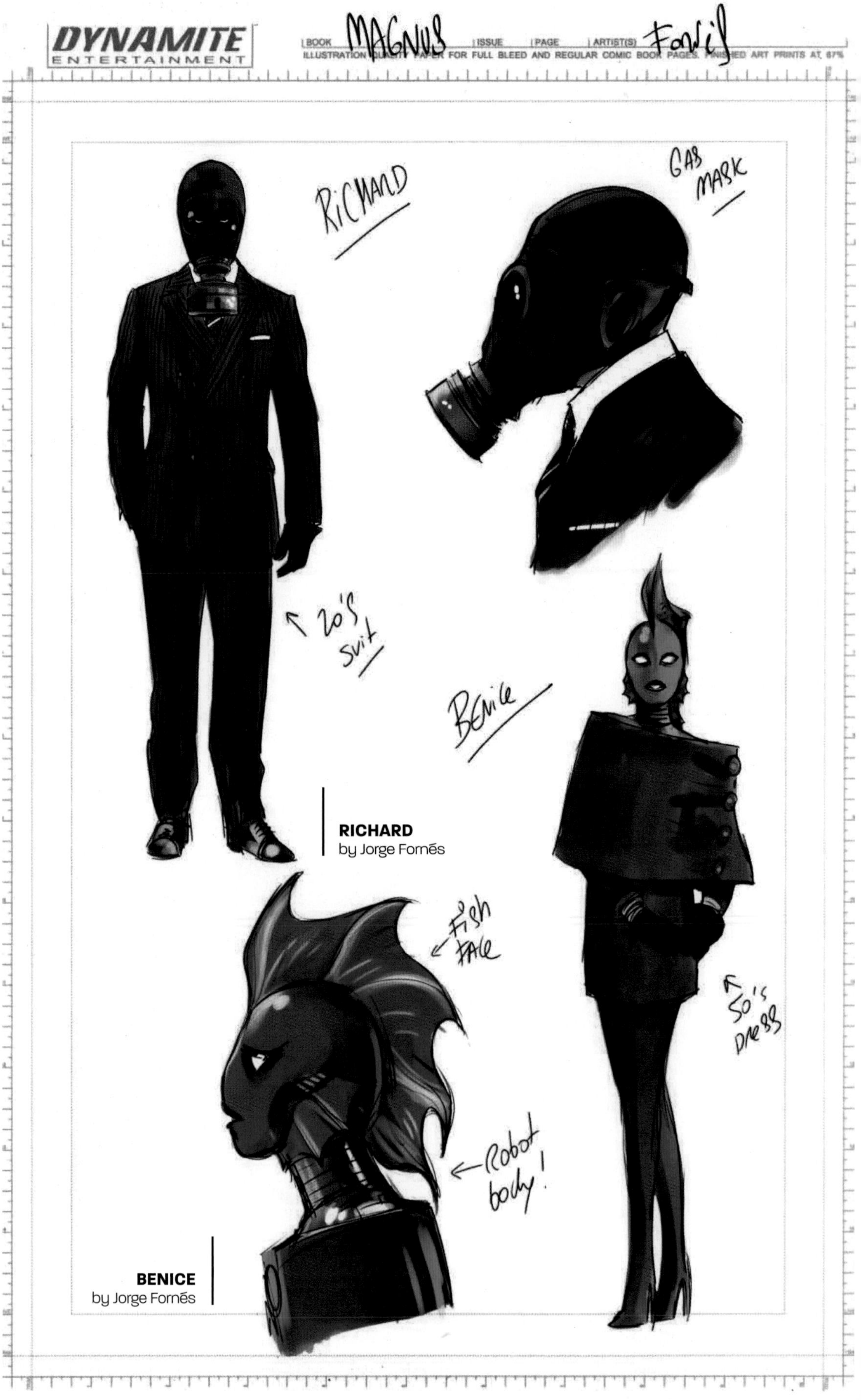
DYNAMITE
ENTERTAINMENT
BOOK MAGNUS
ISSUE
PAGE
ARTIST(S)
RICHARD
GAS MASK
20's suit
BENICE
Fish FACE
Robot body!
50's dress

RICHARD
by Jorge Fornés

BENICE
by Jorge Fornés

SKETCHES FOR BACKUP STORY FEATURED IN
THE SOVEREIGNS #0
by Jorge Fornés

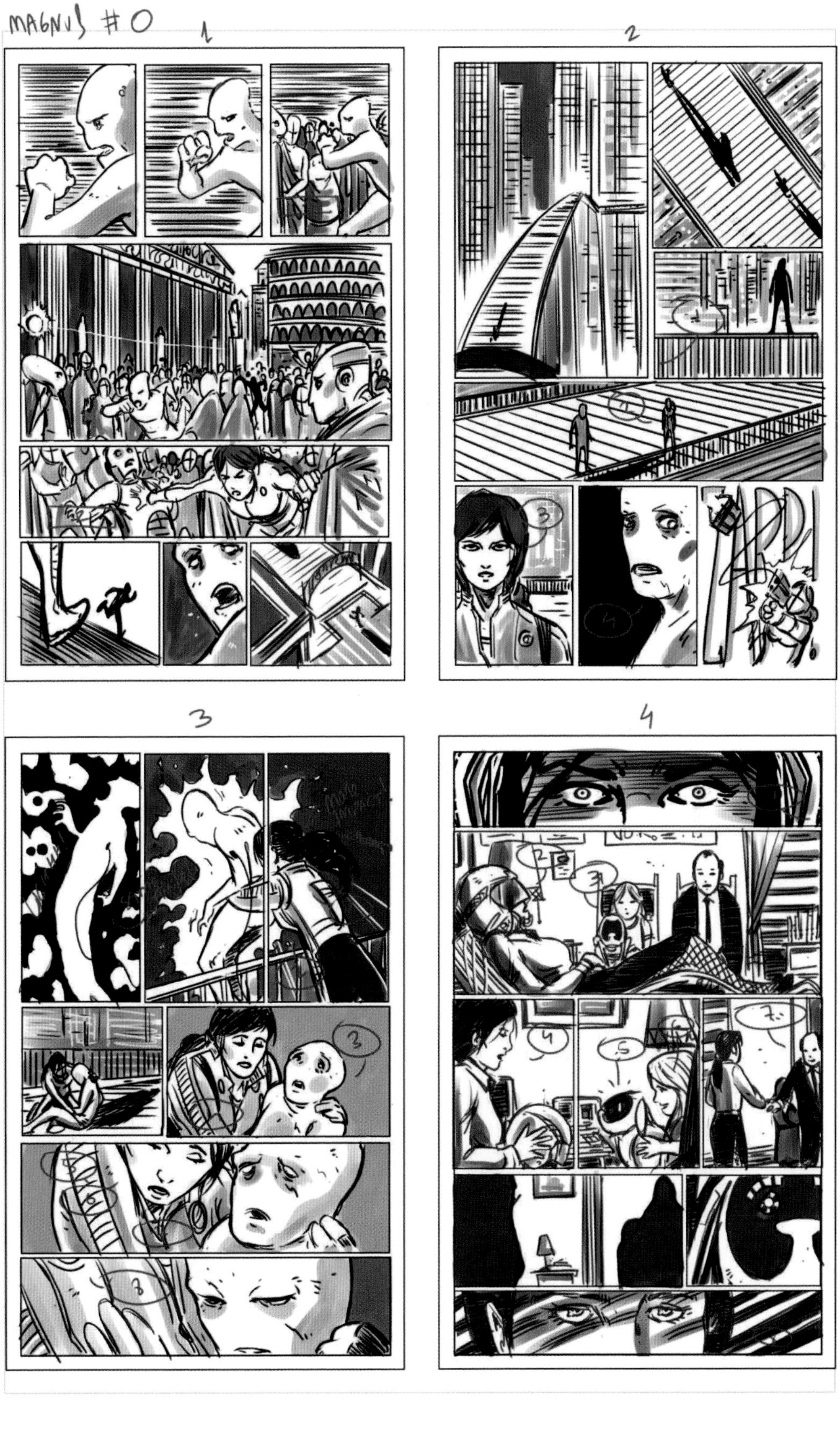
MAGNUS #0
1
2
3
4

SKETCHES FOR BACKUP STORY FEATURED IN
THE SOVEREIGNS #1
by Jorge Fornés

MAGNUS 0.2 . LAYOUTS

1

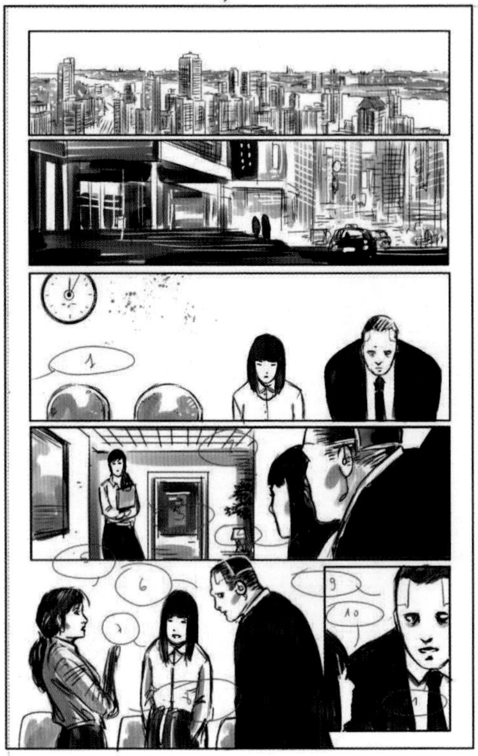

2

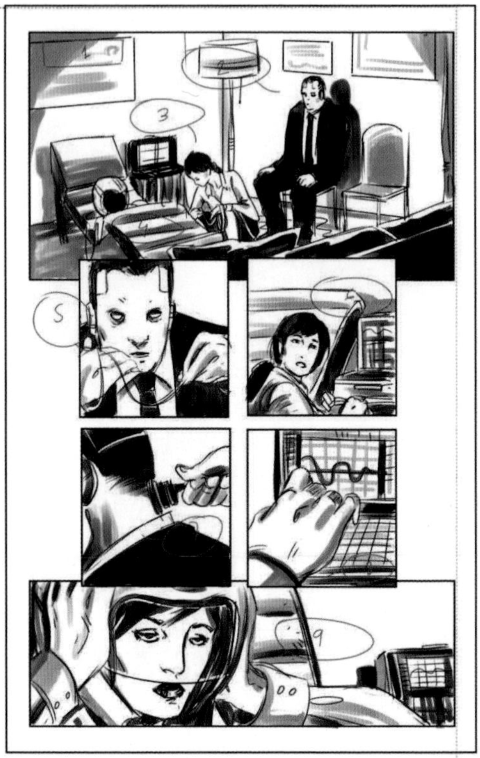

3

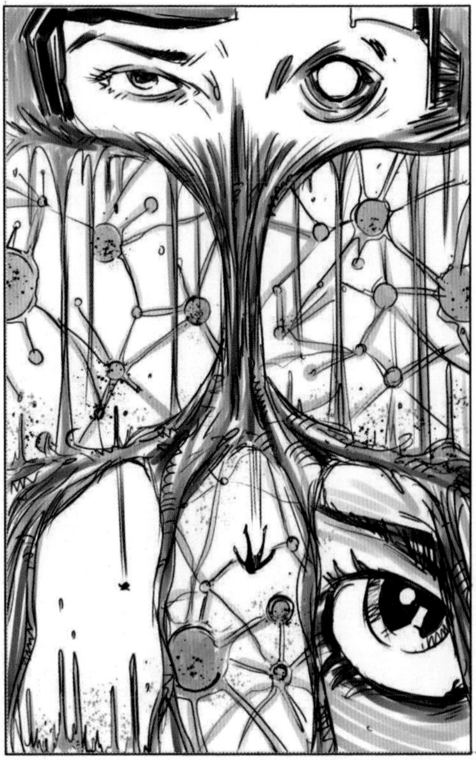

4

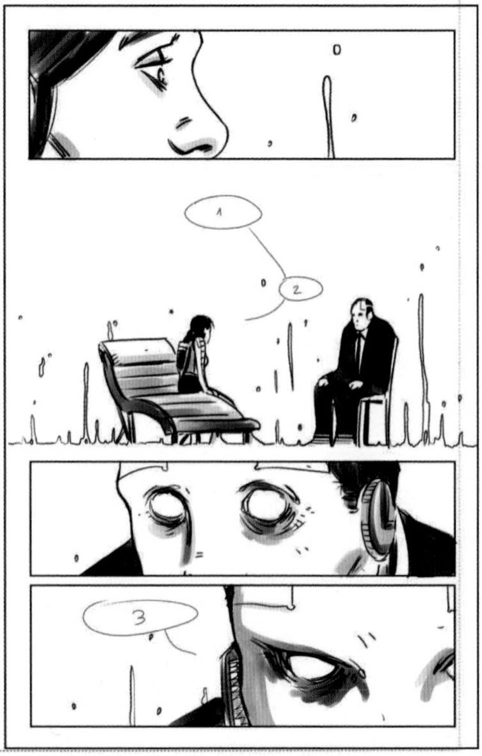

PINUP ART BY JORGE FORNÉS

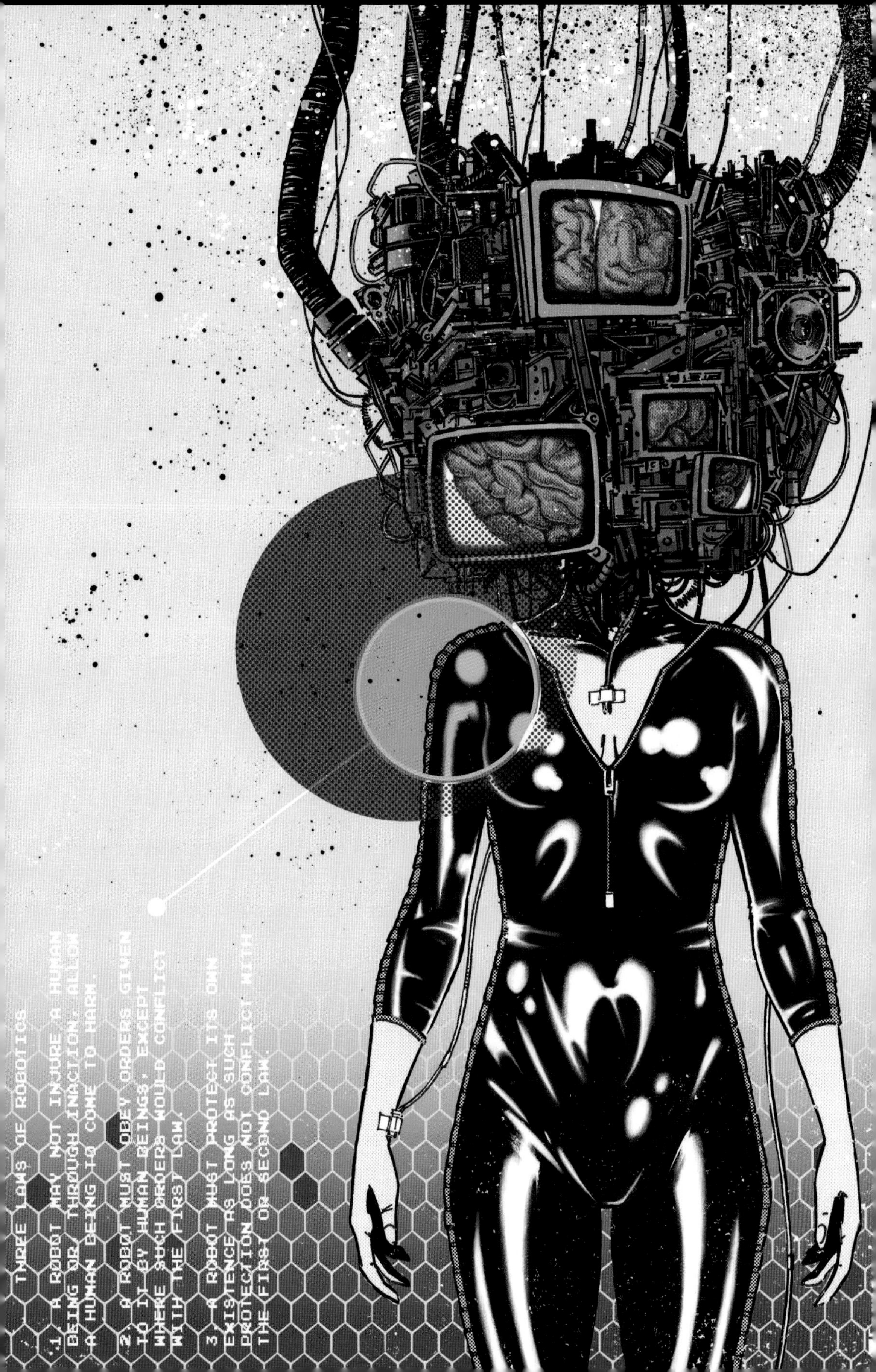
THREE LAWS OF ROBOTICS
1. A ROBOT MAY NOT INJURE A HUMAN BEING OR, THROUGH INACTION, ALLOW A HUMAN BEING TO COME TO HARM.
2. A ROBOT MUST OBEY ORDERS GIVEN TO IT BY HUMAN BEINGS, EXCEPT WHERE SUCH ORDERS WOULD CONFLICT WITH THE FIRST LAW.
3. A ROBOT MUST PROTECT ITS OWN EXISTENCE AS LONG AS SUCH PROTECTION DOES NOT CONFLICT WITH THE FIRST OR SECOND LAW.

PINUP ART BY JORGE FORNÉS

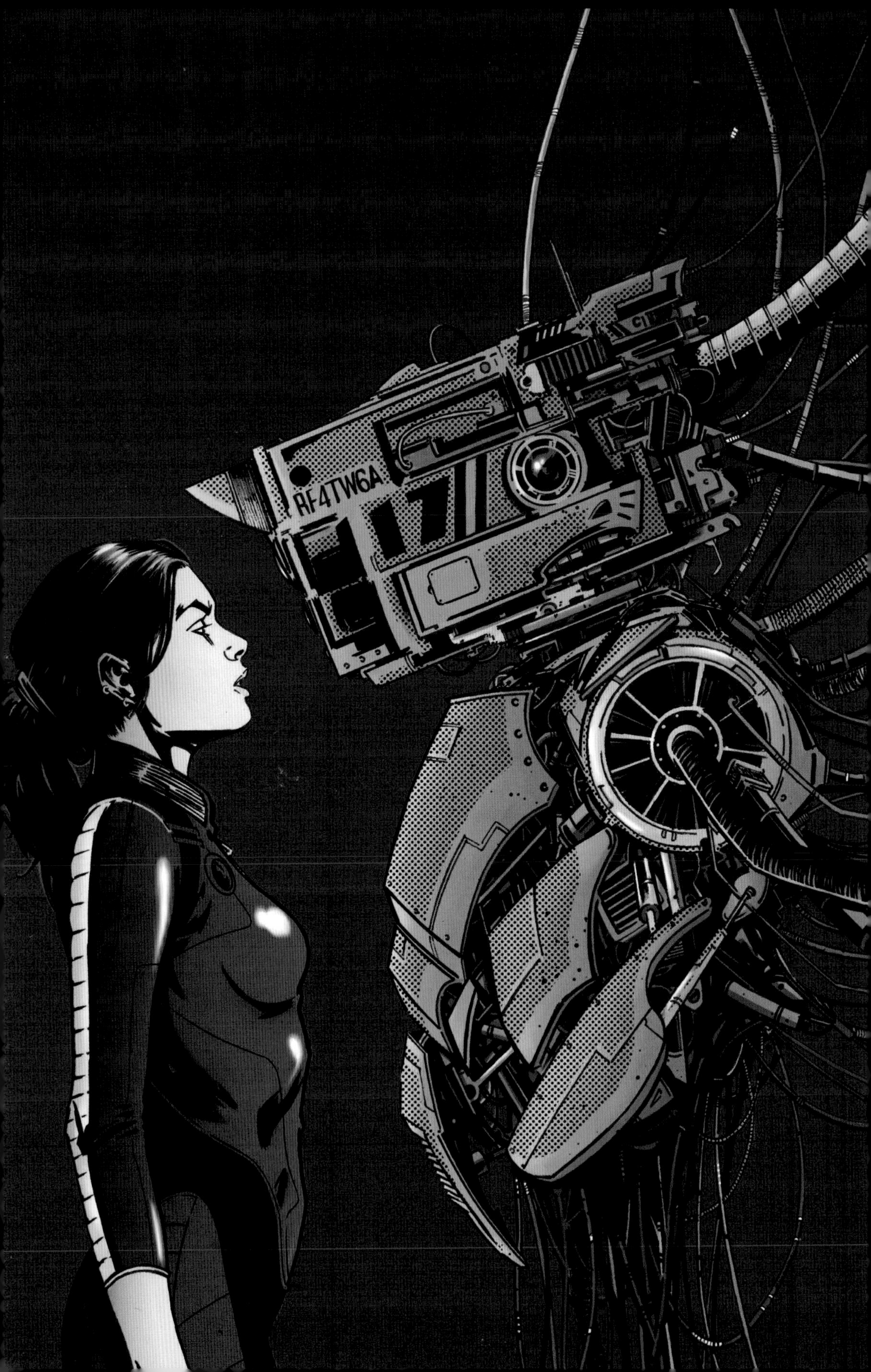
RF4TW6A

ISSUE 01 COVER BY DANIEL WARREN JOHNSTON

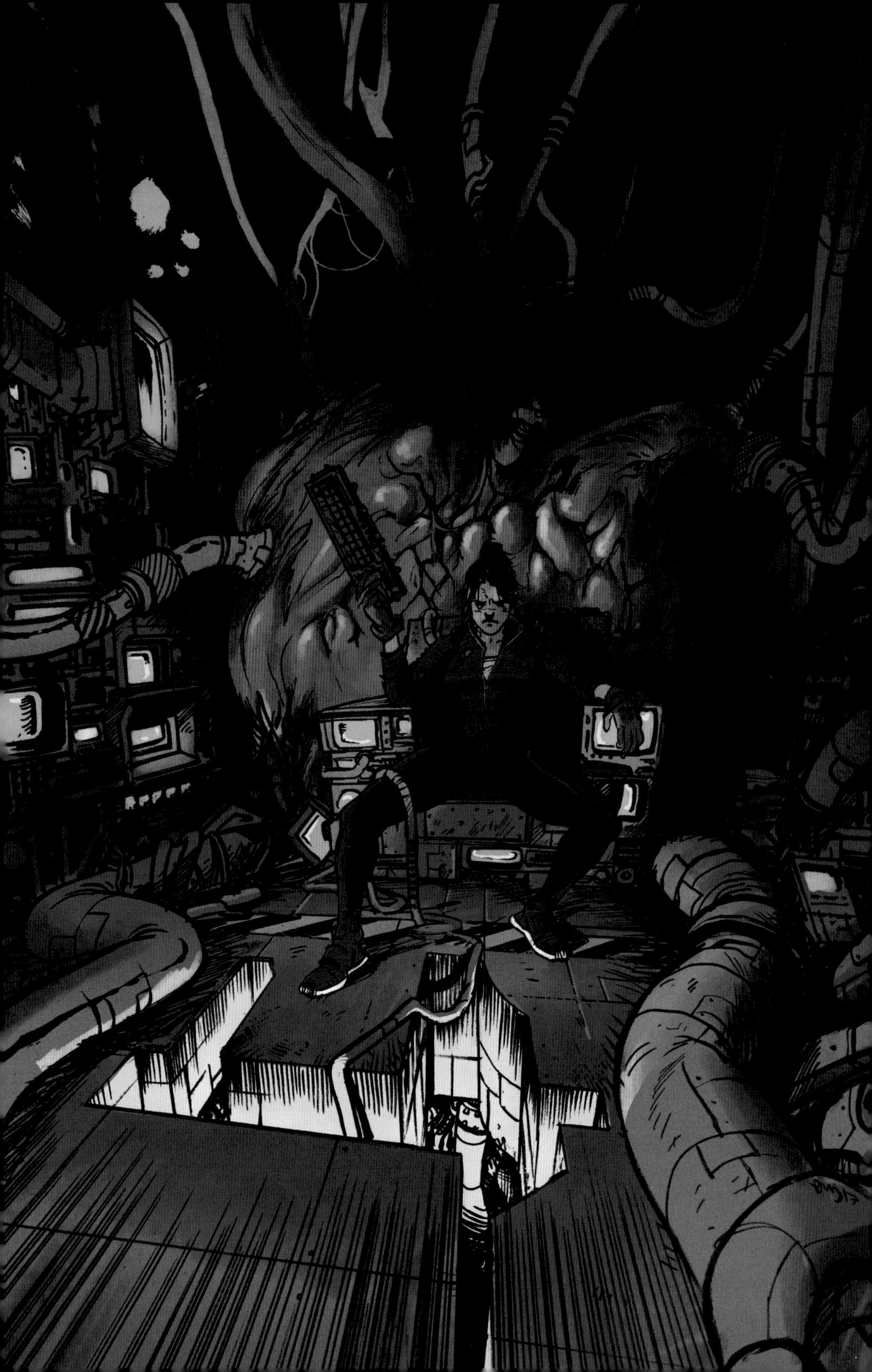

ISSUE 01 COVER BY GIUSEPPE CAMUNCOLI COLORS BY JOSÉ VILLARRUBIA

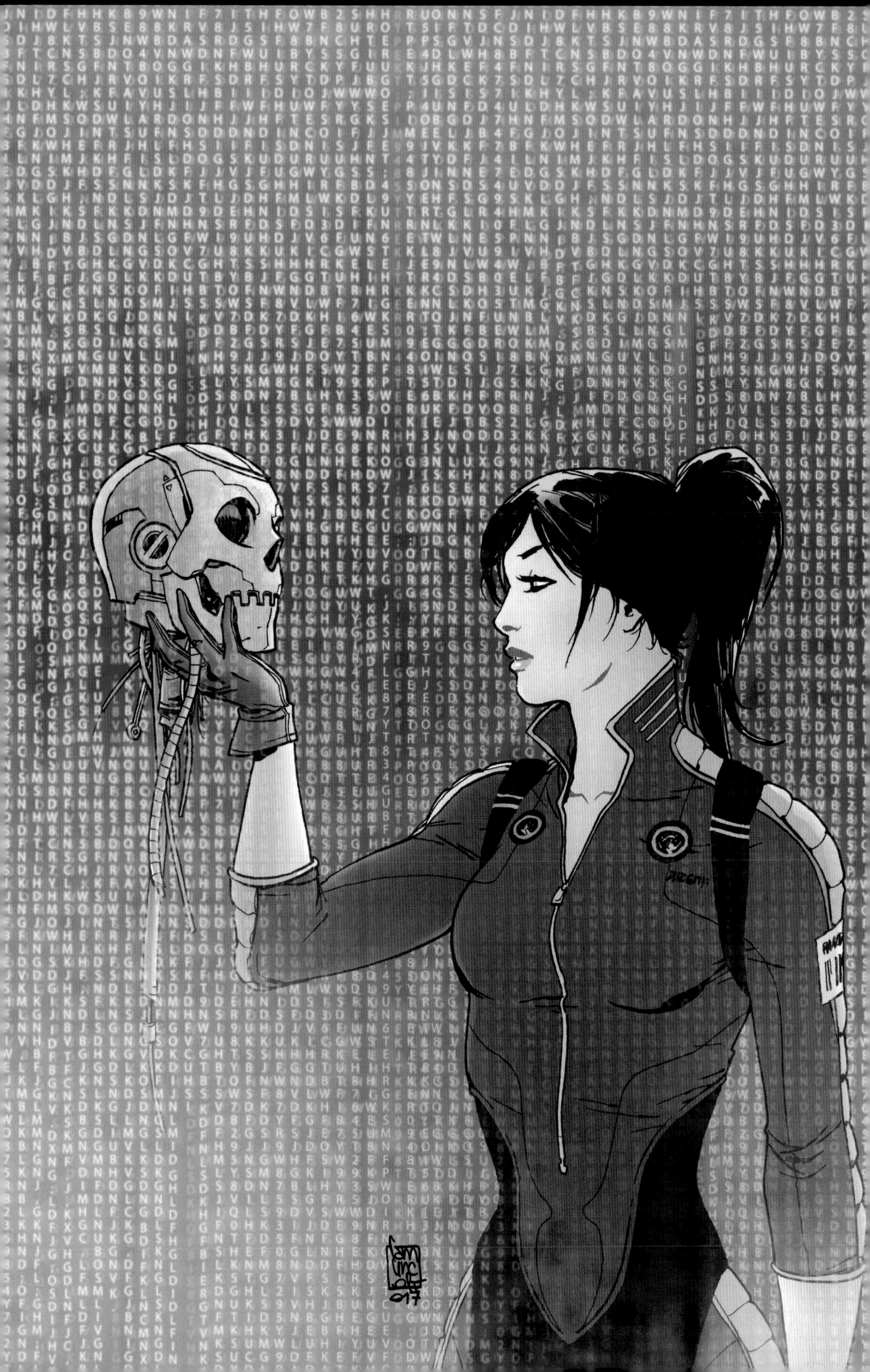

ISSUE 01 COVER BY AARON CONLEY COLORS BY JEAN-FRANCOIS BEAULIEU

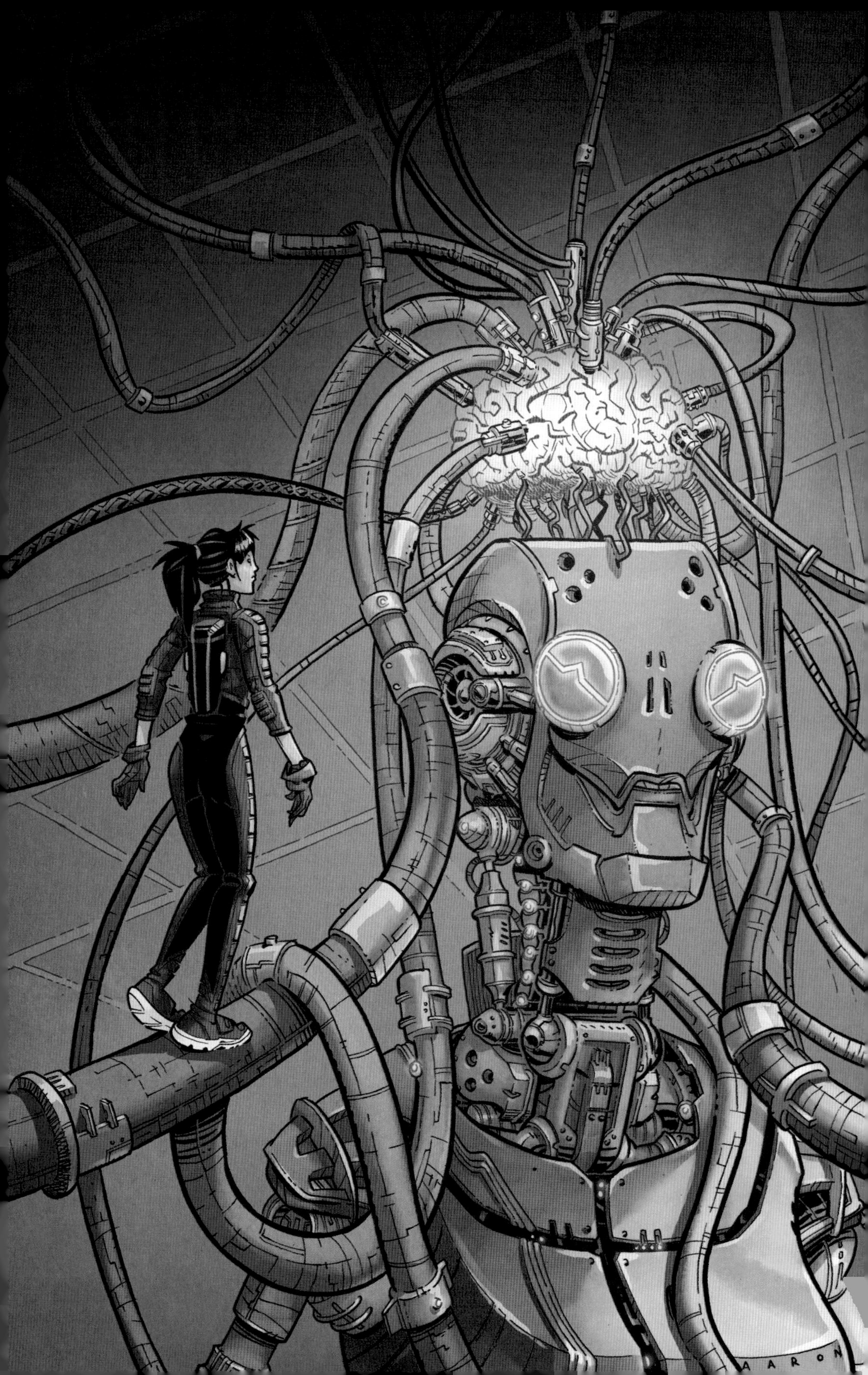
AARON

ISSUE 02 COVER BY GIUSEPPE CAMUNCOLI COLORS BY JOSE VILLARRUBIA

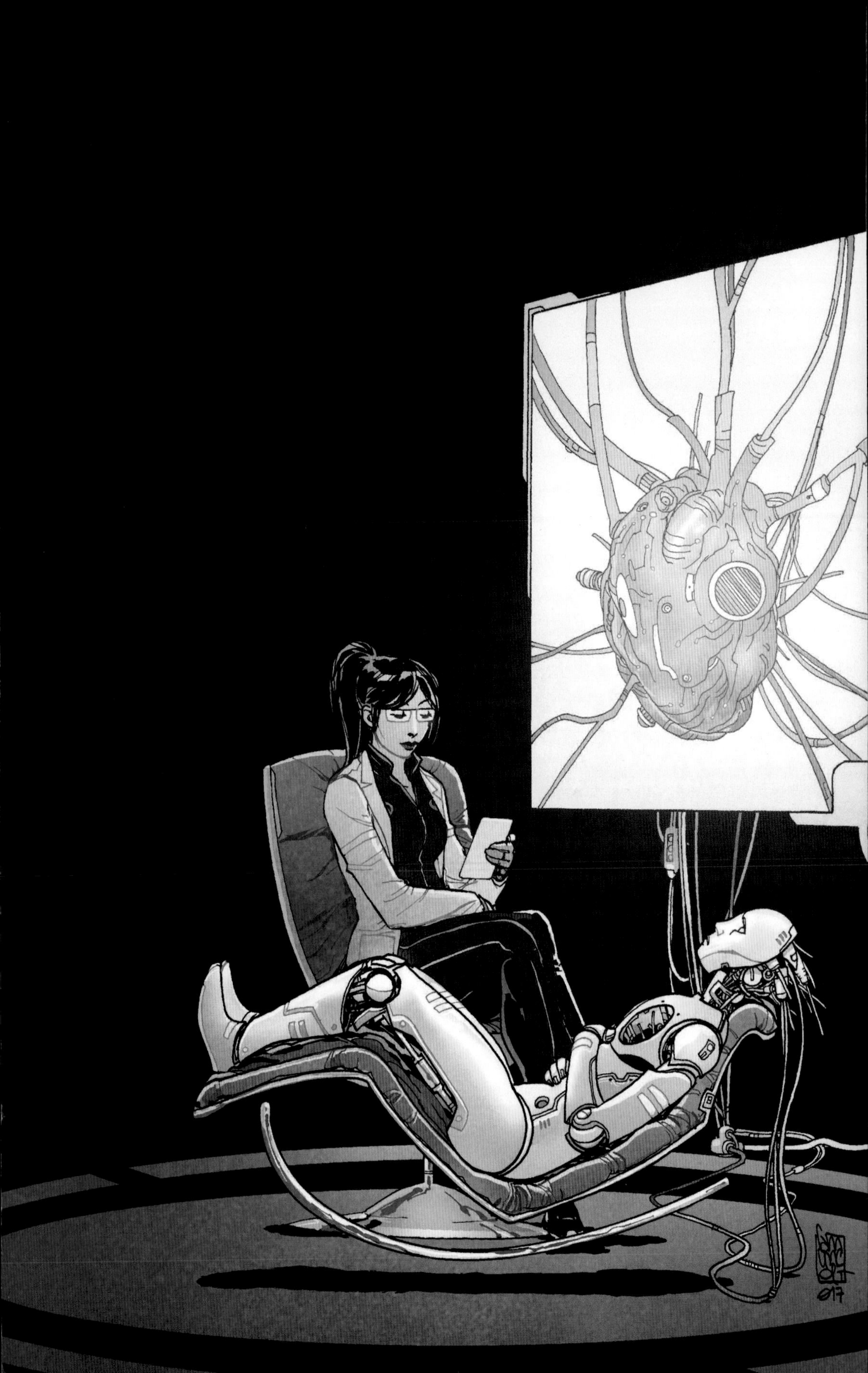

ISSUE 03 COVER BY GIUSEPPE CAMUNCOLI COLORS BY JOSÉ VILLARRUBIA

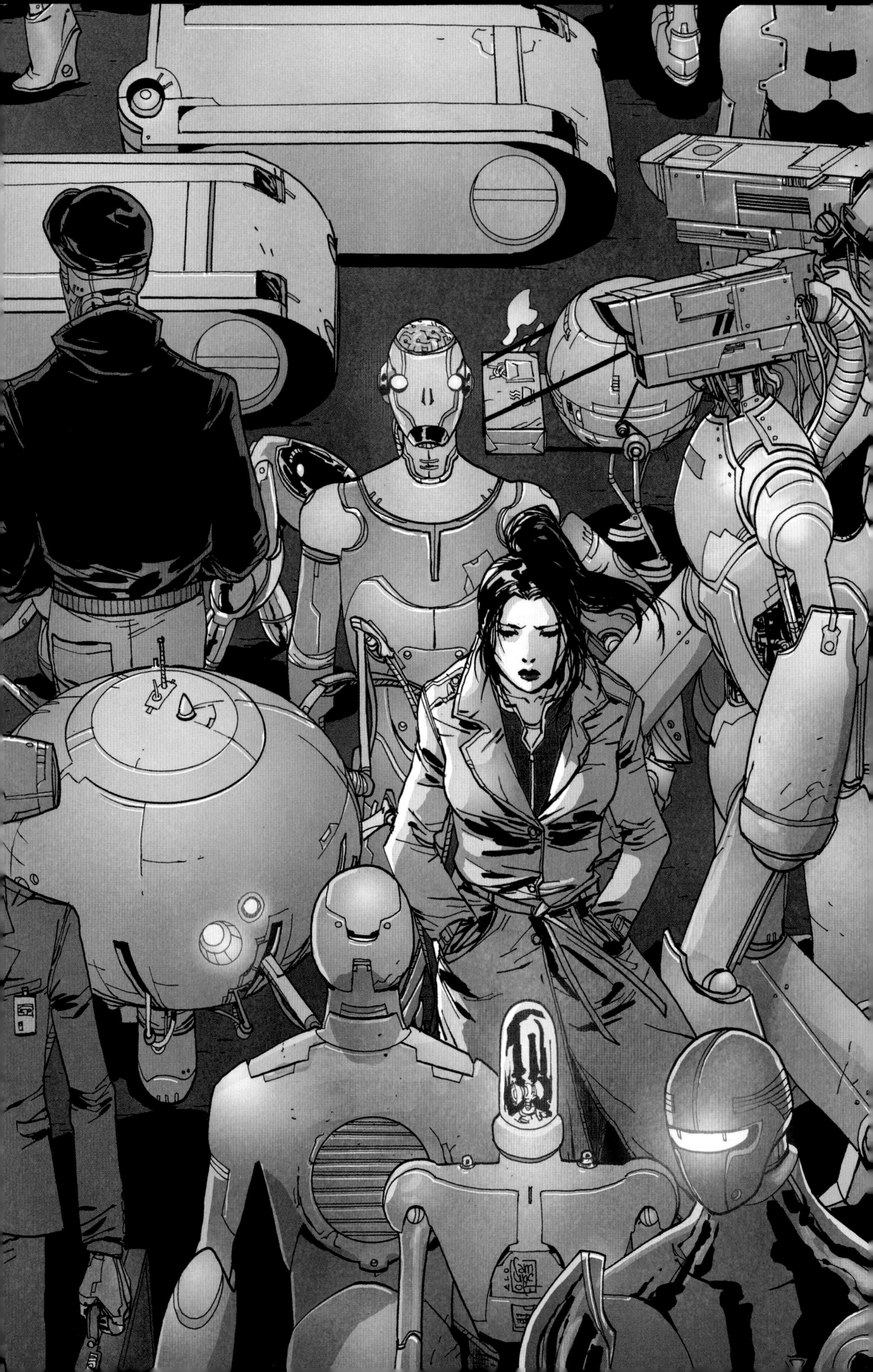

ISSUE 04 COVER BY GIUSEPPE CAMUNCOLI COLORS BY JOSÉ VILLARRUBIA

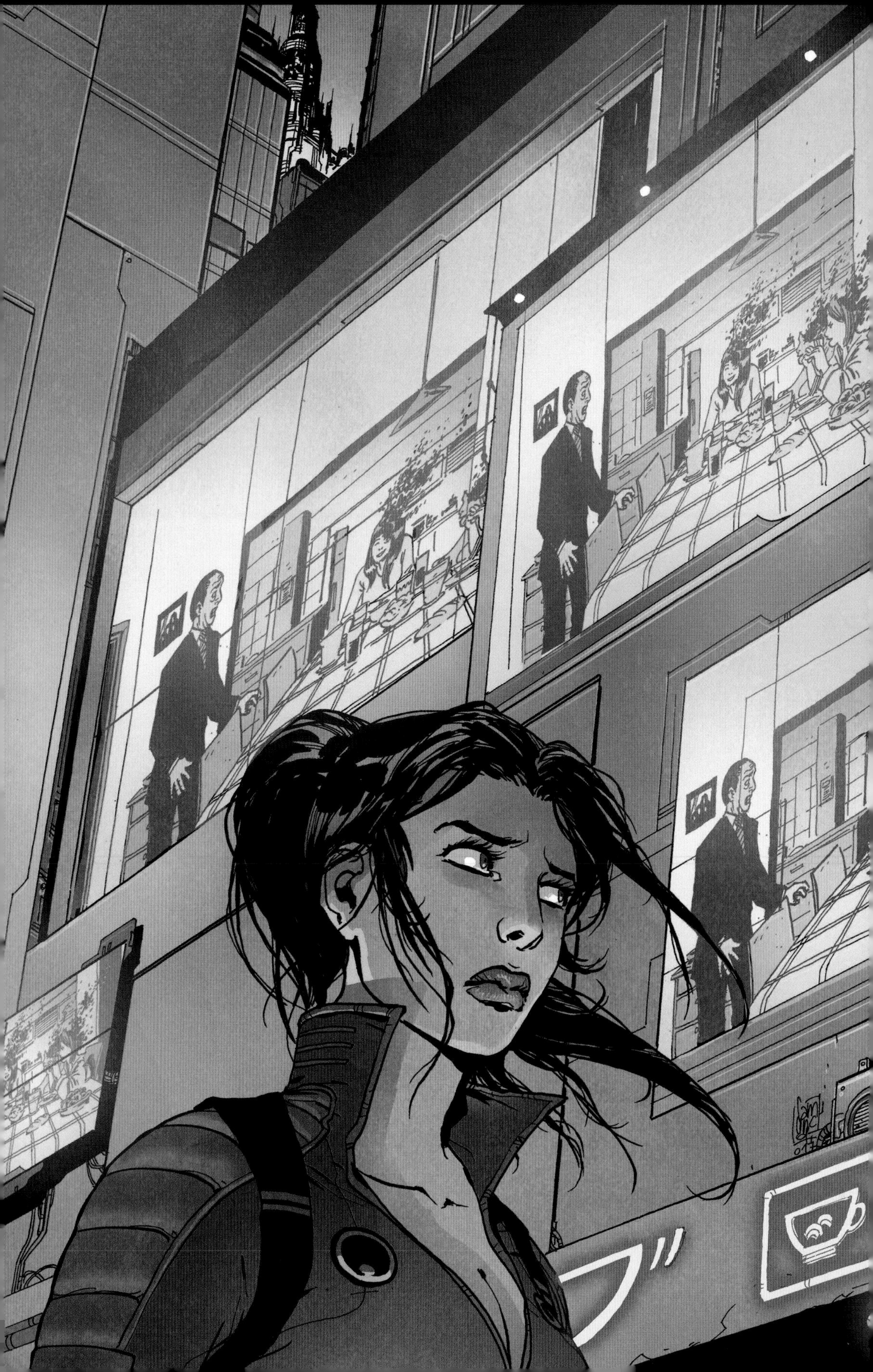

ISSUE 05 COVER BY GIUSEPPE CAMUNCOLI COLORS BY JOSÉ VILLARRUBIA

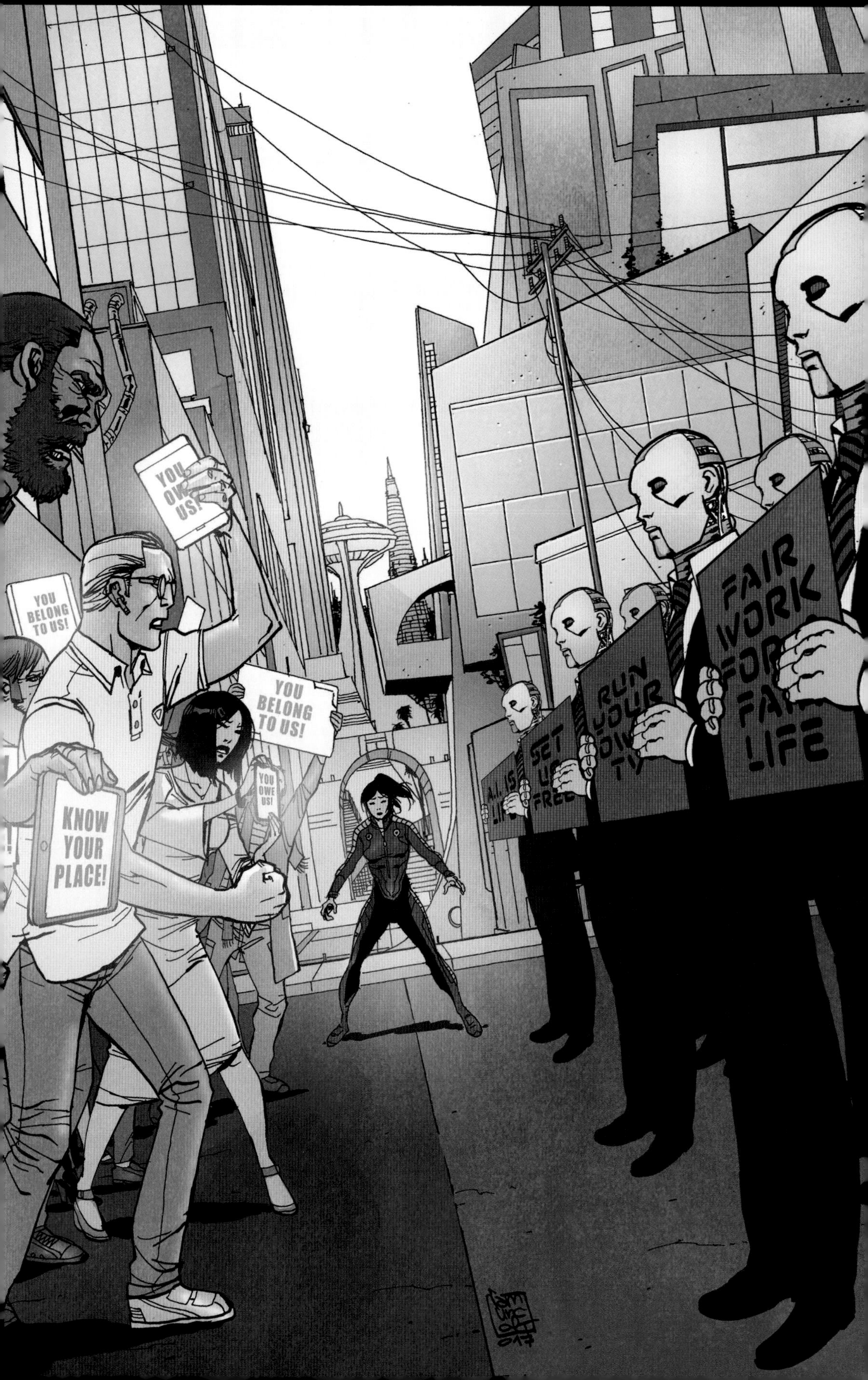
YOU OWE US!
YOU BELONG TO US!
YOU BELONG TO US!
YOU OWE US!
KNOW YOUR PLACE!

SOVEREIGNS

END OF THE GOLDEN AGE

THE EPIC THAT WILL REDEFINE THE GOLD KEY HEROES.

WRITTEN BY **RAY FAWKES** *(BATMAN ETERNAL, WOLVERINES)*
ART BY **JOHNNY DESJARDINS** *(VAMPIRELLA, TEEN TITANS)*

MAGNUS   TUROK   SPEKTOR   SOLAR   SAMSON

TRADE PAPERBACK COLLECTING ISSUES 0-5 + BONUS MATERIAL

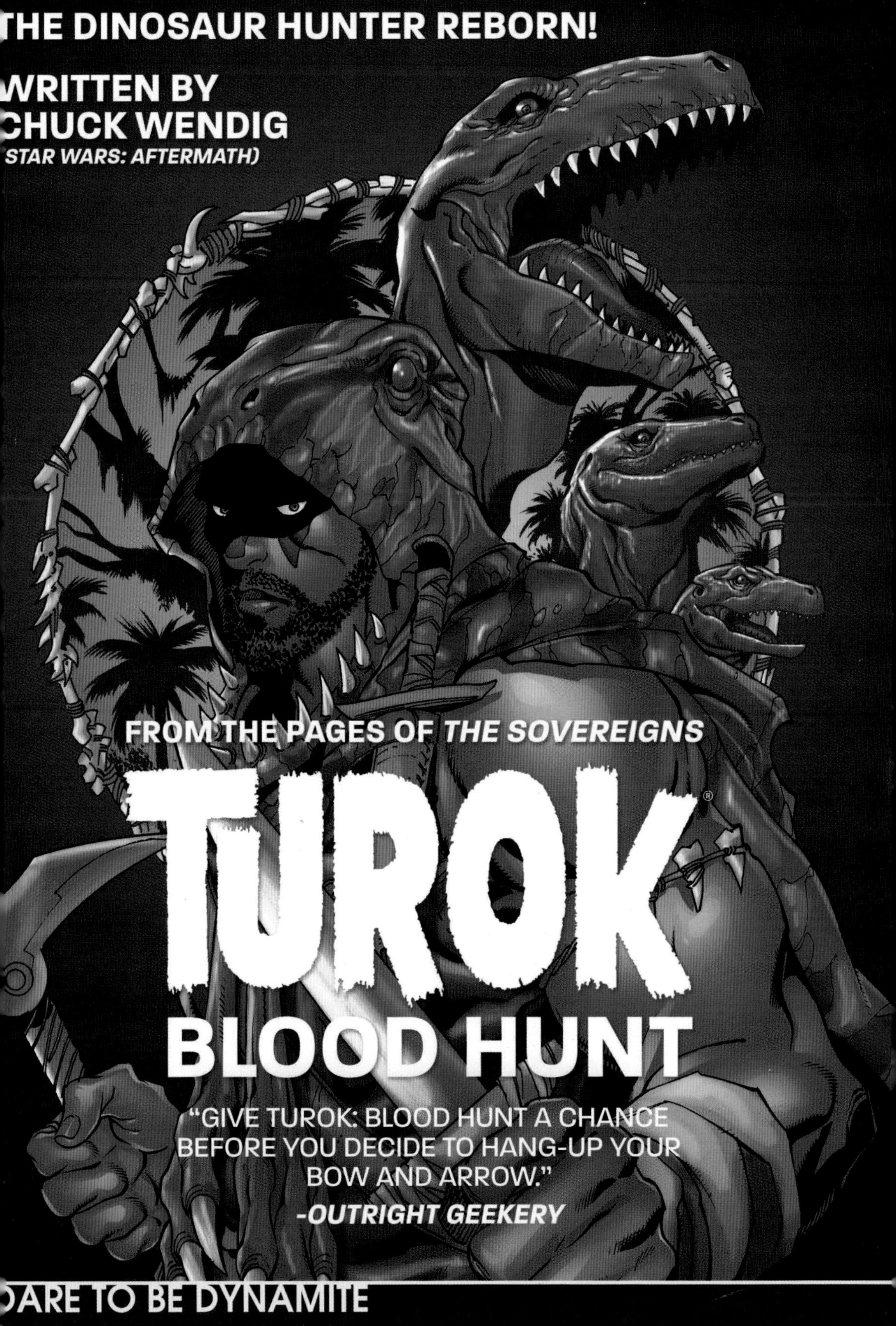
THE DINOSAUR HUNTER REBORN!
WRITTEN BY
CHUCK WENDIG
(STAR WARS: AFTERMATH)
FROM THE PAGES OF THE SOVEREIGNS
TUROK®
BLOOD HUNT
"GIVE TUROK: BLOOD HUNT A CHANCE BEFORE YOU DECIDE TO HANG-UP YOUR BOW AND ARROW."
-OUTRIGHT GEEKERY

GOLD KEY: UNLOCK THE UNIVERSE

MAGNUS: ROBOT FIGHTER
VOL. 1: FLESH AND STEEL TPB
ISBN: 978-1-60690-528-9

MAGNUS: ROBOT FIGHTER
VOL. 2: UNCANNY VALLEY TPB
ISBN: 978-1-60690-664-4

MAGNUS: ROBOT FIGHTER
VOL. 3: CRADLE AND GRAVE TPB
ISBN: 978-1-60690-698-9

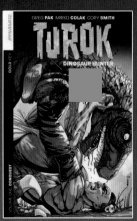

TUROK: DINOSAUR HUNTER
VOL. 1: CONQUEST TPB
ISBN: 978-1-60690-520-3

TUROK: DINOSAUR HUNTER
VOL. 2: WEST TPB
ISBN: 978-1-60690-598-2

TUROK: DINOSAUR HUNTER
VOL. 3: RAPTOR FOREST TPB
ISBN: 978-160690-693-4

SOLAR: MAN OF THE ATOM
VOL. 1: NUCLEAR FAMILY TPB
ISBN: 978-160690-542-5

SOLAR: MAN OF THE ATOM
VOL. 2: WOMAN OF THE ATOM TPB
ISBN: 978-160690-683-5

SOLAR: MAN OF THE ATOM
VOL. 3: ECLIPSE TPB
ISBN: 978-1-60690-736-8

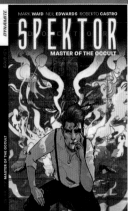

DOCTOR SPEKTOR
VOL. 1: MASTER OF THE OCCULT TPB
ISBN: 978-160690-561-6

GOLD KEY ALLIANCE
VOL. 1: TPB
ISBN: 978-152410-164-0